Attachments

WHY YOU LOVE, FEEL,
AND ACT THE WAY YOU DO

Attachments

WHY YOU LOVE, FEEL
AND ACT THE WAY YOU DO

Unlock the Secret to Loving and Lasting Relationships

DR. TIM CLINTON
& DR. GARY SIBCY

INTEGRITY
PUBLISHERS®

Published by Integrity Publishers, a division of Integrity Media, Inc., 5250 Virginia Way, Suite 110, Brentwood, TN 37027.

HELPING PEOPLE WORLDWIDE EXPERIENCE *the* MANIFEST PRESENCE *of* GOD.

Published in association with Yates and Yates, Orange County, California.

Cover Design: David Uttley

Interior Design: Inside Out Design & Typesetting

Library of Congress Cataloging-in-Publication Data

Clinton, Timothy E., 1960–
    Attachments: why you love, feel, and act the way you do / by Tim Clinton and Gary
      Sibcy.
    p.cm.
    Includes bibliographical references and index.
    ISBN 1-59145-026-8
        1. Interpersonal relations—Religious aspects—Christianity. I. Sibcy, Gary.
      II. Title.
BV4597.52 .C55 2002
158.2–dc21

                                           2002027370

Printed in the United States of America
02 03 04 05 06 BVG 9 8 7 6 5 4 3 2 1

Dedication

Tim: To the ones for whom my love and attachment know no bounds: Julie and our children—Megan and Zachary. You bring such joy to my life.

And to my greater family, both the Clintons and the Rothmanns.

Gary: To Lory and our children, Jacob and Jordan, the family I love most deeply, and to my father, Gary Sibcy Sr., with love and respect.

Contents

CONTENTS

PART II: UNLOCKING THE SECRETS
TO LOVING AND LASTING RELATIONSHIPS

FOREWORD

The Secret to Loving and Being Loved

I know what it is like to feel unloved and have no emotional connection or attachment to the people who are supposed to be the most important ones in your life. That's because I spent a significant portion of my early childhood locked in a closet by my mentally ill mother. My dad was gone a lot, and when he was home he was exhausted and barely "there."

Because of the condition of my primary relationships, I never felt loved or attached in *any* relationship. At least not until I received the Lord. Then I started reading the Bible and learning about God and His ways. I came to see that He is a God who loves us more than we can imagine. I was amazed to learn that He loves even me. And although I had always lived with fear, depression, loneliness, and anxiety, God's love was powerful enough to penetrate my brokenness and take all those negative emotions away. God's love made me into a whole person.

Through all that, I learned that we will never be able to find any degree of wholeness in our lives without love. It is the air that keeps us breathing. We have to be able to take it in, and we have to know how to give it out as well. That's what this book will help you to do. How I wish that back in those early years I had had a book like *Attachments* to help me understand the secret to loving and being loved.

If you have come out of a painful, damaging, or traumatic past; if you have experienced too many empty, broken, or unfulfilling relationships; if you are tired of feeling unloved, disconnected, or lonely; then you are going to love reading this book. It will connect you with the true Lover of your soul. It will help you experience the love and closeness you want to feel. It will teach you how to find loving, fulfilling, rich, and satisfying relationships. Reading this book will be a refreshing, encouraging, enlightening, comforting, and life-transforming experience. There is healing within its hope-filled pages. Who in the world doesn't need that?

—*Stormie Omartian*

I

RELATIONSHIPS ARE EVERYTHING

1

THE HEART OF THE MATTER:
ATTACHMENTS IN EVERYDAY LIVING

Why We Love, Feel, and Act the Way We Do

Anyone who goes too far alone . . . goes mad.
—JEWISH PROVERB

I*t's not good.*

What's not good?

His being alone. Look at him, wandering around the Garden of Eden by himself.

God saw that it wasn't good for man to be alone. So He caused a deep sleep to fall on Adam, and He gave him someone he could relate to, someone who would share the glories of earth with him—a woman, Eve. And later He would give Adam and Eve more humans to relate to—children.

It's clear, right from the beginning of the Bible, that God created us to be attached to others. But maintaining and nurturing those attachments, those relationships—ah, that's the tricky thing.

Relationships start out easily—and sometimes wonderfully. God hardwired us that way right from the beginning, right in the Garden. We were made for intimacy with Him, and according to the opening passages of Genesis, intimacy with each other. Have you ever wondered how Adam felt the first time he saw Eve? The first time he held her, kissed her, made love to her? The Bible says "and they were both naked, the man and his wife, and were not ashamed" (Genesis 2:25 NKJV). Free . . . loved . . . intimate . . . one flesh . . . For a while, it was perfect.

But you don't have to read far in the Bible to realize that even in paradise things can go wrong. Evil lurks, tempts. Eve bites the apple. Adam caves in. Soon they're blaming each other—and this is *before* their children

3

arrive on the scene, entangling them in an entirely different set of relationship problems.

Isn't that our way? Our relationships start out so beautifully, and the next thing we know we're hurting or being hurt by those around us, especially the ones we love the most. Why does this happen? How can we prevent it from happening? And how can we repair the relationship once it has been damaged by this breach of trust?

Teaching you those secrets is the focus of this book. You *can* learn to build and maintain (or restore) strong, nurturing, loving relationships with those closest to you. It's what God has intended for you all along.

GOD DESIRES INTIMACY

When God came to the Garden and said, "Adam, where are you?" God already knew what had happened and where Adam was hiding. Yet He was inviting Adam to walk with Him—to continue to be in relationship with Him. Finally, out comes Adam wearing a couple of fig leaves, trying to cover what was plainly seen—his ways, his sin, his fears. Sadly, when queried, he even blamed God for what happened, saying, "It was that woman You gave me."

As counselors, when we reflect on this story, what jumps out at us most is not the eating-the-apple part but God's desire for intimacy with us. The Genesis story reminds us of the power of His love and of love itself, as well as the fact that He's given us other intimate relationships like those with our spouses, our children, our parents—those who are supposed to be there for us through thick and thin—to help fill our hearts and our longings.

Unfortunately, so much today competes for and tears at our love in relationships. And over time these vital relationships can become challenging, even seriously flawed. When these relationships sour, our sense of well-being can sour as well. Filled with hurt, and maybe with rejection and aloneness as well, we pull inward to protect our hearts. Distancing takes root. Empty yet expecting, we'll work to fill the holes in our souls with other things like work, play, or entertainment, which may become other "lovers" to give us purpose, meaning, and value. "Modern man is drinking and drugging himself out of awareness," psychologist Ernest Becker wrote, "or he spends his time shopping, which is the same thing."[1] Before long, we only intensify our aloneness, magnify our broken selves, and maybe even deny our God and cause more hurt to our "others"—our Eves, our Adams, our kids.

Just look at those others. Look into their eyes. And look at yourself.

Do you dare even look inside?

Yes. We can't help ourselves. Why? Because the persistent human cry is simply for someone to love us, to hold us tight. Our need for relationship is even more powerful than our need for food. In today's time-starved world, we need each other *more,* not less.

If you are tired of empty relationships—tired of giving and not getting anything back—or if you just wish you felt closer to those you love . . . you're not alone. Unlocking the secrets to loving and lasting relationships is our goal in *Attachments.* We'll start by looking at two types of relationships that are most commonly strained: a marriage in serious trouble, and a parent and child on a rocky, deeply declining road.

Trouble in Paradise . . .

"Where have you been?" Sandra Light's voice was harsh, accusing, and claw sharp. "Do you have any idea how late you are?" The mother of two, Sandra was thirty-four with quick, blue eyes and brown, highlighted hair. She was wearing her new bathing suit and a bright, floral coverup as she scolded her husband, Mike, who stood framed in the hotel-room doorway, his expression both taken aback and laced with weariness. Had they been at home in Virginia, he would have expected to be accosted at the door like this; here, though, he had expected a pass.

You see, he and Sandra were in Hawaii—a perk of Mike's success. And what's more, it was February, and the rest of America was locked in ice and snow. Even Virginia had been pitched into a deep freeze, cursed by unusually icy temperatures and whipped by nail-sharp winds. Had he thought it would make a difference, Mike would have pointed out—again—that they were missing all that and that the world they were in was perfumed by orchids, hibiscus, and royal tuberoses, all carried on warm, balmy sea breezes.

They were at a luxury hotel on Poipu Beach, Kauai, an island Mike treasured. He was a computer systems engineer who'd decided a decade before to go into computer sales. He was good at it. Every year since then, he'd "made his numbers," and Sandra had accompanied him on one of these sales award trips. Last year it had been a week in Cancun, the year before some resort in the Dominican Republic, and the rumor was, next year it would be a seven-day cruise.

Why isn't she happy? Mike wondered incredulously. *How can she not be happy in Hawaii? The place even* smells *happy.*

Sandra herself believed she should be happy. But she wasn't. And the longer she'd waited for Mike the less happy she'd become—and the angrier. After all, what good was it to be in a place like Kauai and spend it alone? Well, okay, she wasn't always alone, but she might as well be. Like this morning, when they were scheduled to go snorkeling. A boat was leaving in less than fifteen minutes. And only now did he show up. And he knew how much she loved to snorkel. The first time she'd gone was nearly six years ago when the award trip was to the Virgin Islands. Since then, snorkeling, when offered, had been the highlight of her trips. And he'd ignored all that and been late—too late for them to go. Why? Because of a stupid meeting. A hastily called thing that had already interrupted their lanai breakfast buffet and now threatened to ruin not only her afternoon but her whole Hawaii experience.

Mike recoiled. "It's not my fault."

"Sure, it's your fault," Sandra fired back, turning her back on him and stalking back into the room. "It's certainly not *my* fault."

"It's nobody's fault," Mike deflected. "It's just a meeting. An important meeting. Very important, actually."

"You know how I like snorkeling with you. It gives us a chance to do something together." Then her voice turned bitter. "But I should have known you'd put your meeting first."

"My boss wanted to talk to me. It was important."

"Important," she spat. "What's important about you and the guys swapping computer-sales war stories around the solid silver coffee urn? Real important."

"There are rumors the company might be sold," Mike volleyed.

"There are always rumors," Sandra said. "And you're always doing this to me. Putting me second, third, or fourth to everything else. You didn't know snorkeling would be delayed. And they wouldn't fire you if you had gotten up and left. You could hear about your silly rumors tonight at dinner. But you chose coffee over me."

"Coffee? Is that what you think I do? It's that meeting and a bunch more like it that got us here. Anyway," he said, taking a step or two away from her, his tone withdrawing into a don't-hurt-me-again place, "we can still go."

"No, we can't."

"Sure we can. With the meeting going so long they delayed the departure."

"It doesn't matter."

"Doesn't matter?" He nodded and shook his head in sequence. "Of course it wouldn't matter to you. It never matters how much I do for you. Look around you. You're in Kauai, for cryin' out loud. Flowers. You love flowers. The place stinks of flowers. You know what you are? You're an ingrate."

"An ingrate?" She stepped toward him aggressively. "I should be grateful that you ruined our day together?"

Mike expelled a huge, accusing jet of air through his tightly drawn lips. "I'm done. If you don't want to go, don't go. It's better anyway." Mike grabbed a folder from the open briefcase on his bedside table. "I'm chairing a meeting in the morning. I need to get ready for it."

"Another meeting? Why'd you bring me in the first place?"

He just waved a dismissive hand and stomped into the bathroom. He closed the door just as she stepped up to it. It nearly hit her in the nose.

"It doesn't matter," she bawled at it. "You've done this to me for the last time. The first night we were here you left me waiting for you in the hotel lobby."

"Go by yourself," he called through the door.

"No," Sandra cried to the door. "I'm too angry, too hurt."

"Do what you want. I'm going to the Jacuzzi."

"I might be an ingrate," she said, falling against the door. "But you're an abuser. You get my hopes up and then you dash them. You smash them to smithereens. You're cruel—cruel and insensitive." She took a deep breath as if loading her emotional guns. "You're just like your father."

In the bathroom Mike was stepping into his bathing suit. The instant he heard the words, he felt Sandra's emotional fist bury itself in his stomach. Pulling up his swim trunks, he all but fell against the marble counter, thinking, *Relationships just don't work. Women just don't make sense, so how can you figure them out? No matter how hard you try to please them, nothing works. No wonder Dad left Mom. Mom drove him crazy just like Sandra's driving me crazy. Nothing could please Mom, and nothing pleases Sandra.*

The business papers clutched in his hand like a lifeline, Mike grabbed a towel with his other hand and tossed it over his shoulder, then stepped from the bathroom to the hotel-room door.

"That's the way it always is, isn't it?" Sandra fired her final shot as Mike opened the door. "You go your way; I go mine. I think you enjoy deserting me."

Do You See Yourself?

Yes, even in paradise, relationships go wrong. Marriages conceived in love and blessed in heaven develop severe fissures and begin to crumble. As many as 40 to 50 percent of today's marriages end in the brokenness of divorce.

Do you see any of yourself or your marriage in what we've presented about Mike or Sandra? Have you ever felt betrayed and abandoned as Sandra does? Or battered and withdrawn like Mike? Or have you and the one you love had a fight that's ended unresolved, leaving the two of you emotionally further apart than ever?

As Mike and Sandra's story unfolds, we'll show how seeds planted early and throughout their lives mature into these lost, frightening, and deeply destructive moments—seeds planted in all of us and at work in all of us. We'll also follow them—and others—as they're guided to a much better place.

Abandoned Parent, Abandoned Child

Two of those "others" are Hannah and her seven-year-old son, Darcy, who came for counseling about a month after Darcy started second grade, a notorious time for behavior problems to surface in children. Hannah was twenty-six, blonde, and wore slacks and an untucked blue blouse. Darcy was built like a bear cub—dark hair, wide shoulders, and quick, searching hands. Hannah was a single mother. "My divorce became final just three months ago," she said. "My ex lives in Florida now. He's training to be a police officer there. He's also got a new honey and rarely sees Darcy anymore. The girl-friend's got a baby that takes all his time."

"His baby?"

She shook her head. "No, but he treats it like it is." She gave Darcy a con-cerned glance.

She went on. "I'm a nurse. In the emergency room, the ER. Like on the TV show. I'm babbling, aren't I?" She took a deep breath to calm herself. Then she slumped. "I'm just overwhelmed. I've got people bleeding all over me during the day and sometimes half the night, and I've got Darcy screaming at me when I'm home."

"Sounds awful. How does this usually unfold? How does it happen that Darcy ends up screaming at you?"

"He just won't do what he's told," she explained. "I come home exhausted and ask him to pick up his toys or his dirty clothes, and he explodes." She sighed as if just the memory of it was tiring. "He's so angry all the time. Talks back, throws tantrums—even kicks things. And he argues about *everything*. It rained the other day. I ask him to put on his jacket before going out, and we end up in a big battle. 'I don't want to wear a jacket!' he screams. 'But it's rain-ing,' I say. 'Who cares?' he says. He just argues to argue. And he argues with other adults, not just me. My next-door neighbor gets the brunt of it: 'Don't swing on that branch; it'll break,' she'll say to him. 'I'll swing if I wanna,' he yells back at her. 'Don't throw that ball so close to my house. You'll break a window.' 'I won't break no window.' 'Don't throw the ball.' And he just itches to keep throwing the ball. He's annoying—purposely annoying—and I'm exhausted. I'm tired from work, and then I come home and walk into this hur-ricane. Right away everyone is yelling—but no one can hear.

"He walked over to a kindergartner the other day at school and stepped on his lunch. Mashed both the sandwich and the Twinkies. It was his third time doing something like that. Yesterday he deliberately wrote with a black marker on a little girl's white dress. Wrote A-C-B. He couldn't even get the alphabet right. That's one of the reasons we're here. They told me I needed to have him evaluated."

Helping a Child Feel Loved and Cared For

We strongly believe that before more structured behavioral techniques are used to help a defiant child, the parent-child relationship must first improve. Darcy was filled with a lot of anger. If a child is angry, if he feels unloved and uncared for, no parenting technique can *make* him behave. To help improve Hannah and Darcy's relationship, during their third session with us, we assigned "special times."[2]

Special time is a command-free, concentrated investment of parent-child time. It's command-free in that you're not allowed as a parent to give any commands. If you say, "Let's play army," you just blew it. A good analogy for the parent in command-free time would be an announcer at a horse race. You're involved in the moment together . . . watching, describing, *being with,* but you're giving no commands. Consistently. For Hannah this would mean spending one-on-one time with Darcy for twenty to thirty minutes at a time. In our counseling practice we have found the results of this kind of special time to be phenomenal.

But this kind of relating can be difficult for parents, because they may not be used to connecting with their children during playtime. And what makes it even more difficult for parents is that they have to refrain from asking intrusive questions or giving commands during this time. Hannah had to let Darcy take the lead, then follow him. If he should become excessively disruptive during special time, she was to simply discontinue and return later. And, of course, she wouldn't tolerate unacceptable behavior.

But when they came for their fourth session, Hannah admitted she hadn't found time in the previous week to do daily special times. She had been too busy. "My life is so crazy," she said. "And anyway, what are we supposed to do during special times?" She had tried once, she said, but it had turned into a huge battle. After only a few chaotic minutes, she angrily withdrew from the activity.

"Let's do special time here in the office," we suggested.

Although there was reluctance in Hannah's eyes, she agreed, and a few minutes later she and Darcy were on the floor of our playroom.

Hannah tried to start out on a positive note. But then Darcy took off across the floor with a Hot Wheels car. Hannah, unwilling to chase him, called him back. "You're always doing that," she accused. "I'm not going to run all over the place after you." Suddenly he turned, looked at her for an instant, then pushed the car at her. It spun across the floor like a hockey puck and zapped her in the knee. She shot a piercing glance back at Darcy and grumbled, "You'd better cut it out, *now!*"

Darcy turned away from Hannah and played with his cars in the corner of the office. Hannah, still noticeably angry, just stared off into space. This was a stunning example of anger and distance between a stressed-out mom and her angry, defiant seven-year-old son.

It would have been easy for us to frame Darcy's problem in traditional terms: just a brat in need of some good, hard discipline. But we saw, and we're sure you do too now, that Darcy and his mom's issues have intersected. She is a single mom and a deserted wife, left behind by a deadbeat husband and exhausted with her two full-time jobs: work in the ER and motherhood. Later we will learn that she has a harsh history filled with abandonment, anger, and abuse. Darcy has also been abandoned. His father has virtually disappeared from his daily life, a situation faced by millions of kids in America who live in a home apart from Dad. Many of them haven't even seen their dads in the last twelve months.

Overwhelmed by the demands of single motherhood, Hannah is barely able to muster the energy and focus to get dinner on the table, let alone sit down on the floor and center her attention on Darcy's world. Obviously, help must not only include some new discipline techniques; it also must address a more central issue.

The Fundamental Issue: Attachments

Although these cases seem different, the recovery of all involved hinges on the same fundamental issue—the way they perceive the answers to these questions:

Are you there for me? Can I count on you? Do you really care about me? Am I worthy of your love and protection? What do I have to do to get your attention, your affection, your heart? These are questions of *attachment*. When they cannot be answered positively, your psychological, relational, and even spiritual foundations can be shaken. Throughout this book, we'll look at how Mike, Sandra, Hannah, Darcy, and others we will meet later view themselves, the world, and other people in their lives, and how they form, maintain, and sometimes end close relationships—relationships with wives, husbands, children, God, parents, and others close to them.

Relationships define the quality of our lives. If we have safe, secure marriages, we're generally happy and fulfilled; if our marriages are tortured seas of strife and mistrust, we're generally sad, confused, in pain. If our relationships with our children are sensitive, open, and loving, woven together with strong, resilient filaments, they can weather the storms of teen rebellion and those awkward years that follow. But if our relationships with our children are forced and dissonant, each side mistrusting the other, rebellion can become open warfare, and the years that follow can deteriorate into permanent estrangement. *Attachment* is an overarching system that explains the principles, the rules, and the emotions of relationships—how they work and how they don't, how we feel when we're with the ones we love the most.

How about Yours . . . ?

How are the relationships in your life? Do you feel close to your loved ones? Alone? If you're married, do you feel safe and secure, or do you find yourself frequently angry with your spouse, or withdrawn? Have you been married before and find the elements that tainted your first marriage creeping into your present union? Or have you been divorced several times and find you've chosen the same kind of person each time, dooming your marriage before it even began? Do you keep finding yourself in one abusive relationship after another? Or drawn into relationships that you know will turn out to be destructive? How are you with your kids? Feel any distance? What about God? Do you believe He is there for you? Can you trust Him?

There's a fascinating reason that you love, feel, and act the way you do. It's the same reason Mike and Sandra, and Hannah and Darcy feel pain in their relationships, and the same reason many of us experience difficulty or joy in our relationships, even our relationship to God.

Attachment Styles: How the Relationship Rules Work

In this book we're going to explore that reason. It's comprised by those "relationship rules" that are at work in all of us. We call those rules our *attachment style*.

First, we'll explain in detail what an attachment style is and how it is formulated during the early years of life. We'll explain how it helped us survive emotionally, even physically, in those early years and how it continues to shape key elements of our lives.

Second, we'll introduce you to the four primary attachment styles. We'll explain how they develop within us and why, then we'll help you identify yours. Next we'll show you easy ways to identify the attachment styles at work within those closest to you, and we'll share insights on how the styles interact. Coupling that information with descriptions on how each style impacts some of life's important issues—marriage, parenting, dealing with loss—we'll help you relate more comfortably and securely to those closest to you.

But we won't leave you there. Next, we'll look at the negative influences attachment styles can have on our lives so you can quickly see the need for change. Then we'll show you how to reshape the relationship rules into a positive influence, one that helps form healthier relationships. Remember, though: Change takes courage; but courage grows with knowledge. By following the case studies, by seeing what Mike, Sandra, Hannah, Darcy, and the others have experienced and how they have improved their relationships, we'll share how you can put new life in your own attachments.

Finally, we'll examine the spiritual implications of the attachment styles and explain how they relate to God and you.

So you see, this is important stuff! And if your current relationships are bringing you more heartache than joy, every minute counts.

It's time to get started. In the next chapter, we'll introduce you to another case study then give you a look at how this research began. If you haven't already done so, we think you'll meet yourself pretty quickly.

2

SHAPING OUR VIEW OF OURSELVES AND THOSE WE HOLD DEAREST

Attachment Principles and Dynamics

Unthinking confidence in the unfailing accessibility and support of attachment figures is the bedrock on which stable and self-reliant personality is built.
—JOHN BOWLBY

There's not a more touching image than a newborn baby nestled chubby, pink, and warm in her mother's arms, her tiny hands clenched tight in little fists. The attachment between mother and child is made up of a thousand threads connecting heart and heart, hope and what *will* be, desire and what *is*. How could anything corrupt this relationship?

Of course something can, and often does. Why? Because mother and child are human, and in many cases they are living lives in very new and unfamiliar roles. If she's the first child, the mother is thrust into an emotionally, relationally, and physically challenging environment. And since we're talking about the mother's effect on a human being's life, it's a high-stakes environment as well.

Even if the child is the latest of several, the mother now has one more challenge. The new baby puts one more ball in the air to be juggled: The mix of personalities and jealousies is just that much more intricate and unpredictable, intuition is just that much less useful, and the work is just that much more exhausting. A mother can do only the best she can.

But unlike many of God's creatures, a child is born into a world where it is utterly dependent on its mother for survival. It can't even keep itself warm, much less fed and comforted. We are discovering increasingly each day how dependent a child's developing brain is on its mother's sensitive, attuned, and responsive care. Our earliest relationships are profoundly important. They literally shape the chemical processes in the brain responsible for how we control our impulses, calm our strong emotions, and develop our memories of our early family life.

In the previous chapter, we met a marriage in trouble and a single mother coping with a difficult child. Those visceral images of people locked in conflict and confusion couldn't seem further from the tranquil image of mother and child we've just drawn. Yet, in fact, they couldn't be closer. The seeds of that troubled marriage and the difficult mother-child relationship were sown in the hospital's maternity department, and they grew and matured over the next few years. From their earliest relationship experiences, the mother and child developed their attachment model, which shapes how they view themselves and those they love the dearest.

Relationships Are Everything

It's time to step back. We want you to understand this fascinating model by first giving you a little background on how it was discovered.[1] Our basic premise is "Relationships are everything."

Suppose that it was 1948 in England, and raven-haired, green-eyed, three-year-old Annie Swan was going to a sanitarium for tuberculosis patients. She had a persistent cough and other symptoms that concerned her parents and her doctors.

In those days, conventional wisdom said raising children consisted of keeping them fed, dry, warm, and away from traffic. If you provided these fundamentals, kids would grow up just fine. Nowhere was that attitude more on display than in Annie's parents as they checked her into the sanitarium. The children's ward was a long, narrow room filled with beds protruding from the walls on either side like teeth. Even though Annie would be in the sanitarium for an extended stay, her parents merely dropped her off with a nurse at this ward and left. Their three-year-old daughter wouldn't see them again for about a week, and even then for just a short period.

Annie didn't understand being left. The moment her mother turned to leave, Annie's little face twisted, and she began to cry. Her little hands reached out, and she tried to run and grab her mother's skirts. The nurse restrained her and carried her screaming to what would be her bed.

STAGES OF SEPARATION

Suppose that watching this scenario was John Bowlby, an English psychiatrist, and his colleague James Robertson. Bowlby had begun to study children in Annie Swan's situation a few weeks before and was beginning to see patterns. Annie reacted just like the other children had done, and as the weeks and months progressed, he saw two more stages in Annie's behavior that mirrored stages he and his associates had seen in the other children when separated from their mothers.[2]

Stage One: Protest

Like Annie, the moment the children were dropped off in this sterile, cold environment, they began to express real, distressful, even desperate anxiety, then anger at being left. For Annie this meant tears and reaching out to others; it also meant throwing things and stomping around, even lying down and beating her fists and feet on the floor. Toddler rage. And it was nearly universal. Almost every child behaved this way, regardless of the other children around or how the nurses who took care of them reacted. They wanted their mommies, and the nurses, though they were well intentioned and took care of the children's physical needs, were no substitutes.

Stage Two: Despair

Several days after her mother and father left, Annie slipped into what looked like a state of mourning and despair. Dr. Bowlby watched her huddle in her bed. When other children tried to play with her, she looked at them with dull eyes then just shook her head listlessly. When her tray of food appeared for breakfast, and again for lunch and dinner, she paid little attention to it. At one point, she lifted her spoon as if it weighed a ton and let it slap on top of her milky cereal. Now and then, seemingly out of the blue, she would just start to cry. Her puffy little lips would push into a painful frown, and her little eyes would squeeze out huge, wet tears.

As with the anger, this stage of Annie's reaction to being left was like every other child's. They all eventually lapsed into melancholy—their sense of abandonment and loss taking deep root. The nurses, having seen this a thousand times before, paid little attention to it. In fact, they welcomed it as it marked an end to the more florid emotional tantrums of the previous stage. They felt the children just needed to understand that things will not always go their way and that they just needed to stiffen their upper lips.

Stage Three: Detachment

Over the next several months, Annie appeared to be snapping out of it. One day a little girl with a big, floppy Raggedy Ann doll coaxed her from her bed, and they began to play. Although Annie wasn't 100 percent right, she began to show signs of recovery. Soon she fit easily into life in the sanitarium's children's ward. Annie enjoyed coloring. Like any three-year-old, she rarely stayed in the lines, but she had an eye for colors, and each time she finished a masterpiece she'd show it around proudly. She found which kids liked her art as much as she did, and she limited her exhibitions to them only. All seemed well with the children again; their anger and depression were gone. As "normalcy" eased through the ward, the doctors and nurses alike believed their method of dealing with children had been proven correct once more.

But then Annie's mother showed up for a Sunday afternoon visit. You might think Annie would grab her favorite artwork and run happily toward her mother, merrily shrieking, "Mommy! Mommy! Look what I did." You'd think she'd leap into her mother's arms, and after her mother smothered her in kisses, they'd pore over her colorings excitedly. You'd think so. But you'd be wrong.

Not only didn't Annie run to her mom, she did just the opposite. She hardly looked up. And the picture she was coloring at the moment got turned over while others she'd done that day were pushed under her covers—hidden.

When Mommy came to her bed and kissed her, Annie actually pulled away. Some might say she was just angry—and she was. But Dr. Bowlby saw more than that. He saw that Annie had detached from her mother. Of course she still wanted her mother's goodies—a toy and some of Mommy's home-baked cookies. But she had walled herself off from her mother at an emotional level.

Annie was not unique. Many of the children in the hospital ward detached from their parents in some way. Some, like Annie, avoided their parents, detached emotionally, and were indifferent to their mothers' presence. Others, who were relative newcomers, became punishingly clingy, pleading to be held and taken home. But they learned they weren't going home, at least not any-time soon. Each week they were left behind, feeling angry, overwhelmed, and helpless. At the end of each visit they were pried from their mothers' necks, then they watched powerlessly as their parents hastily scurried out of the hospital ward.

In response, Annie and many others like her developed a calloused self. Repeatedly wounded emotionally, they weren't about to let themselves be hurt again. Instead they developed a system of replacing *things* for relationships. Annie realized that if she allowed herself to really want her mom she would be profoundly hurt. So she switched her desire from Mom to things—toys, knickknacks, candy, coloring pencils. She buried the need she had felt for trust, intimacy, and closeness. Never again would she willingly reach out to anyone for emotional comfort. Instead she relied only on herself and the material things she now loved.

We believe you can trace the genesis of addiction patterns in our lives back to this process, known as the "replacement defense."

Not only did Annie use the replacement defense, but she also learned how to "wall off" her emotions. She no longer expressed or acknowledged her feelings to anyone, including herself. This helped her not to feel so vulnerable and helpless. No longer did she feel compelled to cling to Mommy's neck. No longer did she have to worry about whether Mommy was coming to visit. No longer did she have to get angry when Mommy left. She eradicated her need for Mommy, and consequently, she eliminated her negative feelings about being separated from her.

Now think back to the two relationships we visited briefly in chapter 1. As we will see later, replacement defenses were a part of Mike's makeup. He had become a workaholic. His mind was focused on making the next deal, not on his wife, not on enjoying their vacation together. What drove him was his work, his success, and his prestige. He was unable to attend to his wife's needs because he was cut off from his own. As we will see later, Sandra's pleas for closeness and intimacy utterly confused him, because he had buried his own needs for them long ago.

THE ATTACHMENT BEHAVIORAL SYSTEM

In an effort to explain what he'd seen in many children, Bowlby developed what he called the *attachment behavioral system,* which is diagrammed below.[3]

The Attachment Behavioral System

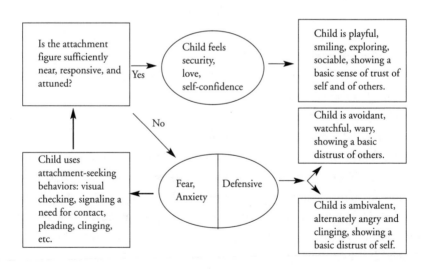

Shaping Our View . . .

Attachment Behaviors

From about the sixth month of life, children begin asking some critical questions: "Is my mom close-by? Is she available to me? Can I get to her quickly if I need her? Will she be there for me if I need her? Will she comfort me?"[4] These questions reflect what we call the *proximity principle*. It works much like a thermostat. You set your thermostat at home to a "set point," say seventy-two degrees, and when the temperature goes too far below this point, the furnace comes on until the temperature returns to the set point. Then it shuts off.

Likewise, proximity, or closeness, is the set point for the attachment behavioral system. If a child believes Mom is close enough, the child feels safe and secure. With this security, she is willing to enthusiastically explore the world around her. If she believes Mom is not close enough, the attachment behavioral system turns on. Attachment behavior is any behavior that results in getting mother and child physically closer. Usually in infants this behavior is crying, crawling, or screaming. Once Mom has returned to a safe distance, the child feels secure again, the attachment system turns off, and the child begins to explore and play.

Older children don't necessarily have to see their parents to feel secure. They may just need to be within earshot. Gary's dad often tells the story of how he was frequently mortified when he took Gary to Rinks, a store similar to Wal-Mart. Gary was about seven or eight years old—a child who marched to the beat of his own drum, as it were—and he would wander off, browsing through various toys and things he wanted to look at. However, if Gary became concerned about where Dad was, he'd just let out a high-pitched scream—"DAAAAD!?"—right in the middle of the store at the top of his lungs. Dad, of course, felt like crawling under a tire rack, but he knew if he didn't answer loud enough for Gary to hear, he'd belt out another window-rattling scream.

It's fascinating that children do not have to *learn* this behavior. It's just there. Have you ever seen a parent saying to her young infant, "Now listen, Junior, if Mommy isn't close-by, you make sure you do whatever it takes to get my attention, okay?" No! Thankfully, God programmed it into us from birth to somehow know that when our caregivers are not nearby, danger lurks. This illustrates a crucial point in our discussion: *Fear of abandonment is the fundamental human fear.* It is so basic and so profound that it emerges even before we develop a language to describe it. It is so powerful that it activates our body's autonomic nervous system, causing our hearts to race, our breathing to become shallow and rapid, our stomachs to quiver, and our hands to shake. We feel a sense of panic that will not be assuaged until we are close to our caregivers—until we regain a feeling of security.

This attachment system is not just part of *human* behavior; it's evident throughout the animal kingdom. The next time you see an Animal Planet documentary on bears, observe how both mother and cub are exquisitely sensitive to proximity. The cubs know how far they can roam from Mom. When they move beyond that point, they scurry to get closer. And when danger appears, both mother bear and cubs work together to get closer. Seeking closeness during times of stress is a survival mechanism, both in other animals and in humans.

Defensive Behaviors

If parents repeatedly fail to respond to their child's attachment behavior, as in the case of little Annie's mom and dad, the child develops a pattern of defensive behavior. *Ambivalence* is one defense. It occurs when the child desperately clings to the parents and yet wants to punish them for having left her. Bowlby's team observed this pattern when parents would take their young children home from the hospital after a shorter stay than Annie's. These children would not let their parents out of their sight. They would throw frequent temper tantrums and were quite uncooperative and defiant. Interestingly, when doctors and nurses heard that these children behaved this way, they blamed it on poor parenting. They had no inkling that the separation had anything to do with the child's anger and anxiety.

Avoidance is another defense. It is exhibited in the detachment we saw in Annie's case. These children decide, *I don't need you, and I don't want you.* They become islands unto themselves, isolated from their own feelings as well as the feelings of others. They replace their need for others with the desire for things.

They live on the periphery of relationships and see others as means to an end (material goods) rather than as ends in themselves.

Attachment Styles: How We Develop Our Core Beliefs

It is easy to observe the attachment behavioral system at work in the first few years of a child's life. Over time, the many interactions between a mother and her infant become internalized by the child and form what Bowlby called the *internal working model,*[5] or *relationship rules.* We simply call this system an *attachment style.* It's a mental model, a set of basic assumptions, or core beliefs, about yourself and others. Right now we'll quickly overview the core beliefs that make up the attachment styles. Later in the book, we'll go into these styles in greater detail so you can identify your own personal style and learn how the different styles interact.

The first set of core beliefs, or relationship rules, form the *self* dimension. It centers around two critical questions:

1. Am I worthy of being loved?
2. Am I competent to get the love I need?

The second set of beliefs form the *other* dimension. It also centers around two important questions:

1. Are others reliable and trustworthy?
2. Are others accessible and willing to respond to me when I need them to be?

Based on your responses to each set of questions above, your sense of *self* is either positive or negative. Likewise, your sense of *other* is also either positive or negative. By combining the four possible combinations of *self* and *other* dimensions, a four-category grid (illustrated on the following page) emerges.[6]

These combined beliefs about your *self* and your *other* dimensions shape your expectations about future relationships. They act as a pair of glasses that color the way you see others, and they inform you about how to behave in close relationships. In other words, they determine your *attachment style.* Various names have been given to the four primary attachment styles. In this book we refer to them as *secure, avoidant, ambivalent,* and *disorganized.*[7] We'll examine each of these styles in greater detail later; for now, we want to give you a quick overview of how they operate in our lives.

Secure Attachment Style POSITIVE SELF/POSITIVE OTHER	Avoidant Attachment Style POSITIVE SELF/NEGATIVE OTHER
Ambivalent Attachment Style NEGATIVE SELF/POSITIVE OTHER	Disorganized Attachment Style NEGATIVE SELF/NEGATIVE OTHER

Sandra, for example, showed an ambivalent attachment style. Her basic assumption about others was positive: They are capable of providing love and support. But her negative *self* dimension also made her believe that those others might choose not to help her because of her flaws. Thus she saw them as unpredictable. Mike's showing up late was yet another example of what she had come to expect. Sandra's attachment style also assumed that the only way to get others to respond appropriately to her needs was to punish them with anger. Thus, she lit into Mike with a fury, unleashing her anger in the form of verbal insults.

In contrast, Mike had an avoidant attachment style; he assumed he was self-reliant and capable of comforting himself and handling his own needs. And he tended to think others were generally unwilling or incapable of loving him and meeting his needs. So he tended to find solace in his work and his success more than he did in Sandra. Thus, working late and showing up late for an extracurricular snorkeling expedition was no big deal to Mike. Sandra's grilling of him helped confirm his core beliefs about others as being virtually incompetent at understanding him and meeting his emotional needs.

Shaping Our View . . .

Measuring an Infant's Security

You may wonder, "How is this relevant to me? My parents didn't abandon me to some sterile hospital for several years. In fact, no one leaves their kids like that anymore."

You are partially right. The kinds of separations that Bowlby studied were not terribly common then and they are much less common today, though you would still be surprised how frequently they *do* occur. Yet Bowlby made the critical link. He saw how early childhood experiences affected the way children relate to others in the future. The difficulty was that Bowlby did not have a way of studying parents and children in their home environment. He also did not have a way of reliably measuring attachment security.

This is where we should introduce you to another giant in this field of study: Mary Ainsworth. Living in the United States, Dr. Ainsworth became interested in Bowlby's ideas. But she was more interested in studying them in the day-to-day lives of mothers as they cared for their children. She wanted to see how mothers interacted with their newborn infants: how they responded to their children when they cried, how they looked into their eyes when they played, how they comforted them when they were upset. She wanted to see these interactions as they unfolded in the home, not in some university laboratory. So she trained researchers and sent them into the homes of families with infants. They meticulously coded how the mother interacted with her baby and how sensitive she was to his or her cries and other bids for comfort.[8]

As her work progressed, Ainsworth developed a method for measuring an infant's security. Her way of thinking about security grew out of her understanding of Bowlby's attachment behavioral system. However, she added something new, which she called the "secure-base" phenomenon. The idea is straightforward: Securely attached children, when they are emotionally upset, will seek comfort and closeness from their parents. Thus, they use the parents as a secure base. Once they are calmed, they will begin to explore and play. Insecurely attached children will not rely on their parents in this fashion. Instead they either avoid them or cling angrily to them.

To measure this secure-base phenomenon, Ainsworth designed a procedure called the *strange situation*. Instead of measuring it at home, though, she brought Mom and her baby to the university lab. This sounds odd, but the rationale was that attachment behavior only occurs when the child feels anxious. Bringing the child to a strange environment should trigger some anxiety. To raise the stakes a little higher, she added two more components. First, she had Mom and her baby sit in a room with a stranger sitting in a chair nearby. Second, she had Mom abruptly exit the room for short intervals, leaving her baby alone with the stranger.

Ainsworth focused a lot of her attention on how the infant responded to Mom when she returned to the room. Keep in mind, the infant was very distressed about Mom's departure. The key question was, How did the baby use Mom to calm his or her feelings when she returned?

What Ainsworth found was astonishing, and it has literally revolutionized the fields of child and developmental psychology, family therapy, and personality development. Her work led to the identification of the four distinct types of attachment styles, which are named for the infants' responses (one of them a secure response and the other three insecure).

The Secure Response

Secure infants were very upset when their moms departed, and when their moms returned these babies generally made a beeline to them. Both moms and babies were happy to see each other. The babies wanted to be picked up, and once they were held in their mothers' arms, they were comforted and all signs of distress melted away.

Obviously, these infants' attachment styles were already well developed. Their *self* dimension was that they were worthy of comfort and protection. They also believed they were capable of seeking comfort effectively. Their *other* dimension was that their moms were available and willing to comfort their emotional upsets. They did not hesitate to go toward their moms, implying that they believed their mothers were trustworthy and reliable during times of distress.

Shaping Our View . . .

Ambivalent Response

Babies showing an ambivalent attachment response also were clearly upset when their mothers exited the room. However, the intensity of their cries was several notches higher than that of the secure babies. They were angry, and they let everyone know it by producing full-fledged, fall-on-the-floor-and-thrash-around-violently types of tantrums.

When their mothers returned, they also went straight to them, but not all was well as it was with the secure group. Even though their mothers held them, these babies were not comforted. They were ambivalent: They mixed their attachment behavior (getting closer to Mom) with anger. They reached up to their moms, wanting to be picked up. But once picked up, they were not settled. They squirmed, they kicked, they threw toys, and they even took swings at their mothers. Yet if their moms tried to set them down, they became even more distraught.

The attachment style of these youngsters was different from the secure group. Their self dimension implied that they were not worthy of love and that they were unable to get their mothers' attention effectively. Their other dimension was that their moms, while capable of giving comfort and protection, needed more than just a simple whimper to get their attention. They needed florid, tumultuous tantrums—almost punishing behavior—before they would respond effectively.

The Avoidant Response

Unlike the first two groups, the babies exhibiting an avoidant response showed very little, if any, distress upon their mothers' departure. As an observer, you would be tempted to think these children were emotionally comfortable with themselves in their mothers' absence. However, studies have repeatedly shown that when these babies are hooked up to physiological measures of emotional distress they are just as aroused as the other babies when their mothers leave. They just suppress their feelings.

27

Similarly, when their moms returned, these babies did not seem to care. Remember, physiologically they were just as upset as the secure and ambivalent children, but they did not seek their mothers for comfort and support. Some just looked away; others literally turned their backs on their mothers and moved toward the corner of the room. Their self dimension was that they were self-sufficient and they did not need the care of their mothers when distressed. Their other dimension was that their moms were not reliable, accessible, or trustworthy, so they considered it a useless mission to seek them out for reassurance and fortification. This combination of self and other dimensions resulted in a baby who looked disinterested, even blasé, on the outside but on the inside was overwhelmed by anxiety and distress.

The Disorganized Response

Follow-up studies that used the strange situation to observe attachment in children who were from abusive families discovered the disorganized response style.[9] These children had no consistent style of relating to their mothers when they returned to the room. They showed a combination of secure, ambivalent, and avoidant responses. For example, one child began approaching her mother as if she wanted to be picked up, then she stopped in her tracks and fell prostrate on the floor. Another child first picked up a toy and approached his mother with it, handing it to his mother while averting his gaze to another part of the room. Some of the children classified as disorganized showed frank fear of their mothers when they returned, standing motionless for ten or more seconds as if they were terrified or even disoriented. Others sought refuge in the stranger seated in the room.

The attachment styles these children demonstrated showed that they questioned their sense of self and other. Like the ambivalent group, they did not consider themselves worthy of comfort and protection, and they were not confident in their abilities to effectively get their mothers' attention; and like the avoidant group, they did not regard others as trustworthy, reliable, or accessible.

Moms Matter

What made these four patterns of response even more astonishing was that Ainsworth systematically linked each to a distinct style of parenting. Mothers of secure children were very responsive to their needs. When their babies cried, they picked them up more quickly. They were also inclined to hold their babies longer, and they showed more affection and positive emotion when doing so. In short, these mothers were more sensitive to their children.

Mothers of the insecure infants appeared, on the surface, to be good parents. They were nice people who were very well intentioned. They changed their babies' diapers, they fed them, they provided them a warm home, an adequate environment. They even enjoyed talking about their children and expressed their love in various ways. However, the difficulty arose when their babies needed to be comforted: Mothers of insecure children were less responsive, less sensitive, less attuned. Their babies' cries became a source of conflict. Power struggles repeatedly emerged, and the mothers became more frustrated, rejecting, mean-spirited, and even hostile.

The hallmark of mothers with ambivalent-response children was inconsistency. At times they were very responsive and attuned to their babies' needs, but then, for no apparent explanation, they became distant and aloof. Or they became exceedingly intrusive and interfering. For example, one mother we worked with had a habit of finding her baby playing peacefully and then swooping him off the floor, trying to smother him with hugs and kisses. When he became fussy and uncooperative, she turned up the heat, getting nose to nose with him, staring deep into his eyes, and screeching in a high-pitched baby voice, "What's wrong, Baby? Don't you love Mommy anymore?" As he become increasingly agitated by her intrusiveness, she complained of feeling unloved and unappreciated by her baby.

Rejection was the key theme displayed by mothers of avoidant-response children. They had great difficulty expressing sensitivity to their children's cries. Frequently they would snub their children and refuse to offer physical contact when their children were upset. They tended to view crying as a form of manipulation and weakness rather than a legitimate expression of neediness.

While we were writing this book, one of our clients, Erica, the mother of a six-month-old girl named Rachel, showed she was clearly interested in the topic. But when she read the section on avoidance, her eyes clouded over, and she looked puzzled.

"You must have made a mistake here," she said. "The avoidant kids didn't get as upset as the secure kids. You'd think just the opposite would happen. If they were insecure they would get upset. And what about this part here—this is crazy—why would a secure child come crying to his to her mom after she had left the room for just a few minutes and then returned? That sounds like a spoiled kid to me."

We tried to assure her that it wasn't a mistake. But our words fell on deaf ears. She rolled her eyes as if she were annoyed and said, "I just think if you keep picking up your baby every time she cries, you'll spoil her. She'll never learn how to deal with not getting every little thing she wants."

"Okay, Erica, no mother wants to spoil her child," we said. "But the goal during the first year of life is to create a sense of security. You do that by being responsive and sensitive. You can't really spoil a child in the first year by being too responsive."

She snapped back, "Well, you're wrong again. My Rachel is already spoiled. All she does is cry, wanting to be picked up all the time. But I'm teaching her better now, while she's still young."

Later in the day we were all eating a meal together. Erica was trying to bottle-feed Rachel, who was growing sleepy and grumpy. Erica was getting noticeably irritated with Rachel as she gruffly shifted the infant from one position to the next. Finally Rachel broke into a full cry, pushing the bottle away and squirming in her mother's arms. She didn't want any more food, but her mother insisted that she consume the whole bottle.

Erica looked embarrassed by her daughter's fit. She picked her up by the armpits, held her at eye level, and tried to stare angrily into her eyes. "You quit that whining. You're being a little brat," she scolded. Then she announced to everyone at the table that the reason she wanted Rachel to finish the bottle was that if she didn't, she'd wake up during the night. But Rachel was full and wanted to go to sleep. Erica, however, had turned this into a power play. She saw her daughter's tears as signs of manipulation and defiance, not as a form of communication, possibly saying, "Mommy, I'm full and want to go to sleep now."

The Great Paradox

Erica's parental mind-set was like that of many parents in Bowlby's time. Even Ainsworth's initial studies were met with sharp criticism, especially from behavioral psychologists who believed that an infant's cries were a learned behavior. They did not see crying as a preprogrammed behavior, designed by God as a form of protection or as a way of communicating emotional and physical needs. Attachment behavior (seeking a stronger, wiser person for protection) was seen as a form of dependency, and it was believed that reinforcing this behavior by too much responsiveness would lead to an overly dependent, whiny crybaby, who would be afraid to face the world with bold confidence and self-reliance.

Dads Count Too!

While the emphasis of this chapter is on Mom, we believe Dad has a profound attachment influence too. While many dads these days are stepping up and getting invested in their kids, without question the grave social ill of our day is the absence of Dad from the home—and the effects are showing.

The way a dad develops a secure attachment to his kids is different than the way a mom does. According to noted "fathering" expert William Pollack, "Fathers are not male mothers."[‡]

Dads differ in that they have a more action-oriented love and thus need to play more with their kids. Roughhousing (pillow fights, wrestling), tag, hide-and-seek, kickball, hunting, and fishing are just a few examples of what we mean. When a dad connects with his child in this way, the bonds of love are formed. He becomes a harbor of safety, someone who is warm and can be trusted, especially in times of trouble.

But Bowlby saw it differently, and Ainsworth's studies scientifically supported this claim: A baby's cry is hardwired. It is not a sign of weakness or overdependency. And a mother cannot be too responsive to her infant. Infants of mothers who were most responsive and most sensitive during the first year of life were much more likely to become securely attached. As we will discuss in detail later, secure babies become just the opposite of what folks like Erica expect: They are more autonomous, and they cry less, explore more, and are much less clingy than their insecure counterparts.

On the other hand, insecure babies were more likely to have insensitive, poorly responsive parents—parents like Erica, who is well intentioned but views her baby's cues as signs of defiance and manipulation ("She's just trying to get her own way"), not as a way of communicating needs. These kinds of parents usually have infants who grow up to be more demanding, more whiny, more defiant and even aggressive, and less likely to be appropriately dependent in relationships.

Paving the Pathway to a Loving Relationship with God

Later we will also see how sensitive, responsive parenting paves the way for children to seek God as a refuge during times of distress. Think about it. Before we are able to speak, we have learned whether or not the stronger, wiser others in our lives really care about how we feel. Listen to any sermon that speaks of God's love and hear it said that God understands us, He cares about how we feel, and He protects us, provides for us, and soothes our worries and fears. For those with secure attachment, this message comes as no surprise.

But for those who have been imbued with a message that their emotional needs are not legitimate—that to feel upset, to feel hurt, and to feel helpless are signs of weakness—the message of God's everlasting love is a difficult one to accept. Some can do it on a rational, cognitive level, but emotionally they feel otherwise. To make matters worse, they are challenged to believe that if they don't emotionally feel accepted by God, if they doubt His loving-kindness and benevolence, then they should question their salvation.

Interestingly, a study conducted on Christian college students found that those with insecure attachment styles felt anxious, overwhelmed, and angry.[10] Those with an ambivalent attachment style tended to doubt their salvation very frequently, wondering if they had really said the right thing to God when they were saved or if they had somehow committed the unpardonable sin. Those with avoidant characteristics were more likely to have given up on God and had begun following sinful habits—idols of the heart.

The good news is that our early attachment styles don't have to sentence us to lifelong relationship difficulties. With redemption, knowledge, and courage, we can reinforce the positive aspects and overcome the self-defeating tendencies of our attachment styles. Then we can begin again, renewing and enriching our attachments to the ones we love with strong, more enduring relationships woven together by love and trust. Interested? Read on!

3

SOUL WOUNDS

How Attachment Injuries Occur

A child can be the object of much affection and still not feel loved.
Feeling loved and being heard are so similar,
it's difficult to distinguish between the two.
—FRAN STOTT

Being made fun of, teased incessantly, laughed at, ridiculed, lied about, pushed, put down, used—who hasn't been hurt by another person? And, oh yes, it *does* hurt. But when you are hurt by someone who is supposed to be there for you, someone like a parent, grandparent, spouse, someone you are "attached" to as your caregiver or other loved one, it's different. That kind of hurt causes pain that goes deeper. Pain that feels like it won't ever go away. Why? Because an attachment relationship is more than just someone who is close to us. A lot more is at stake in these relationships. More investedness. More vulnerability.

Mary Ainsworth gives five criteria that help distinguish attachment bonds from other close relationships.[1] While Ainsworth's focus was on the infant's attachment to his or her caregiver, it's easy to see how her descriptions can also apply to adult attachments, such as a spouse or other loved one you (the adult "infant") trust as a vital source of love and comfort:

1. The infant seeks proximity, or closeness, to the caregiver, especially in times of trouble.
2. The infant sees the caregiver as providing a "safe haven."
3. The infant trusts the caregiver to provide a secure base from which he or she can explore the world.

35

4. The threat of separation from the caregiver induces fear and anxiety in the infant.

5. Loss of the caregiver induces grief and sorrow.

When a relationship means so much to you, it only makes sense that when that relationship goes bad, there is more to lose—and more hurt than normal.

ATTACHMENT INJURIES CAN LEAVE SOUL WOUNDS

According to the dictionary, an injury is "an act that damages or hurts a person, a wound . . . an offense against a person's feelings or dignity . . . a violation of another's rights . . . a sustained loss in value to a business or reputation." In the context of attachments, an attachment injury is an injury to the *self*, an emotional or relational injury—a soul wound.

Attachment injuries occur when, in times of stress, we expect a loved one to be there for us, and for whatever reason, he or she is not. Finding the loved one absent, our fear doesn't subside but increases and can eventually paralyze us as our pain is magnified. And if the loved one remains unavailable or hurtful in other ways, the injury pollutes our soul.

How ironic—and how sad—that the person who says he or she loves and cares for us may be the source of our greatest pain. Our lover/caregiver may be the one who injures us the most, the one who manipulates our love to torture and abuse us for his or her own warped satisfaction. This kind of malevolent injury is far too prevalent today; it is the source of much pain and madness in the modern world.

Most simply, an early attachment injury results when someone we love, someone who we think should love us, like a parent, fails to provide our fundamental safety and security needs. In the attachment bond, anything that stands in the way of our ability to access our support figure and threatens our sense of security—whether that threat is real or perceived—has the potential to cause an attachment injury. And such injuries can ignite life's core pains: anger, anxiety, fear, grief, and suffering of various kinds.

Attachment injuries can result when:

- *The caregiver or loved one is simply not available, physically or emotionally, due to his or her own emotional distress or discomfort with closeness.* We had a client who, as a parent, was frequently depressed and became unavailable for her children. Another client was terrified to show his feelings when he was under stress, and as a result he made himself unavailable when his children needed his support.

- *The caregiver is willing to be available but is not able to be there.* For example, a parent becomes ill and is either in the hospital or is incapacitated by the medication or by dealing with the illness, making him or her emotionally unavailable to the child.

- *The caregiver wants to be available and normally would be there, but is absent at a crucial developmental phase or during a time of crisis.* For example, a mother may go back to school when her children become teenagers, so she has little time or energy to help them deal with the turmoil of adolescence. Or a husband may be thrust into a difficult and prolonged project at work and thus becomes unavailable to his wife when she has to deal with the death of one of her parents. In these cases the loved one may be there physically, but the closeness is blocked or limited to only arm's-length proximity. The loved one may even push the needy one away physically or emotionally.

- *The parent or loved one is there, but instead of providing a safe haven, he or she uses insensitive, off-putting, embarrassing, or sarcastic language toward the needy child or adult.* This can be an insensitive parent who rebuffs her children when the youngsters get upset about day-to-day stressors. Or it can be a husband who ignores his wife's complaints about her stressful day at work and her physical and emotional exhaustion in dealing with the children at home. Instead of listening or offering sympathy, he gives unsolicited advice and trivializes her emotional reactions.

- *The caregiver is there but is smothering and overdoes safety and protection, which doesn't allow the child or loved one the freedom to explore the world and gain confidence mastering life's skills.* For example, a parent who rushes in and tells her children what to do without really listening to their feelings sends this message: *You can't take care of yourself or know your own feelings, so I have to do all that for you.*

Ryan's Story

Children may incur attachment injuries despite the parent's best intentions—and without the parent's realizing it's happening. For example, consider Patti, who was considerably upset when she came to see us about her ten-year-old son, Ryan.

"I'm afraid he's been abused or something at school. But the school counselor can't find any significant trauma in his life. I'm not sure what's going on here. What am I going to do?" She sounded like she was gripping the end of her rope with raw fingertips.

After a few more questions, we learned that Ryan had become depressed and withdrawn in recent weeks. He was suffering falling grades and was driving his mother nuts by clinging to her constantly. "He won't leave me alone. If I turn around too quick I trip over him."

We had our concerns about Patti, as well as Ryan, but she told us all was well with her, and we had to take her word for it.

Ryan came in a few days later; he perched on the edge of his seat, a hand tucked under each thigh. He looked ready to launch himself for the door at the slightest provocation. To calm him, we talked to him about baseball and movies. Our conversation with him culminated with this strong pronouncement on his part: "*Shrek's* a lot better than that *Atlantis* movie," he told us firmly.

Figuring it was time, we eased into our concerns.

"We need to ask you something, Ryan."

"Shoot," he said, relaxing and signaling his readiness to get down to business.

"We all know you're here because your mom's worried about the things going on in your life recently. We also wonder if you're worried in any way about your mom." We were pursuing a hunch. Clinginess in children this age is often indicative of separation anxiety. Was he afraid he was going to somehow lose his mom?

The question hung suspended in the room for a moment. Then his expression tightened, and a look of frightened confusion came over him. He blurted out a big "No!" in protest to the question, but his lip quivered and he started to cry.

"Okay, why don't you just tell us about it," we invited softly.

After another moment, Ryan started talking.

A year earlier, his mom had been hospitalized for a month with depression. And recently Ryan had noticed she had been getting "sad" again. His observation confirmed a suspicion we'd had when we first saw her. A few weeks before, Ryan had overheard her talking about death to someone on the phone; she had mentioned how death might come as a welcomed relief. Making matters worse for Ryan, his dad's job had been keeping him on the road a lot lately, which left Ryan very much alone to face something quite frightening.

Later, when we told Patti of Ryan's fears, she cried. Then, brushing away the tears, she told us she'd been battling depression for a few months but had been denying it and trying to hide it from her family. When Ryan and his mother talked about his fear, it was good to see them reconnecting—and just as good to see the wave of relief wash across both their faces. But there was more work to do. Still concerned, Ryan was consumed with his mother's moods, fearing that she might dive into depression and leave him again. And if she left, who'd be there for him? Not Dad. And if not Dad, who? Can you imagine the anguish and dread in that poor child's heart? It was impossible for us not to empathize with him.

We acted quickly, making sure Patti worked on her depression so she wouldn't be rehospitalized. Then we worked hard to get Dad back into Ryan's picture. This wasn't as easy as we'd hoped. Although he was eager to get involved in relieving Ryan's problem, he believed he had no choice but to be on the road as much as he had been. "It's the only way I have of making a living," he told us. But he began praying and searching for new opportunities—a positive start. Fortunately, Ryan's mom worked her way back quickly enough to compensate for his dad's reluctance.

When we look back on Ryan, we realize that he was a normal kid in abnormal circumstances: a mom dealing with depression and a dad who was away a lot. When his mom got depressed, Ryan had no one to turn to. His attachment security was threatened, stirring up intense anxiety and sadness. Clinging to Mom made perfect sense. It kept him close to her, where he could watch over her like a mother hen.

Attachment Injuries Grid

	Short Duration	Long Duration
Minor Injury	**Childhood Attachment Injury** • Parent shows up late to pick up child. • Parent is upset, tense, and stressful because of work stress. • Parent has flu and is temporarily unavailable to the child. **Adult Attachment Injury** • Often shows up late for work or appointments. • Occasionally fails to keep a promise. • Spouse goes out of town for week.	**Childhood Attachment Injury** • Insensitive parenting. • Caregiver is constantly unavailable, not there for the little things. • Child withdraws emotionally when daycare becomes necessary as parent goes back to work. • Parent is never there for the big things: first baseball game, school play, karate practice, dance lessons, etc. • Parents divorce amicably without post-divorce conflict. **Adult Attachment Injury** • Spouse works too much to avoid home life. • Emotionally distant. • Demonstrates ongoing insensitivity. • Uninvolved in family life.
Severe Injury	**Childhood Attachment Injury** • Parent goes to hospital for a week. • Child is sick, and parent is unavailable. • Child gets lost for brief period of time. **Adult Attachment Injury** • An extramarital affair. • Intense arguments involving verbal abuse. • Physical or sexual abuse that occurs more than one or two times. • Complicated grief after loss of parent(s).	**Childhood Attachment Injury** • Abusive parenting. • Parents involved in abusive marriage. • Parents divorce with ongoing conflict post-divorce—e.g., custody battles. • Sibling gets chronic illness such as diabetes, stealing parents' time and attention. **Adult Attachment Injury** • Marriage ends in divorce. • Gets involved in frequent extra-marital affairs. • Chronic domestic violence • Chronic addictive behavior • Long-term life-threatening illness

Soul Wounds

The Effects of Attachment Injuries

As Ryan's situation shows, not all attachment injuries are dramatic or traumatic. Many soul wounds are much more indirect, subtler in their injuring effect, and are often downplayed or denied by both the injured and the caregiver. On page 40 we map these varied injuries on a grid that considers both how strongly and how long the injury can be experienced—whether the injuries are high-intensity or low-intensity, and whether their effects are short- or long-term.

As the grid shows, childhood attachment injuries aren't always easy to see. And also as the grid shows, they may lurk inside us and reveal themselves later in our lives in subtle ways that only hint at their existence.[2] Moreover, what constitutes an attachment injury can change according to one's stage of life. What never changes, however, is how strongly and intensely we react to these injuries.

Why We React the Way We Do

Our strongest emotional expressions are tied to our closest relationships. God has programmed us this way. Feelings like anxiety, anger, sadness, and guilt are designed to help us deal with attachment injuries.

Remember the three phases—protest, despair, detachment—identified by Bowlby and his colleague James Robertson when children were separated from their mothers? Amazingly, these reactions to attachment injuries continue from cradle to grave. Whenever we feel that our attachment figure's availability is threatened, we experience anxiety or anger. Anxiety drives us to seek closeness. For an infant, it may mean the baby cries to get her mother's attention or crawls closer to Mommy. For a ten-year-old like Ryan, it may mean he refuses to go to school and instead wants to hover over his mother, not letting her out of his sight.

The anger of protest is often called an "anger of hope."[3] It's designed to reprimand the caregiver for abandoning us. Remember Darcy, described in chapter 1, whose defiance and irritability was, in part, protesting his mother's busyness? Think about the last time you were angry with someone you counted on for comfort and support. Were you angry because he wasn't there for you when you needed him? Perhaps he was late getting home from work?

Or maybe some other infraction made you angry. Why did it? In part, it's because of the meaning we attach to the other person's being late or to the other infraction. If we see lateness as a sign of unreliability, a sign that the person is not trustworthy and that in times of trouble we can't count on him or her, then we get angry.

But when we're angry with someone we love, our anger is risky: If we express our true feelings, we might drive the loved one even further away. So we turn the anger inward, telling ourselves that we are selfish and inconsiderate. Or we hold our anger in and express it indirectly by using the cold-shoulder treatment, by becoming critical, or by "getting even." Then let's just see if he or she dares to let us down again!

When injuries are more prolonged, our anger of hope may turn into the "anger of malice."[4] In our fury at the injustice that's been inflicted upon us, we may feel we hate the person and as a result we want to lash out at him or her. As one client put it, "I want to make him hurt like he hurt me."

Or our anger and anxiety may turn into sadness and despair. In this state we stop caring about the events occurring around us, and life loses its meaning and purpose. Our bodies show the result of this listlessness as our energy and concentration wane. Eventually we can lose hope and may even question whether life is worth living.

At some point, coping with prolonged loss means detaching from it. We disguise our attachment needs with a mask of independence and self-sufficiency. We may say, "I don't need her; she means nothing to me. All I need is me." In this detached state, we may turn inward, finding comfort in a fantasy life. Or we may turn to addictive behavior and replace our need for relationships with drugs, alcohol, the Internet, shopping, and/or pornography.

The bottom line is that our most intense feelings are tied to our attachment bonds. When these bonds are threatened, passions run hot. As we will see later in this book, our earliest relationships are crucibles where we learn to handle our feelings and use them to build bridges of intimacy to the ones we love.

Of course, not everyone reacts to a given situation the same way. Some people are mildly irritated when their spouses show up late; others are infuriated. A child who is sexually abused by a neighbor may not experience any long-term consequences while another may be completely devastated. Some children adjust well to a parent's illness and temporary unavailability; others struggle with it. Why? Let's take a look at why we react the way we do to attachment injuries.

Healthy Communication: The Great Immunizer

We all desire relationships that allow us to talk openly and honestly about our feelings, even negative ones. This healthy communication helps immunize us from the sting of what could otherwise be an attachment injury. In Ryan's case, for example, when we opened the lines of communication between his mom and him, Ryan's pain eased. We also encouraged conversation between his mom and dad. Patti had become depressed, in part, because her husband was gone a lot and she had no one to turn to. She understood his absence, but she still felt alone and isolated.

Unhealthy Communication: A Raging Ride in the Wrong Direction

When we can't talk through our feelings with the ones we love and care about, it only intensifies the stress we feel. John Gottman, renowned scientist and family psychologist, found four kinds of unhealthy communication that interfere with our ability to resolve negative feelings following an attachment injury. He calls these the "Four Horsemen to the Apocalypse" (in other words, a ride toward the end).

• *Criticism.* To explain what we mean by *criticism,* we'll compare it to a *complaint.* Complaints are generally specific: "I don't like it when you tell me you're going to take out the trash and you don't do it." Criticism, however, is much more global and is sometimes packaged as a question that implies the other person has a character flaw: "Why do you always do that? You never do what you say you're going to do. This is just another example of how I can't count on you for anything."

• *Defensiveness.* When we receive criticism, it's easy to retaliate with counter-criticism: "What do you mean I never do what I say? What about the dishes?

When's the last time they were piled up all over the counter? Is that all you can do, whine and complain? No wonder you can't get anyone to do anything for you!" Countercriticism and an "I'm-a-victim.-Why-does-everyone-always-pick-on-me?" attitude are both forms of defensiveness.

• *Contempt.* When criticism and defensiveness are ratcheted up several notches, they can lead to derogatory remarks, put-downs, and extreme disrespect. For example, not mowing the grass can lead to "You make me sick! You never do what you say you'll do. You're a big talker, just like your mother, but you never follow through. I've grown used to not being able to rely on you, so I'll just do everything myself, like always."

• *Stonewalling.* When the intensity gets too strong, a person can shut down and decide he or she will no longer participate in the conversation. The person may walk out of the room or just stop talking and stare off into space. One of our clients called this his thousand-yard stare. In the heat of the argument it would, understandably, drive his wife crazy, intensifying her rage and setting up the battle for another round of criticism.

Unhealthy communication, while intended to protect oneself, may intensify the original attachment injury instead. In fact, it can actually become an injury in itself. Constant criticism, defensiveness, contempt, and stonewalling can wound the soul, piercing us emotionally like poisoned arrows to the heart.

REPAIRING THE DAMAGE, PREVENTING THE SOUL WOUND

Gottman's research shows that all couples engage in some forms of unhealthy communication. We've all doled out criticism or retaliated with defensiveness or shut down communication from time to time. (Of course, healthy couples seldom, if ever, are contemptuous or disrespectful of one another.)

Accepting Influence

What seems to distinguish healthy from unhealthy couples is their ability to repair the damage done. We might start out by being critical or defensive in response to an attachment injury, but we catch ourselves and recover. For example, a wife might start to say to her husband, "You never do what I ask you to do." But then she might stop herself midsentence and add, "I'm sorry. It just makes me mad. I was hoping it would be done so we could spend time together this evening. I know you really do a lot of work around here. Sometimes I just don't pay enough attention." Or after saying, "All you ever do is complain" a husband might throw in, "I guess I do tick you off sometimes when I say I'm going to do something and then don't do it. It's a bad habit of mine. But, please, you have to see why I didn't do it."

Healthy couples repair damage before it becomes permanent. They make an attempt to repair the damage and reconcile in the middle of a heated discussion. This willingness to accept a loved one's repair attempts is called *accepting influence.*[5] When you accept influence, it helps insulate your relationship from attachment injury. On the other hand, when you reject repair attempts, and the cycle of destructive arguing continues, the relationship can fragment, deepening the soul wound and weakening the relationship.

Establishing a Healthy Family Context

How you feel about behaviors and events can be influenced by your family context, the overall climate of the household surrounding you as you react to the situation. For example, we've worked with many children who have been sexually victimized by someone outside the family: a neighbor, a family acquaintance, or even someone in the church. When the family responded with concern and comfort for the child and took immediate action to stop the abuser, the children seemed to recover and adjust pretty well. However, when an unhealthy context created family circumstances that kept parents from responding appropriately and sensitively—marital conflict, financial stress, family illness, one parent struggling with depression or crippling anxiety—the children did not fare well.

When we look at family contexts, we consider two factors: closeness and structure.[6]

• *Closeness.* How involved family members are with each other is described as closeness. Some families are too involved and set poor boundaries. Other families are too distant. Both extremes can be unhealthy for children and for couples. Healthy families balance their closeness; they respect each other's need for closeness while making room for each person's individual physical and emotional space.

• *Structure.* A family's structure has to do with the roles, rules, and rituals of family life. Again, structure can be too rigid, with strict, inflexible rules and roles. Or it can be chaotic, where no one knows what to expect from day to day. Both extremes are unhealthy.

When healthy, these two factors, closeness and structure, work together to create a family context that helps buffer its members against attachment injuries. When these factors fall into imbalance, attachment wounds occur more easily. For example, a school counselor referred to us a nine-year-old named Katie. The counselor had discovered that the family baby-sitter was mistreating Katie. She would often scream obscenities at the child, put her in hourlong time-outs, and sometimes refused to feed Katie dinner.

Katie's mother was completely taken aback when she heard about this mistreatment. She had had no idea Katie was being treated this way. As we talked more, however, we found that Katie's parents had noticed some changes in their daughter's attitude over the last month, but they hadn't asked Katie about them. They had just assumed she was getting the "normal" preteen attitude. They also had never asked the baby-sitter how the day had gone, just assuming that no news was good news.

Katie, unfortunately, had taken her parents' silence as an endorsement of the baby-sitter's actions. As a result Katie felt betrayed and began to act out more at school.

Katie's family context lacked closeness. Family members were left to fend for themselves, and even dramatic changes in Katie's emotions were dismissed. Katie had coped with the structure, but she felt her parents didn't care about her when they'd "failed" to investigate the "why" of her struggle.

ATTACHMENT STYLES AND OUR VULNERABILITY TO SOUL WOUNDS

In the last chapter we introduced the four different attachment styles—secure, ambivalent, avoidant, and disorganized—and explained how they are formed in our earliest relationships. Our personal attachment style creates a template through which we view future relationships. They also shape whether we avoid attachment injuries—or feel their effects later in our lives.

Remember, people with a secure attachment style believe they are worthy of love and believe their caregivers are able and willing to meet their emotional needs. Those people are best prepared to avoid or quickly repair the damage inflicted by attachment injuries.

Those with an insecure attachment style (ambivalent, avoidant, or disorganized) tend to question their self-worth and don't expect their caregivers to be there for them when they are needed. The insecure attachment style can make them hypersensitive to attachment injuries. In fact, people with certain insecure attachment styles almost expect to be betrayed and abandoned, because in the past, their support figures have repeatedly let them down.

For example, a young couple, Jim and Sheila, came to see us after only six months of marriage. Within a couple of weeks of their honeymoon, Sheila became obsessed to constantly know Jim's whereabouts. Anytime he'd leave the house, even to go to the grocery store, she would call him on the cell phone a half-dozen times. If she detected even the slightest irritation in his voice, she'd erupt in a rage. She was convinced he was having an affair. Confused and overwhelmed by her jealousy, Jim retreated further from Sheila emotionally, afraid she'd "swallow him up" in her obsession. They were on the brink of separation when they came to see us.

Sheila's story was entangled with preoccupation and anger from her past. Her family context had been one of chaos and betrayal. Her father had been chronically unfaithful to her mother, but her mom could never find the strength to leave, fearing that she would never find another man to take care of her. For comfort, the mother turned to Sheila, who had to listen to her mom's tirades about how men are "worthless and untrustworthy."

Sheila was determined not to follow in her mother's footsteps, but now she could easily see that she was headed down the same path. She was furious with herself—but still obsessed with Jim. It was as if her past had set the stage for how her current relationship would unfold. She believed the only way she could protect herself from abandonment and betrayal was to hover

over Jim and spy on his every move. Unfortunately, her method was leading to madness.

KNOWLEDGE IS POWER

Sheila and Jim's situation seemed almost hopeless, but just in the nick of time, they took a crucial step toward resolving their problems and restoring love and trust to their relationship. The step they took was seeking out professional help. They came to us with a willingness to learn and an eagerness to acquire the skills that could not only save their marriage but also strengthen their attachment to each other. Armed with knowledge about their personal attachment styles and how these styles interact, they soon learned the secrets of developing a loving and lasting relationship.

The rest of this book will show you how you too can acquire the relationship tools that will enrich your attachments and protect you and your loved ones from inflicting—and incurring—soul wounds.

We'll begin by studying the four attachment styles in greater detail and showing you how you can identify your own personal style. Then we'll give you the tools for using your relationship strengths and tempering your injurious tendencies so that your relationship becomes all that you dreamed it could be.

4

THE HARDENED HEART

The Avoidant Attachment Style

The ability to trust others is at the heart of intimacy.
—CLINTON AND SIBCY

Arnold pushed out his chest, leaned back into our floral sofa and threw his arms over the back of it, then crossed his legs. He was a guy who took command; that sofa wasn't going anywhere. Then, in measured, deliberate tones, he explained to us how exhausted he was in his marriage—that his wife was entirely too demanding.

"She's everywhere I am. I can't get a break. She can't even make a decision without me. What do I care what color the new drapes are? As long as I can close them, that's all that matters. Honestly, I don't have time for stuff like that. I've got a congregation of twenty-five hundred people to lead—my sheep—and I've got to stay focused. It's what I'm called to do. God's work." He emphasized *God* as if there were stone tablets involved somewhere. "Time," he finally said. "It's all about time. I don't have enough of it. Everyone is so demanding, and it seems like my wife and kids just don't understand. And things are just getting worse."

In fact, a few days ago the time with his wife had become a bit hot. Tempers had ignited, and threats were made, driving this pastor to our office. His request was simple: "You people are in ministry. You know how important the work is, how many lives we're responsible for. What do I do about her? I'm sure you've faced this at home. I need some pointers on how to communicate with her. Let her know just how important my work is. How can

Comparison of Attachment Styles

Secure Attachment Style	Ambivalent Attachment Style
Self Dimension	**Self Dimension**
• I am worthy of love. • I am capable of getting the love and support I need.	• I am not worthy of love. • I am not capable of getting the love I need without being angry and clingy.
Other Dimension	**Other Dimension**
• Others are willing and able to love me.	• Others are capable of meeting my needs but might not do so because of my flaws. • Others are trustworthy and reliable but might abandon me because of my worthlessness.
Avoidant Attachment Style	**Disorganized Attachment Style**
Self Dimension	**Self Dimension**
• I am worthy of love. • I am capable of getting the love and support I need.	• I am not worthy of love. • I am not capable of getting the love I need without being angry and clingy.
Other Dimension	**Other Dimension**
• Others are either unwilling or incapable of loving me. • Others are not trustworthy; they are unreliable when it comes to meeting my needs.	• Others are unable to meet my needs. • Others are not trustworthy or reliable. • Others are abusive, and I deserve it.

picking the material for those drapes compare at all to counseling a young woman about not getting an abortion? I deal with *real* issues. I'm sure if she only knew, she'd understand my schedule and the extra time I have to be away from her and the boys."

Arnold was a sea of practical contradictions. Known far and wide as a fine pastor and family man, we quickly learned how much he loved his family, but he was locked away into his world of ministry and was anything but "in touch" with his own family. In the pulpit he sermonized about families, even about dads spending more time with their kids. And he tried to practice what he preached. But even when he was home, he was just unable to connect. Good to his wife and kids? Yes. In touch with them? Nope. Emotionally, he was cut off from his family and had little idea of what his wife and children really needed from him. In fact, there were times when he even saw their pleas for his time and attention as part of Satan's plans to sabotage his ministry.

You'd also think that a man as steeped in faith as Arnold was, a man who so often had counseled other fathers to do what he was avoiding, would respond positively when confronted with his behavioral contradictions. You'd think he'd say, "Something is wrong!" But he didn't. You know why? He couldn't see it. In fact, discussing the possibility with Arnold that he was misconnecting in his relationships and was using a number of substitutes for closeness was like speaking to him in Navajo, a language used in World War II in coded messages. The code was never broken; neither was Arnold's hold on his own sense of being right. Yet until Arnold could face the real problem—his fear of intimacy—his life was going to remain very stuck.

The Components of a Loving Relationship

Research, confirmed by our own experience, tells us that those who connect lovingly with others are able to

- have an emotional connection with others,
- disclose private thoughts and feelings, and
- participate in nonsexual touch.

Emotional Connection

A wife tells her husband about her difficult day with the children. Even though she's frustrated and shares her feelings in harsh tones, her husband is able to sift through the emotion, hear what's said, and sensitively respond to her immediate needs—without becoming overly defensive, retreating into his own world, or simply capitulating to the moment. Conversing and relating in this way, showing sensitivity and responsiveness to the feelings expressed by others, creates an emotional connection. Such a connection implies understanding and, even more, empathy, the ability to see the world through another's eyes. As a result, there is relational warmth and enjoyment that only comes from knowing others.

Disclosure of Private Thoughts and Feelings

Connecting lovingly means we open ourselves up to our loved ones. We all have private parts of our lives that we want to keep to ourselves. That's normal. However, the ability to reflect on and share parts of your past—the nitty-gritty—with the people you love is meaningful because it creates understanding and helps you join the other persons' world.

Disclosure is the cornerstone of intimacy. (We think of it as *in-to-me-see*.) We make ourselves vulnerable when we are able to share our most intimate, personal thoughts and experiences with the person to whom we're connected. It's being able to tell a funny story about a difficult time in your past. It's the ability to understand how your past largely influences who you are. It's the enjoyment of knowing yourself and of being known.

In contrast, the person with an avoidant attachment style does not enjoy being known or knowing others because it awakens his or her repressed feelings of loss and of anger about not being known, or emotionally connected, as a child. Helping those with an avoidant attachment style find the courage to acknowledge these feelings can free them up to face intimate relationships. It's what fathering expert William Pollack describes when he talks about fathers getting a second chance at intimacy with their own sons. By getting close to their sons they work through the pain they had as young boys when they were "abandoned" by their own overly industrious or workaholic fathers.[1]

Nonsexual Touch

It's said that kids need physical touch, on average eleven touches per day. Noted Christian psychiatrist Grace Ketterman believes kids need at least one hundred touches per day! Touches like high-fives, wrestling, handholding, warm hugs, tender caresses, cuddling, and gentle kisses. It's parent-child touching, and it's also part of the warmth and tenderness of a romantic relationship in adults. Everyone needs touch.

Interestingly enough, this nonsexual touching is linked to the release of oxytocin, a chemical also released during those tender moments when mothers nurse their babies. It's believed to enhance the child's attachment to the mother, the mother's bond with the child, and her drive to be a sensitive caregiver. This substance is also released during the climax of sexual experience and in the tender cuddling afterward—the afterglow.[2]

We didn't include sexual intercourse in our definition of intimacy because people can, and often do, engage in sexual intercourse without experiencing intimacy. Prostitutes are prime examples. When practicing their trade, they generally avoid any kissing on the mouth, caressing, tender hugs, or face-to-face contact.[3]

THE FEAR OF INTIMACY

Persons with the avoidant attachment style often struggle with at least one of these three areas of intimacy.

Avoidant Persons Struggle with the Emotional Connection

People with an avoidant attachment style find it difficult to listen sensitively to the thoughts and feelings of those they're closest to—their spouses and their children. Like Arnold, they're too busy or see this kind of listening as a distraction from their true, God-given purpose. Or they may see such sensitivity as a weakness—or as "thumb-sucking," as one avoidant husband saw it. By showing it, they picture themselves as being overly mushy or childlike.

Obviously, this is very sad for everyone involved. The avoidant person can be very desirous of a relationship, even loving, yet those around this person may not know how much love he or she is giving or sharing. Instead, loved ones may feel very unloved and abandoned.

Avoidant Persons Struggle with Disclosure of Private Thoughts and Feelings

Those with the avoidant attachment style also don't like to disclose their private thoughts and experiences. Why? Because when you grow up feeling abandoned and rejected, you learn to hide those thoughts and experiences. You learn to distance yourself from your own feelings, even your own desire for emotional closeness.

By disclosing intimate thoughts and feelings, one becomes vulnerable to being hurt all over again. This vulnerability opens up one's thoughts and experiences to criticism and misinterpretation. And that is difficult and even scary to avoidant individuals. When they share their private thoughts and feelings, important parts of themselves can be seen differently than they really are. This would ordinarily *not* be a big issue, but for those who have built up a thick, protective shell, exposing parts of themselves can arouse feelings they had long ago tried to bury.

Think about the millions of children who grow up in families with depressed parents or an alcoholic mom or dad. Often kids describe these homes as being very lonely. In this family context there was rarely any support and usually no one to turn to. A typical comment is, "Mom couldn't help. She was depressed about everything else going on in her life."

Or those with avoidant attachment styles may come from homes where the kids had to make it on their own. They had to "suck it up" because their moms and dads had little room for their children's fears, hurts, and frustrations. These feelings were taboo. Signs of weakness. Failure was not tolerated, and success was always applauded.

No wonder avoidant people want to keep all their "personal stuff" locked up and hidden away from themselves and others. For them, the bottom line is that the way they handle or deal with their emotions mirrors their relationships with others. If you keep your feelings at a distance, they believe, you keep others' feelings there too.

Avoidant Persons Struggle with Nonsexual Touch

Have you noticed how a lot of people today struggle with touching other people? Even people they love. Recently on a live radio talk program, a caller told us how proud he was of his brand-new son. He said he found himself wanting to kiss his newborn a lot. His question was, "Do you think it's healthy? I mean, will it have an adverse affect on him? You know, will it make him effeminate, or something like that?" We couldn't help but laugh with him. He was relieved to learn that it was not only okay, but it was critical for him to be crazy about his son and to "love on him."

Interestingly, many avoidant people are turned off by tenderness and touch. Arnold is one of them. He puts it this way: "I enjoy being close to my wife, but too much of that touchy-feely stuff drives me crazy."

We pulled for an example of what he meant by touchy-feely stuff. "What really gets me is when she tries to rub the back of my neck. To her it's romantic; to me—I really can't stand it! It doesn't work for me. I know I shouldn't feel this way, but my mind-set is that if it doesn't feel good, don't do it."

To Arnold, time is better spent on the Internet planning his next family vacation. "Now, that makes sense. If I can save a couple of bucks on the fares, it's that much more money to spend on good dinners." Arnold approached his relationships functionally. He believed in doing what needs to be done. "All that intimacy stuff is window dressing. A relationship is about the two of you making it through life without killing one another." He laughed after saying this, but it was a laugh that said, *I might be exaggerating, but you can see the truth in what I say.*

Some counselors call this type of attachment "the protected self" because these people appear, and generally are, tough, and even hard, on the outside. Oh, they may be personable enough. Some are even the life of the party. But all this life and energy are used to keep people at a distance. You've seen them—maybe even when you look in the mirror. Breaking through all that veneer and actually penetrating to where true emotion and vulnerability live can be difficult; and the closer you might get to avoidant people's hearts, the more threatened they may feel and the more defensive they may become.

No one could have been nicer, more congenial, than Arnold. At times he even spoke as if we were part of his inner circle. But when he left our office, we were no closer to him emotionally than when he'd entered.

The Relationship Rules of the Avoidant Attachment

People with an avoidant attachment style have two basic relationship rules.

The Other-Dimension Relationship Rule

First, regarding their *other* dimension, those with the avoidant attachment style assume, *Other people are not reliable, dependable, or trustworthy when it comes to my needs.*

You may be asking, *How did this happen? Why did this person come to believe this way?* The answer: In close relationships, this individual was often turned away, rebuffed whenever he made bids for comfort and safety. He was given the message that to be needy was to be weak. As a result he came to learn that reaching out would often be met with hurt, shame, and rejection.

Imagine living in a home with a depressed mom or dad. These parents just don't have any emotional energy to give. They can be irritable, dismissing, and rejecting because they are so absorbed with life's troubles. So the child, like a turtle, slowly envelops his heart with a hard, impenetrable shell to protect himself from the feelings of abandonment and rejection.

The Self-Dimension Relationship Rule

Second, regarding their *self* dimension, those with avoidant attachment styles also assume, *I must rely on myself alone in order to meet my needs.*

Again, why? This assumption flows naturally from the belief that *I can't rely on others, so I must turn to myself.* The child learns to bury his or her feelings of weakness and vulnerability and replaces them with an inflated sense of self-confidence, an "I-don't-need-you, I'll-do-it-myself" mentality. As one avoidant mother said, "I learned to suck it up, to just get over it and go on with my life. Just stop whining and move on." She had long ago given up on others to be there for her and had become a female version of John Wayne. She had a good heart and a well-meaning soul, but she had hidden her sense of vulnerability and was impatient with the neediness of others, including her children.

With these relationship rules, it only makes sense that the person with the avoidant attachment style becomes hardened. If those near her can't be trusted, why let anyone in?

However, avoidant persons are typically not paranoid. After all, Arnold knows his wife, Sheila, isn't out to hurt him. He knows Sheila doesn't sit around all day looking for ways to make his life miserable. The opposite is true. She works tirelessly to make his life a lot better, and he knows this. She does all the cooking, cleaning, and washing; she takes care of the kids, does his errands, and when he needs someone to complain to, she's there. No, she wouldn't deliberately hurt him, but still, he can't bring himself to trust her *not* to hurt him inadvertently. In his mind he can't count on her to be there every time he needs her. She's not perfect. She might make the wrong decision or say the wrong thing at the wrong time. In fact, she has. And Arnold took this "failure" as just another confirmation of his relationship rule: *Others always let you down, just when you need them the most.*

Because avoidant persons don't have anyone who's qualified to be let in, especially when they are emotionally bruised, they have no one to confide in. There's no one to share the hurt with, no one who'll understand *why* they're hurt, and no one who knows them well enough to help them deal with it. So they're forced to rely on themselves to provide comfort.

What's amazing to us is how much inner strength some of these armored adults and children have. We have worked with avoidant people who are very reliable, capable, and competent. They can make good leaders because of their avid self-reliance and their ability not to be weighed down with emotion.

Below the tough veneer, however, they are also empty, especially when they get hurt or disappointed. They are particularly vulnerable to fragmenting when faced with a professional or public failure. Because they give so much emphasis to success, their world can quickly come crashing in when they stumble. And though they often deny painful emotions, they are prone to depression and even anxiety.

More frequently, they turn to an alternate substance—anything to replace the other person, anything that creates the illusion of intimacy, warmth, or love. We believe, and research suggests, that the genesis of addictions lies within this pattern of relationships. The reason addictions are so hard to break is that they mean so much. They've been used to replace, literally, what can't be replaced—relationships. The man addicted to pornography (i.e., the woman who is always available to him through books, magazines, or the Internet) creates a false intimacy. Even positive addictions and rituals—like studies, sports, and religious activities—can create a false sense of closeness in which habits and things replace our need for relationship.

Think about your relationship with God. First John 5:21 (NKJV) says, "Little children, keep yourselves from idols." When we turn from God to something else for comfort, safety, or security, we have, in essence, turned to an idol for the fulfillment of our deepest needs. If we don't believe God is faithful, it is no wonder that these substitutes have so much meaning and power in our lives. That's why they are so hard to give up. These addictions medicate and temporarily numb the emptiness that only God can work to fill.

Arnold's Wife, Sheila, Speaks Up

Arnold, still sure all he had to do to stop his wife's "nagging" was to just convince her his time was too valuable to waste on life's trivial issues, invited Sheila to attend one of the counseling sessions with him.

The instant she stepped into our office, it was obvious to us she was angry. She was an attractive woman with shoulder-length auburn hair and a gentleness revealed in soft, green eyes and lips that seemed capable of an easy, winning smile. But, of course, she wasn't smiling. Her lips and brows were drawn into tight lines, and her eyes were narrow and expectant. Yet there seemed to be more than anger at work. She walked with a telltale weariness, like someone who was deeply frustrated and losing hope rapidly. After a few minutes, our first impression proved right, and she quickly told us what had brought her to that place.

"He's gone all the time," she said, speaking to us as if Arnold were waiting in the car instead of sitting at the other end of the sofa. "He's either at the church, away at this conference or that, or off at some *important* meeting." *Important* came out with sarcasm. "I'd probably see him more often if I put a podium in the living room. But then he'd complain that it blocked the TV. And when he *is* home he's worn out. He comes in, flops into the recliner like a beaten dog, grabs the remote, and hides in the news channel—or reads the paper. I *guess* he reads it. I can't tell what he's doing behind there. He could be sleeping, for all I know. Unless the phone rings. Then he perks up—like a dog on the scent again. And he'll talk for a half-hour to people he doesn't even know—complete strangers, for crying out loud. I can't get a word out of him, and with them he won't shut up."

"They're my job," Arnold protested, leaning forward. "I'm a pastor. My job is to win people to Christ. Even complete strangers."

"Well, that's only part of your job," she groaned back. "There are two vast wastelands in our house. Only one of them is television—although the other one has a television in it." She turned back to us. "And when he does talk to me, it's not about anything important. It's never about love or the kids or about feelings—his or mine. I don't think he *has* feelings." Managing to add even more sarcasm, she said, "He's successfully weaned himself from having to carry the dead weight of all those emotions around. I just want someone to love me—that's all. I know he works hard. He is a good man . . . a good pastor. But as for me . . . I'm just alone, me and the boys. And he doesn't even know it."

Although Sheila probably had other names for Arnold, she's married to a man with a classic avoidant attachment style. When Arnold is around people he doesn't have to be intimate with, he's social and outgoing, but when he's around his loved ones, he keeps them at a distance—he dodges intimacy. To him it's foreign, uncharted territory. And for most of us, what we don't know, we fear. So the crux of the matter is that Arnold is *afraid* of intimacy.

ATTACHMENTS

THE ADULT ATTACHMENT INTERVIEW

In our clinical work we utilize parts of the "adult attachment interview" first developed by attachment researcher Mary Main. We have adapted portions of this technique that evolved out of the research performed by Main and her colleagues, which found that it is not so much *what* people say or the content of their stories about their childhoods as much as it is about *how* they talk about it or the process they use to convey the story. Main and her colleagues identified some basic principles of coherence and some specific ways that each of the insecure attachment styles violate these principles.

For example, when avoidant people describe their parents they tend to overidealize them, using words like *wonderful, great, warm, loving, kind,* etc., but they are unable to recall specific incidents where their parents behaved this way. This failure is an indication of an insecure attachment style. It's indicative of a person who wants to believe everything was great but has no specific experiences to back up that belief.

Arnold's Attachment Interview

From the start, Arnold saw no need to discuss his childhood. "I don't see any reason to talk about that. It was fine. Look, I came to you to get advice on how to deal with my wife. *My* part has nothing to do with *her.*" It took us some time to persuade Arnold to go along with our request, but he finally shrugged and said, "Okay, I guess there won't be any harm done. But don't take too much time. I've got things to do."

We began by asking him for a general impression of his childhood. As expected, he painted a rosy picture. He told us his dad worked a lot at the family business—a little grocery store on the edge of town—while his mom stayed at home with the five kids, Arnold being the oldest. "Everything was neat, clean, and orderly," he said. "Mother kept us fed, Father kept a roof over our heads, and everything was good. We were all close and very happy."

Attachment to mother. We asked Arnold to describe his relationship with his mom using a number of adjectives. He shared several words that represented

60

grand concepts: *loving, kind, warm,* and *caring.* We asked him to give us specific, concrete examples of each behavior. What specifically did she do that was loving? Did she give you your favorite snack in your lunch bag? we asked. Or did she dry your PJs in the evening so that when you put them on at night they were still warm? Did she do things like that?

Arnold thought for a second, looking to his right, an indication that he was retrieving memories from the brain's left side—the more logical, factual side. He finally gave up. "I can't really recall any specifics, but Mother was just that way."

He said no more about it. However, by what he said he'd violated one of the basic principles of storytelling that Main and her colleagues watched for. He gave general descriptions of his childhood that couldn't be supported by specific memories, a behavior they identified as *inconsistent.* This type of inconsistency is unique to people with avoidant attachment styles.[4] Another inconsistency revealed itself when we asked Arnold about times when he had been upset during his childhood. Since our attachment beliefs lie dormant when we're calm and boil to the surface when we're distressed, it made sense that one of Arnold's attachment issues materialized when he remembered this. As a child, whenever he was knocked into bed by some illness, like the flu, his mom would exile him to the back bedroom then only appear when she brought him meals.

"Did she do anything else?" we asked.

"No," he said, vindicating her by his upright posture. "She was a very busy woman. She didn't have time to sit and cuddle. She just made sure I had what I needed."

Arnold also remembered fracturing a bone in his foot. He had managed to hide the injury from his mom for nearly a week, afraid she'd get mad at him for goofing off and getting hurt as a result. He wasn't sure what she had said or done to him once she discovered the injury, but he did remember it required a cast. Neither story conformed to Arnold's description of his mother as being caring and loving. Rather, both portrayed his mother as being busy and critical, and offering no safe haven for Arnold in times of trouble.

Attachment to father. Arnold described his dad using only two adjectives:

hardworking and *loving.* He had plenty of good examples to show his dad as being industrious but nothing specific to illustrate how he had been loving. "Do you ever remember being hugged by your dad?" we asked.

He shifted his eyes away, almost as if ashamed, and shook his head. "No," he whispered.

This interview was hard for Arnold but very important. Although a strong part of him wanted desperately to believe his parents had been ideally warm and loving, his memories, especially those that remained locked away, unspoken, revealed a different story. But there was a promising sign: the moisture in his eyes when he realized his parents had never even hugged him. Like all of us, Arnold longs for intimacy. Unfortunately, he doesn't know he does. Those tears might show him the truth of what he has hidden inside. Soon, with work, he might begin to understand how much his wife and children yearn to connect with him—and how much he yearns to connect with *them.* It's a yearning Arnold had long ago sealed off. But it was there; he just needed to rediscover it.

Jerry's Connection with Longing

Another client, Jerry, came to us in his late thirties in an attempt to deal with marital problems—and, we discovered a little later, a pornography addiction. Although we suspected his issues stemmed from a longing for intimacy, the proof of it came unexpectedly. He was telling us about a recent phone conversation he'd had with his sister, who was complaining that he didn't visit the family often enough. Ten years earlier he had moved several states away for a new job. Since then he'd been home to visit only a handful of times. One of those visits had been for his mom's funeral. "She died a few months after I moved," he said. "I rushed home for it but had to come back for work right away."

"How'd you feel about your mom's death?"

"We weren't all that close. I don't remember being very sad," he admitted. He went on to tell us that his mom and dad had remained married out of convenience and that as a result, both parents always seemed depressed, probably preoccupied with their problems. "I was alone most of the time. I'd come home from school, and the place would be empty. Mom and Dad both worked second shift, and my older brother and sister took advantage of it and were always out with their friends. I put myself to bed most nights" (like thousands of latchkey kids do every night, we might add). Then one of Jerry's buddies introduced him to pornography. "Talk about being hooked," he admitted. "I couldn't get enough of the stuff."

He'd finally found the drug to feed his intense emotional hunger.

But as Jerry recounted the phone call with his sister, a hint of anger seeped in. "She got after me about not coming home. She said that I really didn't care about her or the rest of the family, that I never really loved Mom or Dad. She said I'd left and become absorbed in my own world and shut everyone else out."

"What did you say to that?"

He paused. Then large, unexpected tears began to sear his cheeks. For a moment he was a stiff, tearful statue, then he took a deep breath. "I asked some questions of my own: 'Where were you guys when I needed you as a kid? Where was the whole sick family when I came home from school? I cooked my own meals, kept myself company, put myself to bed. Where were you and Mark? [Mark was his brother.] Where was Mom? And Dad? Everyone was gone. I was alone. Now I take care of myself because I've always taken care of myself. I envied other kids in the neighborhood when they whined that they had to go home to eat dinner and do homework. At least someone was waiting for them at home, someone who cared. No one waited for me. So if I don't come home and visit the family now, it's because no one cared if I came home then.'"

A rage boiled inside Jerry, one equal to the desire within him that had gone unmet in him as a child—a yearning to be held, cared for, kissed warmly good night. At the time he found a cure for his breaking heart, he armored it and made it unbreakable. Only these many years later, when confronted by the injustice brought by his sister, did his heart soften up enough to let out a small bit of the rage and resentment. This was an important event in Jerry's life journey. It allowed him to connect with, to identify, what he really desired. It was the first step on Jerry's road to healing.

INSENSITIVE PARENTING:
THE PATHWAY TO AVOIDANT ATTACHMENT

Research has identified specific pathways to the avoidant attachment style. Insensitive parenting is the one behavior that most consistently leads to insecure attachment, and dismissive parenting, rejection, and intrusive parenting are distinct forms of that insensitivity.

What Does It Mean to Be Sensitive?

To understand the various forms of *insensitive* parenting, it helps to examine just what it means to be *sensitive* to a child. Sensitive parents, especially parents of infants, adjust their behavior to help the little ones remain calm, or if the babies are agitated, sensitive parents help them become calm as quickly as possible.

Infants communicate by crying. If they're hungry, they cry; if cold, they cry; if lonely, they cry; if wet—you guessed it—they cry. Sensitive caregivers respond to these cries by helping their infants become calm again. If they're hungry, they feed them; if wet, they change them. This kind of caregiving is called *contingent responding.*[5] These parents satisfy their children's needs. And they do not do it angrily or resentfully. They know the little one's not trying to manipulate them or drive them nuts. He or she is just a helpless human being who, in order to survive, needs to be taken care of responsively.

And when infants are cared for responsively and tenderly, they develop relationship rules, such as, *My emotional needs are important, and I can count on others to help me in times of trouble.* Paradoxically, instead of becoming self-centered, as one might expect, this foundation seems to equip a maturing child with empathy, the ability to more fully see and respond to the needs of others. Interestingly, in Ainsworth's study, infants whose mothers were sensitive to their needs within their early months were more likely to be securely attached at the child's first birthday. These children cried less and developed other forms of communication, such as facial expressions and various physical and vocal gestures, to catch their mothers' attention.[6]

In fact, Mary Ainsworth concluded that "an infant whose mother's responsiveness helps him to achieve his ends develops confidence in his own ability to control what happens to him."[7] This is the opposite of what many insensitive parents believe will happen. They generally believe responding sensitively to their children's crying leads to spoiled children who can do nothing for themselves.

Having seen this research into sensitive parenting verified in our practice, a major concern for us is parenting programs that emphasize structure over sensitivity. These programs falsely teach that sensitivity is a form of spoiling a child. They underscore the need for a plan—a sort of cookie-cutter mentality that places infants on rigid feeding and sleeping schedules that ignore the child's basic temperament and physical hardwiring.

We are pro structure, but we are more sensitivity based, especially in the first two years of childhood. The fact is that sensitive parenting creates a foundation; it literally shapes the brain structure[8] that leads to better-behaved kids who can care more deeply about others.

Insensitive parents, however, tend to dismiss their children's crying.[9] They work their own schedules, believing that to respond sensitively to their children's distress is coddling or spoiling, much like Erica believed in chapter 2. When holding their babies, insensitive parents are less affectionate and tend to be physically brusque. Most importantly, they find it hard to respond appropriately to their children's attachment needs. As their children become distressed and upset, insensitive parents become more frustrated and angry, and in doing so, they turn what could be a time of comforting into a major power struggle.

Dismissive Parenting

Dismissive parenting is a form of insensitivity that primarily involves dismissing the child's emotions, especially negative ones. For example, when a nine-year-old girl comes home from school in a grumpy mood, she's gruff with her younger brother and complains to their mom about having to empty the dishwasher, her usual job. A mom who's sensitive to the situation might ask, "What's wrong? You seem to be awfully grouchy today." She invites the child to figure out why she's so irritable.

A dismissive parent, however, ignores the emotion or labels it as a bad attitude. She might say to the grumpy child, "I don't know what your problem is, but you'd better change that attitude right now." The dismissive parent acts as if the child's feelings are unimportant.

Dismissive parenting happens all around us. Go with us to a recent Little League baseball game. After a little guy dropped a short pop-up fly, allowing the winning run to score, he went to his mom, upset and dejected about what he'd done. She replied flippantly, matter-of-factly, her eyes focused out toward the parking lot, "Stuff happens; just go on. Don't whine about it; whining won't do anybody any good."

Rejection

Rejection is a much stronger type of insensitivity than dismissiveness and brings an almost complete disengagement from the child. These parents aren't just cold. Rejecting parents are emotionally disengaged from their infant children, sometimes mocking, even ridiculing them. When their babies cry, these parents can become noticeably angry and troubled and tend to criticize the infants. Such parents push away emotional closeness and dislike close physical contact. In one of the Ainsworth studies, even though mothers of avoidant children held their children as frequently as other mothers, the quality of that contact was much different. It was brusque, sometimes abrupt, and rarely, if ever, tender, warm, or gentle.

Intrusive Parenting

Intrusive parenting provides too much of a good thing. Infants and children need to be held, hugged, and talked to in comforting tones. But intrusive parents overdo it. They fail to read the child's subtle, nonverbal cues that say, *Okay, Mom, I feel better now. I want to go play.* The intrusive parent may dismiss or "guilt-trip" these requests to be left alone, saying, for example, "You really don't want to push Mommy away, do you, dear?"

Bugs Bunny comes to mind, as he often does in our practice (just kidding). In one of his cartoons a huge snowman attempts to capture Bugs as a pet. In moments of intense ardor, the snowman snatches up ol' Bugs and squeezes him in his bulky arms while he roughly strokes Bugs's long ears. "I want to hold you," he says, "and hug you, and love you, and squeeze you. . . ." During this show of affection, our poor bunny friend's eyes bug out from being squeezed so hard as he tries to wrench himself free. But the snowman is oblivious to Bugs's desire to escape any more lovin'.

Intrusive parents are like the snowman. They fail to read the child's cues, probably because they don't care to read them; they just run over the child with their own wants.

Consider Alicia, for example, the mother of two children: Debbie, nine, and Nicole, ten. Alicia was irked that neither of the girls shared their feelings with her or came to her when they were upset. In an attempt to observe their family dynamic, we invited all three in for a session. It didn't take long to identify the reason the two kids kept their mother at emotional arm's length. Whenever they brought anything up to her, Alicia began firing off questions like a Gatling gun. And each had the stinging tone of accusation, implying the child's problem was the child herself. "Well, what did you do that for . . . ?" "No wonder your teacher got mad. Why didn't you . . . ?" "How many times have I told you that would happen? Why don't you listen to me?" And then, "Doctor, do you see what I have to put up with?"

For Debbie and Nicole, bringing a problem to their mother was like bringing their head to the guillotine; comfort, empathy, or understanding were nowhere to be found. Alicia thought she was trying to get information so that she could teach them properly. But her district-attorney method gave them no opportunity to express their feelings, their hopes, or their desires.

The Three Shades of Avoidance

Avoidantly attached persons usually share one or more of the parenting environments we've identified here, but they can also have other characteristics that set them apart. Usually those with avoidant attachment come in one of three shades: narcissistic, exiled, or compulsive perfectionist. Let's take a brief look at these characteristics.

The Narcissist or Inflated False Self

Narcissism is a state of excessive, inflated self-love. This sense of self-love is considered a *false self,*[10] because below the layer of superiority festers a deeply rooted sense of worthlessness. Nonetheless, several characteristics about a narcissistic character style can make life difficult for others. Typically this person

- seeks excessive praise from others
- tends to be arrogant and condescending and portrays an inflated sense of self-worth
- fantasizes about fame, fortune, and power
- is very sensitive to criticism and can respond with intense anger
- takes an "I'm-first-and-everyone-else-comes-later" attitude
- manipulates others to achieve his or her own ends
- envies others' success
- associates with "special" people and engages in lots of name-dropping
- shows poor empathy for others
- is externally focused, with a "you-are-what-you-have" attitude

For the more successful narcissists, especially those who engage in entertainment, politics, public speaking, and even Christian ministry, manipulation and exploitation are common themes. These individuals frequently acquire a handpicked staff of extremely devoted followers who have committed themselves to providing their charismatic boss with uninterrupted adulation.

To complicate things, narcissists become even more self-absorbed under stress. When they receive negative feedback, for instance, they become angry and contemptuous. Their pride swells, their defense systems punch into overdrive, and they inevitably alienate those around them as they strongly, even indignantly, defend their actions, no matter how indefensible they may seem. They may even counterattack, challenging their critic for his or her failings or for having the gall to confront them. As a result, their problems go un-addressed and may worsen. Afterward, narcissists will probably avoid their critics and generally continue on in their same harmful behavior.

The Exiled, or Disconnected, Self

Unlike the narcissist, whose ego feeds off the praise of others, the exiled, or disconnected, person[11] is robed in self-sufficiency. These persons do not feel the need for acceptance or approval from others. In fact, they have very little desire to connect at all. Like narcissists, those with exiled, or disconnected, characteristics believe they must count on themselves to provide emotional and psychological support. The following are some of the other common characteristics seen by those with avoidant attachment styles whose selves are in exile:

Extreme introversion. Typically, the exiled self has cut himself off from people. He looks inward to a world of fantasy to find pleasure and comfort. To those around him, the exiled self may look cold, distant, and aloof.

Self-sufficiency. As a child, the exiled self was required to be precocious. Caregivers failed to be reliably available and trustworthy, so the exiled self learned to fend for herself. Latchkey kids are prone to develop this relational style. Having to depend on others for emotional support provokes anxiety, which leads to profound feelings of vulnerability.

A sense of superiority. Unlike the puffed-up superiority of the narcissist, the exiled self believes that only he can provide comfort and safety for himself. He prefers inwardness and fantasy over emotional connection. He has very little drive for external pleasures and derives little, if any, enjoyment from interacting with people.

Emotional desert. To wall off the self from people this person barricades her-self from her emotions. The exiled self experiences few intense feelings about anything. Life appears bland and colorless. But she likes it that way: calm, cool, and without much intensity. Unlike the narcissist, the exiled self remains tranquil when criticized because she doesn't seek acceptance. Like the narcissist, however, the exiled self has little empathy for others. She cannot identify and label her own emotional experiences, let alone understand why and how other people feel the way they do.

Loneliness. Just below the exiled self's sense of superiority lies an inner longing for connectedness. But his fear of being controlled and overwhelmed by others blunts it, so much so that he may never admit to himself or to others that the longing exists.[12]

For example, Billy was a middle-aged, impeccably dressed businessman sent to us for counseling by his wife, Kari. He was depressed, but it was hard to see it behind his big, broad-faced smile and his engaging small talk. But once the smile left his eyes, we could see an emptiness within them.

His wife complained that it was difficult to maintain a conversation with Billy. When friends gathered at their home, Billy would eventually wander off into a corner of the house to strum his guitar and compose new songs. When Kari confronted him about this, Billy said he'd just become bored and wanted to be alone.

His wife became increasingly distraught, putting more pressure on him to open up. But the more pressure Billy felt, the more he believed himself to be trapped in a marriage that threatened his individuality. After all, he was perfectly content in his world of music and ideas. Eventually he began to question whether he needed anyone, including God.

In a way, he'd come full circle. It had been pretty much like this when he was a child. His earliest memories were of sitting in the back room of his house, listening to old 45s, and daydreaming. No one ever checked on him. No one ever came back to the room and inquired about what he was doing. "I just sat back there, lost in my world."

He had walled off his feelings, his longings, and his need for anyone. When his wife and friends tried to become intimate with him, Billy became terrified of losing himself and the emotional control he now exercised. He did what he knew best and what felt safe to him: retreated into fantasy.

The Hardened Heart

The Compulsive Perfectionist

"I can't talk to her about anything," Frank told us, referring to Kathy, his wife. "She complains endlessly. Nothing is ever right, and nobody can please her; she wants everything to be just so. And when it's not, she launches into a hissy fit.

"The kids won't take their problems to her. She starts preaching at them the moment they do, about how they should do this and shouldn't do that. She drives them nuts because she's such a control freak. And I'm caught in the middle. I don't know what I'm going to do."

Frank is talking about a perfectionist. As children, perfectionists achieved attention only for significant successes and were ignored or sternly criticized for anything less. They were discouraged from showing intense feelings, and they were severely chastened for expressing anger or frustration. Their parents were emotionally cold and distant, and they were very uncomfortable with physical expressions of affection or intimacy. Perfectionists value logic and order. For them, feelings and relationships are sort of like ants at a picnic.

Here are some other characteristics of the compulsive perfectionist:

- pays excessive attention to details, order, and organization
- controls others, frequently using guilt
- demands that self and others submit to rigid, moralistic rules with lots of dos and don'ts
- has difficulty sharing; viewed by others as stingy of time, money, and resources
- is uncomfortable with emotions; very constricted
- is uncomfortable with physical touch
- has difficulty displaying affection toward others
- tends to procrastinate because of such high standards for performance
- is reluctant to delegate tasks because others are viewed as incompetent[13]

As with Kathy, many perfectionists come to counseling only after being prodded by family members who are clinging tightly to the ends of their ropes. Perfectionists are prone to depression, especially after losing control of some element of their lives. They are also vulnerable to anxiety problems and worry. And when they are worried about something, their compulsive perfectionism intensifies, and they are quite irritable and cantankerous.

DISTURBING TENDENCIES

Because of the way persons with the avoidant attachment style see themselves and their relationship to others, they tend to be the most likely of the identified attachment styles to develop two especially disturbing tendencies: addictive behavior and/or an angry resentment of God.

Addictive Behavior

As we discussed in chapter 3, addictive behavior stems from turning away from others, especially God, and looking to the self, and only the self, for comfort. This state of inwardness, so characteristic of those with the avoidant attachment style, sets the stage for addiction, where the avoidant looks for intimacy substitutes. The focus of this self-feeding process can include such behaviors as excessive fantasy life, Internet addictions, eating disorders, compulsive masturbation, substance abuse, shopping sprees, and compulsive thrill seeking (driving fast and other types of high-risk behaviors).

Angry Resentment toward God

In our research,[14] we found that the avoidant attachment style was often associated with an angry resentment toward God. This resentment, referred to by Gary Habermas[15] as *volitional doubt,* involves a turning away from God and pursuing sinful habits. Volitional doubt is driven by feelings of resentment, a belief that *God is not really there for me; I've prayed and prayed, yet he never comes through. I don't need Him; I just need me.* In a similar vein, many of the atheists we have met are notably avoidant in their attachment style. They rely on no one, including God.

Many avoidants have dampened their desire to learn about God. They have stopped seeking Him, stopped praying, and given up on the church community. For avoidants, God's purpose is seen as merely making sure nothing goes wrong in their lives. So when things do go wrong in their lives, they blame God. They say to themselves, *See? God doesn't care about me. This just proves He is not involved in my life. I'm definitely not turning toward Him. He lets you down, just like everyone else in this world.*

This mind-set only perpetuates the avoidant's distancing and isolation. First, it assumes that God's purpose is to make sure we don't run into trouble. Second, it downplays God's role in providing comfort during times of trouble.

Often the avoidant's life is so pressed and stressed it's easy just to push on without ever coming to a place of honesty.

Relief from Relational Poverty

As you've read through this chapter, did you recognize yourself or someone you love? If the characteristics of the avoidant attachment style don't sound familiar to you, read on! We'll be examining the other predominant relationship styles in the next chapters. But if you read this chapter, cringing at the descriptions, recognizing the forces that are at work in your own or your loved one's life, tearing apart your relationships, don't despair. Help and hope are waiting for you in the second part of this book. We'll show you how you can break free from destructive tendencies, overcome the background forces that shaped your attachment style, and begin to restore and revitalize your attachments to those you hold dearest.

5

DON'T ABANDON ME!

The Ambivalent Attachment Style

The biggest disease today is not leprosy o r tuberculosis, but rather the feeling of being unwanted, uncared for, and deserted by everybody. The greatest evil is the lack of love.
—MOTHER TERESA

Remember when you first had feelings for that special boy or girl as a child and you played the daisy game? *She loves me, she loves me not.* Sadly, some children grow up continually playing this "game" as they wonder how their parents feel toward them. They are preoccupied with Mom and/or Dad's feelings toward them: *Do they love me or not?*

There is a tentativeness in their minds. They're not always sure of where they stand. Why? Because from early in their lives they have struggled with the notion that their parents might leave them. One client recently said, "It's like Mom can love and hate me in the same breath. It's her way of control, really." As a result, these children become perpetual people pleasers and mold themselves to their parents' expectations and, later, to the expectations of others they love. They become dancers who are always onstage.

The problem is obvious: No one can always please everyone all the time. But these children try hard, walking through their childhoods gingerly, as if on eggshells. Sadly, the slightest misstep seems to destine them for anger, disappointment, rejection. A fragile self develops filled with strong but ambivalent emotions. Sometimes they feel intense love, sometimes intense hate. The comments of three recent clients help illustrate the brittle characteristics of the ambivalent attachment style.

Todd: "I guess you could say Dad loved the game. He loved to watch me play baseball. Get a hit, and he was right there beside me. But if I struck out

Comparison of Attachment Styles

Secure Attachment Style	Ambivalent Attachment Style
Self Dimension	**Self Dimension**
• I am worthy of love.	• I am not worthy of love.
• I am capable of getting the love and support I need.	• I am not capable of getting the love I need without being angry and clingy.
Other Dimension	**Other Dimension**
• Others are willing and able to love me.	• Others are capable of meeting my needs but might not do so because of my flaws.
	• Others are trustworthy and reliable but might abandon me because of my worthlessness.
Avoidant Attachment Style	**Disorganized Attachment Style**
Self Dimension	**Self Dimension**
• I am worthy of love.	• I am not worthy of love.
• I am capable of getting the love and support I need.	• I am not capable of getting the love I need without being angry and clingy.
Other Dimension	**Other Dimension**
• Others are either unwilling or incapable of loving me.	• Others are unable to meet my needs.
• Others are not trustworthy; they are unreliable when it comes to meeting my needs.	• Others are not trustworthy or reliable.
	• Others are abusive, and I deserve it.

or made an error he would lose it. Then he ignored me, wouldn't even look at me. There were times after I'd messed up in some way when he would leave the game and not even come back to take me home. Before long, I quit playing baseball."

Rebecca: "Nothing was ever good enough for my mother. She scrutinized everything I did. Oh, she never called me names or put me down, but she would launch question after question: Why this? Why that? She was always controlling and basically questioning everything I did. All those whys always had a sting of implying that what I was doing was never just quite right. It was like she was living her life through me—her unhappy, unfulfilled existence through me. So I just left. What scares me is that I'm now seeing a lot of my mother in me."

Joyce: "It's like Mom and I are best friends. She tells me everything about her life—her job, her friends (or lack of them), her fears, even her sorrow. Now, it seems like I spend most of my time worrying about her, wondering if she is okay."

These clients' comments set the stage for us to introduce another client, Amy, a college student living three thousand miles from home. Her story shows how the ambivalent attachment style can make a person vulnerable to soul wounds.

Tears seared Amy's cheeks when she came to our office, and she wiped them tentatively, almost fearfully, with a Kleenex wadded in her hand. Nineteen, with short, bleach-blonde hair and preoccupied blue eyes, Amy, during the past few months, had suffered at least a dozen sudden episodes of having the overwhelming feeling that she was going to die or that she was losing her mind. After several trips to the ER, where she underwent a number of extensive medical tests, her family doctor finally diagnosed her as having panic disorder. After breaking the news to her, he wrote her a prescription for Paxil, an antidepressant commonly used to treat the disorder, and sent her in for counseling.

For Amy, these panic attacks seemed to strike out of the blue. She'd never had them before. In fact, her life growing up in a Christian home had been relatively free of fear. Then *bang!* One day her heart began pounding, her insides seemed to rat into a tight tangle, and she was gripped by what she could only describe as acute terror. Now she'd been diagnosed with the disorder and had been told that the attacks wouldn't actually kill her, as she had feared, but she wanted to know more.

"Okay, I'm having panic attacks," she said to us. "What causes them? And how do I get rid of them?" Neither Amy nor her doctor had considered the possibility that these attacks had *relational* roots. But after talking with Amy for a little while, we thought they might.

As it turned out, Amy's six-month relationship with her boyfriend had heated to a point that had put Amy into a moral bind, one she'd been strongly warned about by her parents, her youth pastor, and a score of sermons she'd heard in church throughout her high school years. Her boyfriend was pressuring her to go much further sexually than she felt comfortable with.

"I want to put the brakes on, but I'm afraid he'll get mad," she told us. "I constantly worry he's going to lose interest in me and find somebody else. I don't know what to do. I couldn't handle it if he left."

In her heart we found that Amy's greatest fear was to be abandoned—by her parents, by her boyfriend—eventually by everyone close to her. We say "in her heart" because this *fear of abandonment* goes to the very core of how she sees herself and how she expects others to see and react to her. In this case, Amy's fear of abandonment was leading her toward moral compromise. She believed she had no inherent value in herself, and she felt no confidence that she could stand on her own. So she thought she had nothing to offer her boyfriend except sex and that if she didn't give in to his demands, he would abandon her, leaving her alone and bereft. Now that she was living away from home, she was even more vulnerable.

This concept, the fear of abandonment, is the core of the ambivalent attachment style. The internal war that results is very sobering. In this chapter, we'll explain why.

THE FEAR OF ABANDONMENT

The person with an ambivalent attachment style evolves from an emotionally brittle climate that revolves unpredictably around two opposing poles: At one moment the people we love, those we turn to for emotional and physical support, give us the distinct impression we're in their lives on borrowed time and that at any minute we'll be left on our own. Often they tell us just that, and what's worse, we might even see them abandoning others in their lives— friends and maybe even the spouse, our other parent. Then, moments later, they're in a good mood and all is well. We're smothered in hugs and good feelings, and we know we've never lived in a better, more caring environment.

Momentarily we're reassured, believing, *No one who loves me this much could ever leave me.*

Then, a little while later, the angry finger is shaking in our face again, and the fiery eyes are threatening to throw us out on our collective ears. This kind of ying-and-yang atmosphere corrodes our sense of self and clouds our belief that we have the ability to be loved, to get the love we want and need. This unpredictability is crazy-making behavior. As such, two core beliefs develop. The first is *I'm poor at getting the love and comfort I need* while the other says *I have to please my loved ones or I will be worthless and unlovable.*

Blinded by Romance, Frozen by Fear

Amy's story shows us how these beliefs result in negative behavior patterns that play out in our adult relationships. She met David a couple of days after arriving on campus. Less than a month later, she felt he might be "the one." As she sat in our office speaking about David, it was clear she was smitten. When she told us about him, she talked in one of those cute voices and with wide, expressive eyes. Even when she told us less-than-flattering things about him, she couched them in terms that relieved him of all responsibility. She was literally saturated, pore-by-pore, with romance. Her prince in shining armor glistened, and she certainly wasn't open to questions that might tarnish him.

Which is a problem in counseling. Obsessive romance is diametrically opposed to this kind of help. Romantic images conjure up idealized images of the boyfriend or girlfriend, and place him or her on an unassailable pedestal of praise and adoration. In contrast, when we counsel, we search for truth and balance.[1] Therapy is about bringing people like Amy to a safe place where they see the unvarnished fact that their hero is less than perfect. Talk about a chore!

This goal becomes doubly difficult to attain when the client is looking for a hero, someone to rescue him or her from a persistent, nagging sense of aloneness or emptiness. Persons who are preoccupied with idealized, romantic images take a don't-bother-me-with-the-facts attitude when it comes to their sweethearts. Sound familiar? If so, you probably know the pain this kind of attachment style can cause.

Amy believed her panic attacks were merely a product of bad biology—which *can* be true. We did find out that Amy's mom was also quite anxious and prone to occasional panic attacks. But even though biology might have aggravated Amy's situation, we didn't think it was the total answer. We quickly taught Amy some skills (breathing exercises, how to relax, and ways to change her negative thinking) that would allow her to cope more readily with the attacks when they occurred. We felt this would accomplish two goals: First, it would help Amy deal with the attacks, and second, it would help foster her trust in counseling. Then, ever so delicately, we began to explore Amy's relationships with her parents and with her previous beaux.

Her relationship with her mom had always been turbulent, and that ended up giving her a mixed bag of feelings about leaving home. On one hand she was ready to dance in the streets—she was elated. How great was it to finally be out from under Mom's demanding, controlling ways. On the other hand, she was sad, even anxious about it, worried about her mom's relationship with her dad. He had cheated on her mother in the past, and Amy was convinced that she, the beloved daughter, was the glue that had kept them together—or at least had kept Mom sane. She even felt guilty at times for leaving her mom alone. Amy worried that, now that she (the glue) was three thousand miles away, her parents might separate. She wrestled with the issue a lot.

But that wasn't her only source of concern. Her mother struggled with anxiety and depression, and Amy had become her confidant, the person Mom looked to for support and comfort. Thus a parent-child role reversal, common in the formative years of ambivalent-attachment-style individuals, stifled Amy's emotional and spiritual growth. In a lot of ways, she began to parent, or fill in for her mom—which meant that Amy herself never really had a parent she could turn to. It also meant she desperately wanted someone she *could* turn to, someone she *could* count on.

David, her boyfriend, looked a little like Brad Pitt, had a great sense of humor, treated her like a princess, and was always there when she needed him. So it only made sense that he quickly became Amy's new safe harbor. She came to rely on him for just about everything, especially emotional support, and he came through. For the first time ever, she felt she'd found someone she could trust. But then things began to change. As their relationship progressed, their time together became more passionate. "He wanted to do more than kiss and hold hands," Amy said, staring at her wringing hands. "We both know it's wrong, but his values get shoved aside when he pushes me to get more physical."

"Or his hormones shove his values to the side," we suggested. Then we asked, "What keeps you from putting on the brakes? What have you said to him about your feelings?"

"I don't know," Amy said pensively.

"What do you think he'll do if you *do* say something?" we asked.

"I don't know," Amy repeated, a little irritated that she was being pressed.

"Take a guess."

"He might leave me."

"And that scares you?"

"Of course it does!" Amy fired back, surprised at her sudden anger. "Where will I be when he leaves? What if I'm pregnant when he does?" Fear burned at us from behind those blue eyes.

Asking the Right Questions

Have you ever found yourself in this situation? Afraid to let someone know who you are and how you feel because you're worried you might be rejected? If you have, you can empathize with Amy. And if you can, you need to ask yourself some important questions to help identify what you should do next. Let's take a look, now, at the questions we went on to ask Amy.

"What would happen if you talked to David, straight up, about this pattern you two have gotten into and told him that you were no longer willing to do it?"

"I don't know," she said, avoiding the answer that would terrify her.

"Stick with this one, Amy. Just close your eyes and imagine telling David you want to talk with him about something important. Now imagine telling him that you really care about him and you hope your relationship lasts forever. Then imagine telling him that you really want to save yourself for marriage and that you want to stop getting into situations where you two are so close to giving that up. What would he say?"

"I don't know!" she said, pressing her open hands to her eyes as she began to cry.

"What would happen, Amy? What pictures do you have in your head?"

"I see him getting up and walking away from me."

"And if that happened, then what? What would become of you?"

"I don't know!" Her crying turned to sobs; her breathing became labored. "I'm starting to feel panicky right now."

"Just focus on your breathing; slow it down. But stay with this feeling. It's telling us a lot about what triggers your panic attacks. Your images suggest you feel if you set a boundary with David about your sexual behavior, he will . . ." We left the sentence incomplete, hoping she would fill in the blank.

Which she did: "He'll walk away from me; he'll lose interest in me."

"He'll abandon you?" we said, expressing the root issue.

"Yes! Abandon me."

"And if he did," we asked, "what would happen?"

"I don't know!" she said, facing this fear as she had initially faced the others.

One of the biggest lessons in life is learning to face your fears. When you do, the truth about your life begins to surface. Amy's panic attacks were triggered primarily by her fear of abandonment, and over the years, she'd developed an attachment style that helped ensure loved ones would not leave. That strategy was simple: Perform. Dance. And then just hope everything works out. The difficulty, of course, is that everything might not work out. Others might take advantage of you and, in doing so, violate your most sacred beliefs.

Think about it. When you always have to dance to be loved, who you are is constantly onstage. You're only as good as your last A, your last sale, your last hit. And when your loved ones' view of you can change in an instant, it cuts to the core of your being, tears at your soul. Yet you plod on. Why? Because—you guessed it—we were made for love. We need it—live by it—from the cradle to the grave. So we struggle to dance better and more often. And ultimately, this way of life focuses on what others think, feel, say, and do. As a result, a dependency develops, a sense that you are nothing or of little value apart from someone else. Talk about power! Talk about control! In Amy's relationship with her mom, who had the power? And now, with her boyfriend, who has the power?

Don't Abandon Me!

DEPENDENCY:
THE HEART OF THE AMBIVALENT ATTACHMENT STYLE

Those with the ambivalent attachment style are wonderful people to be around. They have a powerful way of making you feel good about yourself, and they can experience life with intense emotion, love, and laughter. But really they are needy people with some very strong core beliefs:[2]

- I am/feel incompetent.
- I struggle to handle things on my own.
- I need a strong protector to care and do things for me.
- This is a cold and dangerous world where people will hurt me and disaster will strike at any time, so I need to play it safe and stay close to those who are stronger and wiser.

Those who hold to these beliefs will unavoidably develop some pretty negative feelings. If they feel incompetent, when they're presented with a challenge, even a normal challenge of life, they'll be visited by stifling anxieties and nearly debilitating self-doubts. For example, a very delightful and hard-working lady we know was asked to lead devotions at the next week's Sunday school class. The next Saturday she broke out in hives, and by the time she stood in front of the class Sunday morning she had become overwhelmed to the point that after she read the verse of Scripture, her voice shut down and she couldn't even speak!

Can you imagine what it's like for those who need a strong protector to care for them to even think of going on a trip alone, dealing with hotel and plane reservations, figuring out what to do when things go wrong? The mere thought of doing these kinds of activities alone would terrify them. After all, in the eyes of dependent people, the world literally crawls with danger: Cars run out of gas, airline tickets get lost, jobs evaporate. And because they view themselves as needy, they diligently search for someone to rescue them from all these possibilities, all these eventualities. For them, "White knights are not the inhabitants of fairy tales; they are the invited dinner guests."[3]

When you believe you can't survive without the protection of someone you perceive as stronger and more competent, you're willing to go to great lengths to keep that other person around. You simply can't take the chance of driving him or her away. You have to please that person. So the template for living your life is *Make no waves*. If you're hurt, say nothing. If you're afraid, say nothing. If you need the salt, get up and get it yourself. And if you need to be a doormat, lie down, and when he's done, make sure his shoes are clean. Sure it hurts . . . but it's true. In all things, serve with unwavering devotion. Whatever you do, don't let your beliefs, your moral values, or your sense of self get in the way of pleasing that other person. Tuck them away.

Persons with an ambivalent attachment style are terrified that by asserting their own beliefs, desires, limits, and opinions, they will anger their attachment figures, and those figures will run screaming from the relationship. Now, that's a tough way to live. But it's more common than you might think.

The fear of rejection can breed some pretty destructive behaviors and feelings in those with an ambivalent attachment style:

- very low self-confidence
- fear of making decisions, looking to others to make major life decisions
- rarely expressing disagreement with others
- frequently seeking assurance, nurturance, and support
- feeling obsessed with the fear of being left alone (for example, the fear that your spouse will die suddenly)
- feeling helpless when alone
- desperately seeking new relationships when others end
- frequently subordinating themselves to others
- perpetually seeking advice
- often working below their ability level
- accepting unpleasant tasks to please others
- having a tendency to express distress through medically unexplainable physical symptoms rather than emotional pain (For example, they may develop headaches while doing unpleasant activities rather than saying, "No, I can't do this. It's too stressful.")[4]

Don't Abandon Me!

DEPENDENCY DEVELOPMENT:
THE PATHWAYS TO AMBIVALENT ATTACHMENT

You might wonder how this type of dependency develops. Let's take a look at four common scenarios that can produce a dependent personality most likely to develop ambivalent attachment.

The primary goal of good parenting is to help children become autonomous adults who are able to function independently of their parents. But some parents do just the opposite. Their goal is to foster compliant, always-there-for-the-parents kids—dependent children who are discouraged from being independent.[5]

The Cold-Shoulder Treatment

The genesis of the dependent personality can begin in situations like this: (a) The child behaves in a way the parent disapproves of, and (b) the parent refuses to talk to the child or emotionally turns a cold shoulder toward the child. Often uncomfortable with strong emotion, these parents especially learn to unleash their frigid-shoulder demeanor when the children assert their sense of self, their own opinions, and their ways that differ from the parents'. Ice also forms on their shoulders when the children express strong emotions, like anger or frustration.

Don't get us wrong here. We are not suggesting that parents allow their children to be rude or obnoxious when they disagree with their parents. However, children *should* be allowed to disagree, and that disagreement should *not* be automatically interpreted as "bad attitude" followed consistently with the cold shoulder to correct their nonconformity.

Overprotection

Kids should be allowed to be kids. When parents forbid children from participating in age-appropriate, ordinary activities because the parents believe such activities put the children in too much physical or emotional danger, the children never learn to deal with the normal bumps and bruises the world hands out. As a result, they remain dependent.

A couple of examples: A mother of an overly anxious, generally fearful child refused to let him go roller-skating because she thought he would undoubtedly break a kneecap, or worse. Another parent, of an anxious fourteen-year-old this time, insisted she sit next to her at all high school football games because "there are lots of creeps at these events, and I don't want her getting manipulated by one." Her daughter's objections were met with cold stares and emotional withdrawal. The message was clear: *I must protect you from this dangerous world, and I will withhold my approval of you if you disagree.* Safety is one thing. Overprotection is another.

Withholding Affection and Approval

As the name implies, withholding occurs as parents withhold their affection and approval when children get excited or experience joy independently of the parents.[6] As you can imagine, this dampens the children's sense of autonomy and makes it too dangerous to explore outside the parents' world.

For example, a ten-year-old girl told us she and her girlfriend were playing in her room, whispering and giggling about the typical things ten-year-old girls find funny, when the girl's mom poked her head in, interrupted, and accused them of misbehaving. With the mother present, we discussed this incident in some detail. Mom finally admitted she was jealous that her daughter was having fun without her. Mom was sending her daughter the message that it was not permissible for her to have fun independently of Mom.

Invisible Fences

An invisible fence is used to teach the dog to stay in the yard. Here's how the training goes: An electronic "fence" is buried around the perimeter of the yard. During training, when Rover, wearing a special collar, gets too close to the fence, the collar emits a high-pitched sound. As the dog walks closer to the electric field it gets a painful shock. The master then pulls the dog back, away from the shock. The dog quickly learns two things: First, it associates the high-pitched sound with pain, so when it hears it in the future, it stops and retreats. Second, it believes the electric force field continues, infinitely, beyond the perimeter. That's why good doggie parents never let the dog loose beyond the invisible fence's electric field. It will learn its parents have misled him, and may take them out of its will.

Dependency develops in the same way whenever children behave autonomously, express their own opinions or their feelings of anger or frustration, or engage in age-appropriate activities, and the parents display disapproval. Just as the dog associates the high-pitched sound with a painful electric shock, so the dependent person comes to associate painful disapproval with the experience of autonomy and independence. Likewise, just as the dog becomes anxious at the sound from its collar and retreats into the safety of the master's yard, so the dependent person becomes fearful whenever faced with independence and anxiously seeks refuge in the caregiver.

Three Shades of Dependency That Lead to Ambivalent Attachment

Anxiety, uncertainty, and self-doubt rumble like a nearby subway just beneath the surface of dependent people. Their goal is to manage the anxiety. If and how they manage it differs, however. Let's take a look at three shades of dependency.

The Anxious Dependent

Anxious dependents behave a little like turtles without their shells. They feel vulnerable all the time—to the world and to others. All they ever want is security and to be protected, but they never get it, or at least they never feel that they do. Instead, a foreboding sense of danger, of being somehow defective and inadequate, follows them like a little black cloud. If you are married to one of these people, you understand. Caught in a tough spot, this strong dependency is combined with the dismal sense that others will inevitably reject them.

For these people, the greatest fear is that others will get to know them for who they really are—inadequate and defective. And they are sure this awareness will lead to instant and outright rejection.

As a consequence, anxious dependent persons hesitate to start a relationship unless certain that they won't be rejected. And how many relationships like that do you know? To the casual observer, these people appear apathetic and disinterested in relationships, but somewhere inside them a storm of desire clashes with fears of rejection—and the thunder rolls. Some common characteristics include

- a tendency to avoid close relationships because of fear of rejection
- an unwillingness to get involved in activities that require social interaction
- a pattern of restraint and reservation within social situations
- excessive fear of criticism
- an aversion to embarrassment, one of the most feared emotions
- low self-esteem, a feeling that the person is fundamentally flawed or defective
- a tendency to exaggerate risks, especially the risk of being embarrassed socially
- a tendency to be easily sidetracked and overwhelmed by otherwise minor failures or disappointments

Engulfed in this fire, it's very difficult to get out of the flames. Why? Because it's a vicious, self-repeating cycle that is often plagued by a number of negative thought patterns:

- I feel flawed; no one could possibly like me.
- Every failure verifies I am flawed.
- If someone rejects me, it also proves I'm flawed.
- Those who like me must not really know who I am or else they're poor judges of character.
- If I feel embarrassed, it will be overwhelming and unbearable.

What's also difficult is that they tend to behave in ways that invite rejection from others. For example, Gina was an anxious dependent college student who followed her high school boyfriend to college, where they continued dating. But during her freshman year she became depressed because she couldn't develop new friendships with other females due to spending all her time with the boyfriend so that she wouldn't lose him. Faced with all the pressures of her new life, she became clingy and controlling with her boyfriend. As a result he felt smothered and found someone else.

To find a solution to her problem, Gina went to counseling. After several sessions, she was referred to group therapy. Soon after starting the group, her self-defeating pattern of behavior surfaced again. During the sessions, she just sat there aloof and disinterested, rarely making direct eye contact with the others. When she finally opened up and described her incredible fear of embarrassment and her actual desire to connect with group members, many of the group members were shocked. They told her they initially thought she was snobbish and conceited. So they had withdrawn their attention and ignored her. This revelation shocked Gina as well and caused her to see, with the group's help, how she'd fallen into a self-defeating cycle of social behavior.

Just to put a fine point on it, let's review the cycle: Gina felt flawed, and she feared if others knew her true self, they'd reject her. So she withdrew socially to prevent them from knowing her. Others, in response, interpreted her stand-offishness as a sign of disinterest and conceit. They reacted angrily and withdrew from Gina, putting up a wall of indifference. Gina, not to be outdone, interpreted this as confirmation of her feelings of being flawed and worthless.

The Melodramatic Dependent

While anxious dependents deal with the fear of rejection by withdrawing, melodramatic dependents, often women, are far more active about it. They seek attention with great enthusiasm and tenacity.[7] Unfortunately, when trying to achieve their goals of acceptance and social applause, they tend to rely too heavily on their looks and theatrical displays of emotion. As a result others tend to see them as shallow and immature as they live "life as a child, hoping to find a perch on Daddy's knee."[8] Their ambivalent attachment style is characterized by dependency and attention seeking, especially getting attention from men. The following list shows some important characteristics and life themes of melodramatics:

- are "onstage" all the time as they seek to be the center of attention
- tend to perceive relationships as closer than they really are
- are strongly impacted by the opinions of others
- pay excessive attention to their physical appearance
- always want to stay looking young
- dress in sexually provocative ways but get little pleasure from sex, even in marriage
- shift emotions rapidly, often quite dramatically
- speak in a very impressionistic way, paying very little attention to details
- though emotional displays may be quite dramatic, they generally try to downplay stronger emotions (especially about abandonment) and present themselves in a very favorable light[9]

Movies, the secular music industry, and pop magazines strongly reinforce the "beauty" image for our kids. They underscore the message that the more attractive you are physically, the more lovable you are, and if others are more attractive than you are, they're more lovable as well. In addition to basic dependency, melodramatic dependent people struggle with three fundamental beliefs:

- I must be the center of attention or I'm not worthy/lovable.
- I need someone, especially a strong man, to constantly offer me reassurance and praise or I will feel awful about myself.
- In order for others to want to be around me, I must always be fun and exciting.[10]

It's no wonder they're thought by those nearest them as shallow—because they might just be! And for good reason, since they spend so much time and energy on their externals while paying little attention to their internals. Self-knowledge is often just avoided. It feels alien, just plain odd, to look too deeply into their own thoughts and feelings. As children, their parents praised their looks and theatrics, not their thoughts and feelings when they tried to discuss them. In fact, because self-reflection was somehow threatening to their parents, it was shunned and ignored.

Lizzi exhibited many of the characteristics of the melodramatic dependent. Forty years old with two teenage daughters, she attended the same group as Gina and complained incessantly that "no one really cared" about her. She said her daughters were growing up and were more connected to their peers and their boyfriends, and her husband, a successful businessman, was gone almost three weeks a month. "He makes big bucks, which I need—I love to shop. I gotta look good, y'know. I like to glitter when I walk." Everyone in the group agreed she actually did.

But the more she talked, the more everyone, including Lizzi herself, realized her marriage was profoundly dissatisfying and a source of a lot of anxiety and frustration. As the group experience continued for Lizzi, her melodramatic style became more apparent. At one meeting a member confronted Lizzi on her lack of substance, her tendency to focus on wealth and prestige rather than on character, feelings, and thoughts. He wanted to know how she really felt about life issues, how she felt about others in the group. He was tired of hearing about her money, her clothes, and her church activities. The rest of the group chimed in with similar questions, but Lizzi shut them off as she collapsed into a histrionic display of tears. Her face twisted and streaked with mascara, Lizzi squalled, "You guys don't understand me. Nobody understands me." Then she slumped into her seat and withered into sobs. Everyone fell silent and open-mouthed as they glanced at one another with deep discomfort.

To Lizzi's credit, she stuck it out with the group. And over time she gathered some important information about herself and her marriage. Probably most importantly, she came to understand that if she wanted deeper, more intimate relationships and she wanted to dampen her nagging sense of loneliness, she had to get *real*—both with herself and with others. This was rocky, uncharted territory for Lizzi, but she schlogged her way through it.

Next, she learned her looks were not synonymous with her self-worth and lovability. Because she had equated looks with those characteristics, whenever Lizzi's hubby commented on how other women were also attractive, Lizzi went off like a Roman candle. She was sure he was admitting he loved other women. And if he considered other women attractive, then he must consider her "as ugly as an ol' cow"!

Well, on this topic, the group sparked like the Fourth of July. The members held an opposite view, but Lizzi wasn't about to be easily swayed. She was prepared to fight tooth and nail for this belief, because it was a faith to her, an intensely held conviction, so deeply lodged in her mind that she couldn't see life unfolding any other way.

Tom, a middle-aged, pudgy-cheeked member of the group, leaned forward in his chair. "Lizzi," he began, "take a look at us guys here. We're all just regular guys, past our prime, but even when we were at our peaks we weren't all that good looking. Do you think our wives really think we're the best-looking guys they've ever seen? Do you think my wife believes I'm the best-looking thing on the planet? She'd have to be delusional!"

Lizzi smiled. She was starting to get it.

Tom went on. "But she loves me. I know she does. She'd have to, to stay with a guy who looks like me. She's not in it for the looks. That's obvious, isn't it? There's more to me than my looks."

Tears welled in Lizzi's eyes then broke down her cheeks. She'd stopped wearing so much mascara to group meetings, but what little there was of it began to run. Reacting, several in the group expressed concern and asked her why she was crying.

"There's nothing else," she cried, the tears stronger now, "nothing but my looks. I hate getting old. I hate having to worry every day about wrinkles, about weight, about how my clothes fit, about what I eat. I hate it. But that's all there is to me. My looks. Without them, I'm nothing!"

This was an important admission for Lizzi. It distilled on the outside what had been, up until that moment, an internal truism. Now it was out in the open and in play, and over the next year or so, the group helped her deal with it. How? They helped her find more about herself than just her looks to rely upon. Finally, she saw herself as more than just a boy-toy, more than a Christian version of Madonna's "Material Girl." She discovered that others enjoyed hearing about her opinions, her insights, her thoughts, and her feelings. When she shared those elements of who she was, they felt closer to her. And, to her surprise, she felt closer to them and, as such, far less lonely, less clingy, and less dependent.

Her relationship with God also got stronger. She began to realize that no man could meet the deepest longings of her heart—only He can. We witnessed how she started turning to Him for a sense of safety and security and began to rely less on the things she had.

The Angry Dependent

Although anger seems out of place for a dependent person, it's a common characteristic—if we define it right. So before we go any further, let's define two types of anger.[11]

Primary adaptive anger recognizes we've been wronged or mistreated. It is validating anger; some have called it righteous indignation, a sense that *This just isn't fair. I don't deserve what you've done to hurt me.* For example, if a husband comes home from work an hour late without calling, a move that causes the wife's roast to burn, she might say, "I'm mad. You don't care about the work I do around here or my feelings. Do that again, and you're sleeping on the couch with the dog."

Secondary maladaptive anger frequently ignores the event that provoked the anger and suppresses it. Behaviorally, it's repressed anger, tamped down—stuffed and overcontrolled because the person is afraid to be direct about it. However, anger can't ever be totally repressed for very long, because it always finds an expression. In time it will surface—maybe physically, in problems like ulcers or high blood pressure, or perhaps emotionally, through irritability and nagging. In the above situation, consider that the wife, instead of confronting the husband when he gets home, says nothing initially. But later she may begin criticizing him about how he strews his clothes all over the bedroom or how he never completes a project: "You've got half-done projects all over this house," she might continue. The husband fights back, and as the battles between them heat up, she may escalate from criticism to contempt,[12] assaulting his character or his prowess as a father, a husband, or a follower of Christ, and so on.

For dependent people, anger generally takes the form of the secondary maladaptive type. This causes those exasperating, unsatisfying emotional wars of the type we just described, but it can also get even worse. An unfortunate, but all too frequent, scenario bubbles up if the partner, tired of the nagging, emotionally disengages from the dependent person and goes silent. The walls thicken and become impenetrable, forcing the angry dependent person into a vicious cycle as he or she becomes increasingly exasperated by the situation. After all, angry dependents believe themselves unworthy, and when their anger, no matter how indirectly expressed, goes unacknowledged, anger can easily degenerate into rage. Inevitably the relationship deteriorates. When this happens it fulfills the dependent's worst nightmare and a morbid depression or devastating anxiety may consume the soul.

BREAKING THE CYCLE

To be honest, we feel a little uncomfortable sharing these rather dark and disturbing descriptions of the ambivalent attachment style with its clinging dependence and self-feeding tendencies toward anxiety, anger, and despair. We know if you've recognized yourself or a loved one as you've read this chapter, you've probably been hurt by the stinging descriptions and disturbing depictions. If you're one who relates to your loved ones with an ambivalent attachment style, you might even have become embarrassed as you've read these depictions—and we've already discussed how fearful you are of that unwelcomed emotion! But we encourage you to keep reading. You *can* break free of this destructive cycle of dependence. Just as we helped Lizzi and Gina— and many others—escape the negative aspects of the ambivalent attachment style, the information we share in the second half of this book can help you break free to a new life of close, rewarding relationships.

6

THE GRASS IS ALWAYS DEAD
ON BOTH SIDES OF THE FENCE

The Disorganized Attachment Style

Being abandoned, treated with inconsistent love and abuse,
and being subjected to contradictory communications
all contribute to a child's sense of helplessness.
—LOUIS BREGER

Persons with a disorganized attachment style have the ability to find darkness everywhere they turn. As they look out at the world of relationships, the grass is always dead on both sides of the fence. Why? Because they hold a negative view of others *and* a negative view of themselves. The result is behavior that includes a mixed bag of attachment problems. We often describe these persons as having a "shattered self." They can behave like those who have an avoidant attachment style, looking inside themselves for satisfaction as they emotionally wall off those close to them. Then, they can sense some kind of shift in the emotional winds and change strategy without warning, becoming desperately clingy and dependent, like those with the ambivalent attachment style, as they hope a stronger, wiser other will come to their rescue. Surprisingly, at other times, they may appear secure and relate to others in warm, trusting ways.

These sudden shifts from one attachment strategy to another often leave those closest to them confused and frustrated while the "disorganized" persons themselves feel trapped in a chaotic world, one of rapidly shifting emotions, impulsive behaviors, and muddled relationships.

Do you know people like this? We do, and we'd like to introduce one of them to you.

Comparison of Attachment Styles

Secure Attachment Style	Ambivalent Attachment Style
Self Dimension	**Self Dimension**
• I am worthy of love.	• I am not worthy of love.
• I am capable of getting the love and support I need.	• I am not capable of getting the love I need without being angry and clingy.
Other Dimension	**Other Dimension**
• Others are willing and able to love me.	• Others are capable of meeting my needs but might not do so because of my flaws.
	• Others are trustworthy and reliable but might abandon me because of my worthlessness.
Avoidant Attachment Style	**Disorganized Attachment Style**
Self Dimension	**Self Dimension**
• I am worthy of love.	• I am not worthy of love.
• I am capable of getting the love and support I need.	• I am not capable of getting the love I need without being angry and clingy.
Other Dimension	**Other Dimension**
• Others are either unwilling or incapable of loving me.	• Others are unable to meet my needs.
• Others are not trustworthy; they are unreliable when it comes to meeting my needs.	• Others are not trustworthy or reliable.
	• Others are abusive, and I deserve it.

TRAUMATIZED TWICE

"I don't know what's wrong with me," Linda said, pretty much as you'd expect her to say it: confused and worried. Her raspy voice, heavy with a New York-Latin accent, was electric with desperation. "My family doesn't even think it's safe to be around me no more." Right there in front of us, her face, already harshly etched, became tight with panic. She was heavyset and middle-aged, and it was obvious that years of bad choices had taken their toll on her.

96

"I feel like I'm going to explode!" she went on. "All these stupid doctors I've been seeing—they don't know what's going on with me." Linda now became angry. Not only was she struggling emotionally, but she dragged along with her a body plagued by unexplainable physical symptoms: neck pain, lower-back pain, occasional chest pain, tingling in her hands, cramps in her stomach, extreme fatigue. And the doctors' medical tests had found nothing.

"So what brings you to see us?" we asked, almost rhetorically.

We were a little surprised at her answer. "Well," she began, rather sheepishly, pausing for a second or two, "I told my doctor I'd bust his head if he didn't figure out what was wrong with me. He didn't like that too much. So he sent me here. He said if I didn't get counseling he wasn't going to treat me no more. So here I am."

Not exactly the circumstances under which we see most people, but . . . whatever works. We asked Linda to tell us her story.

Two years ago, while working the late shift in a convenience store, a young man came in to buy some beer. When she asked for ID, he reached into his coat, pulled out a shortened broom handle and whacked her across the face with it. She fell to the floor, and instead of just running off with the beer, her attacker jumped the counter and began savagely kicking her in the ribs.

The incident traumatized her—and stayed stuck in her mind. She'd be thinking about something completely unrelated, and suddenly her mind would flash onto the event. Sometimes it was just a momentary flashback, but sometimes her mind would transport her behind that counter again and she'd feel again the toes of his shoes digging into her side, feel again her own death beating on her. In the middle of the night, she'd awaken having just relived the terrible event in a dream so real she could taste her own blood.

"And suddenly, when I'm driving somewhere, or when I'm sitting alone at night watching television, I look at my life, at me, and I feel hopeless. I mean really hopeless. And when that happens, I feel emotionally numb. Like I'm hollow inside. Empty. Just a big hole down in there. But I don't always feel like that. Sometimes I feel so mad—so angry—angry enough to spit nails. It just comes on me, especially if I see something that reminds me of—well, the event. I never go down the street anymore that the store's on. And if I see a young man who looks like the attacker, I break into cold sweats, and I'm sure my life's going to end right there and then."

A full-blown panic attack. But there was more to the story about that terrible night she was attacked. When Linda went to the ER for treatment of her injuries, the doctors found something quite unexpected in the X-rays. The films showed that Linda's body was plagued by a lot of old bone fractures in her hands, her wrists, and her ribs; there were even bone fragments in her face and on her skull. Their first guess was that when Linda was a child she'd been in a car accident. But she had no memory of an accident. Plus, an accident severe enough to cause the kind of trauma the doctors were seeing would have almost certainly involved another visit to the ER—and surely she would have remembered that. So what had caused these injuries, and why hadn't they been cared for?

Dissociation: A Normal Response to Abnormal Circumstances

Eventually we learned that Linda's devastating experience on the floor of that convenience store was the unfortunate continuation of experiences that had been visited upon her as a young teen. But although she grew up in the projects of New York City, the perpetrator wasn't some tough-looking member of a neighborhood gang. The offender was her mother.

Linda's father had died when she was only seven. Two years later her older brothers moved out of state to work the coal mines of Appalachia. Soon after that, her mother remarried a man named Ed.

Ed found Linda attractive, and within months of marrying her mother, Ed began slipping into Linda's room at night after her mother had fallen asleep. But her mother didn't stay asleep. Before long she knew about Ed's evil intrigues. But instead of protecting her daughter by taking the back of a skillet to Ed, she turned the skillet on Linda, enraged by a bonfire of jealousy directed toward her daughter. One of her favorite "skillets" was a broomstick, and she hit Linda with it every chance she got. She also bent Linda's fingers back until they popped. "There were mornings when Mom threatened to kill me if I told anyone that it was her hitting me and not me just falling down. I don't think my teachers believed me when I explained away some bruise by tellin' 'em I just fell down the stairs or something. But they never said anything. No one ever showed up on my doorstep or anything like that." So no one ever knew that Linda was the target of a tragic triangle—her stepfather's sexual abuse and her mother's physical and psychological torture.

THE LOSS OF A SAFE HAVEN

As we discussed in chapter 2, attachment relationships form because we, as needy children, seek someone stronger and wiser to protect us from a dangerous world. One of parents' fundamental roles is providing a safe haven for their children when the children are distressed. As the children mature, they internalize this safe haven as a feeling, a sense of *felt* security. This felt security becomes a template for understanding how close relationships work. The support and comfort they receive in their safe haven makes them confident they can get the support and comfort they need from other attachment figures—a spouse, close friends. They know these attachment figures will be available when they're needed.

In contrast, children like Linda who have been traumatized by their parents are placed in an awfully tough spot. Their parents are both the "source of and the solution to"[1] their fear and anxiety. Which simply means there is no solution, there is no safe haven, no place to go that's calm and reassuring. Yet, in their hearts they know there ought to be. Parents ought to be the safe haven. God programmed these children to believe, *They ought to love me. And I should love them, not dread them.* But no matter what *ought* to be, there still is no solution for them when anxiety calls. And because there isn't, these children become disorganized and emotionally fragmented during stressful times.

Dissociation As a Solution

Linda's only way to manage the volcanic emotions and animal pain triggered by her stepfather's sexual abuse and her mother's physical abuse, abuse so severe it caused the damages seen in those X-rays all those years later, was to go emotionally and psychologically limp. "I just let go," she said, her eyes still full of questions. "I let go of who I was, of who I wanted to be, of—me. And I went into another world. Off to never-never land—to somewhere else even further. I could still see what was going on. But it wasn't me anymore getting pounded, getting hurt by him, by them. It was someone else."

Dissociation is the ability to psychologically cleave off thoughts, feelings, and even physical pain, and shift the experiences to some other part of the consciousness. Young children are prone to use dissociation as a way to cope with life's normal anxieties. Louis Breger put it this way: "The essence of dissociation . . . is to be found in the typical ways in which a child meets a conflict he cannot resolve in reality; that is, by splitting himself off from such reality and 'solving' conflicts in play or fantasy. . . . Fantasy solutions to conflict involve an abandonment of a direct or 'real' solution for a 'pretend' or imaginary one."[2]

Later in this chapter we will outline the types of abuse children suffer. When children are repeatedly abused, they rely increasingly on dissociation as a way of coping. Infants and toddlers exhibit dissociation in odd, sometimes contradictory, and often disorganized behaviors, especially when they're anxious or frightened. Mary Ainsworth found that children she classified in category "D—Disorganized" were unable to coordinate a coherent attachment strategy. For example, when the mother reentered the room following a brief separation, some of these children would dart toward their mothers, then, just before they reached them, they'd fall on the floor. Others would be clearly upset. They wanted their mommies, searched for them, but in the middle of their quest, they'd stop and just stare off into space. Still others put their hands over their mouths then hunched their shoulders in fear. In all cases, these children had no clear, consistent strategy to deal with anxiety in their parents' presence. These were outward indications that these children viewed their parents as both the "source of and solution to their fear."

The disorganized, contradictory behavior of these children in Mary Ainsworth's study was a sign of dissociation. It was also something else: a harbinger, an omen, a dark cloud hovering ominously on the horizon of these children's future—a broken self. These children generally grow up to be adults who have difficulty controlling their emotions.

If you're married to someone like this, no doubt you have found how hard it is to love and comfort your spouse.

The Abusive Family:
The Pathway to the Disorganized Attachment Style

In 1962, the *Journal of the American Medical Association* published an article entitled "The Battered-Child Syndrome."[3] Before this, most Americans, including the medical profession and the church, turned a blind eye to childhood abuse and its devastating impact on a child's emotional development. For example, as late as 1980, one of the nation's foremost textbooks on psychiatry claimed that fewer than one in a million women had experienced childhood incest and that the impact of incest was of little consequence.[4] During the 1970s and 80s, with the Vietnam War and the increasing awareness of childhood sexual abuse and domestic violence, experts began to notice an interesting pattern: Survivors of trauma, no matter the source—war, domestic violence, sexual assault, incest—all had a very similar pattern of symptoms, very much like Linda's.

"Home," according to Bruce Perry, arguably one of the most prominent experts on childhood trauma and brain development, "is the most violent place in America."[5] As Christians, we work from the assumption that many more people than the church realizes, or is willing to admit, are affected by the brutal, savage reality of childhood abuse. While some, like Linda, have been directly affected by it, others have loved ones who've been victimized.

In this chapter as we discuss the different types of abuse that occur in families, from subtle forms of psychological abuse to incest, our goal is simple: to help you understand just how devastating its impact is on developing children's psyche and how it can lead to the most damaging of attachment styles. Our hope is that you'll see just how pervasive child abuse is and how it impacts not only our children but our society.

We also hope you'll consider the prevention of child abuse a critical cause for all of us, especially the church, to invest in—invest our time, talent, and treasure. Why the church? First, because abuse of children isn't confined to nonbelievers, and when a believer engages in it, no matter how subtly or overtly, it's a sin. And the church needs to help its members confront and mortify their sins. Second, because those exposed to the toxic effects of child abuse are often so arrested by fear and so confused about their attachments, particularly about their attachment to God, that they're hardened to the gospel message or stunted in their ability to grow in three important elements of the Christian life—faith, hope, and love. Usually this happens not because of a lack of desire but because of fear—especially a fear of trusting those who are expected to be stronger and wiser. We believe this problem, like no other psychological issue, deeply affects the church and its members.

What Is Child Abuse?

How we end up defining abuse may, to some, seem radical. So it's important that we give you a quick preamble before we begin. As complex as being a good parent is, there are essentially just two goals: Parents help their children grow up to follow rules and live within limits, and they prepare them to love and be loved.

As parents, we want our children to feel secure about themselves and about their ability to offer warmth and support to others. We want to lay the foundation for them to accept love from others and to trust in the ability of others to be reliably available and supportive. When others fail them, we want our children to offer them grace and forgiveness, understanding and mercy. And when they hear the message of the gospel, we want them to gravitate toward God's love and transfer their ultimate hope and security to Him.

That said, we believe abuse is anything we do that intentionally prevents our children from developing these capacities.[6] Some might think that by concentrating on issues like these, the child might end up mollycoddled. Not so! In fact, mollycoddling, or overindulging, children is really another form of abuse. A spoiled child who has not learned how to deal with limits and who cannot tolerate normal day-to-day frustration isn't in a position to love or be loved.

Still others think that teaching a child to love and be loved runs contrary to teaching children limits. Again, the facts prove this just isn't so. Research verifies that children who are treated sensitively and who are prepared for the business of love are more likely to live within the limits God has prescribed for them. There's a saying: Rules without relationship lead to rebellion. And it's love that makes living within the rules, or limits, tolerable and desirable. Remember, the two greatest commandments are to love the Lord with all your heart—and to love others as you love yourself. All other commandments are merely extensions of these two (see Matthew 22:36–40). When we prepare our children for love to come to them and go out from them, we lay the foundation for them to live contently within limits. Love and limits go hand in hand.

SIX TYPES OF CHILD ABUSE

In this section we're going to present six forms of abuse. We've arranged them from the most subtle to the most obvious. And even though each stands on its own as a separate behavior, a common thread runs through each type of abuse. It's that the child is treated merely as an object or a piece of property, devoid of thoughts, feelings, and intentions.

Psychological Abuse

Hard-handed rejection, sarcastic put-downs, callous harshness, confused inconsistency, and unreliable care are but a few forms of psychological abuse. Many parents who are psychologically abusive are in denial about how rude and insensitive they are to their kids. They literally ignore how often they yell at or psychologically intimidate their children.

If you wonder if you're being psychologically abusive to your child, here is a litmus test: Do you treat your children with greater kindness, patience, and understanding and with a softer tone of voice when you're around acquaintances and friends? If you answer yes, ask yourself why. Most parents who do realize there is a marked difference are immediately convicted. They suddenly realize they treat their children harshly and rudely when they're outside public view.

Emotional Neglect

Bradley had but one dream—to get into politics. He ordered his life for it: political science in college, law school, then a run for mayor. The only detour he made was to get married between college and law school; then twin boys were born at the end of law school's first year. By the end of his first term as mayor, when he was thinking about a run for Congress, his wife, Debra, sat him down. "Brad, the boys are six years old, and they're really starting to need a father—a dad to play ball with them, goof around with them at night. They need a man in their life, and you're always gone."

"I'm not always gone. And anyway, when I go to D.C. you guys are coming with me, so we'll be together even more."

"They need you to play ball with them *now.*"

"Okay. I'll play ball." That night Bradley played catch with his sons for fifteen minutes before they went off to bed. The next evening he came home from work with a Nintendo and an electronic baseball game. "When you play this," he told the boys, handing them the controls, "think of me." Then he went into his study and made some fund-raising calls.

Fran Stott once penned, "Children need more than food, shelter, and clothing. They need at least one person who is crazy about them." Parenting that focuses only on the physical needs of the children is called *functional parenting.* These parents make sure their children have food, clothing, a bed, probably a Nintendo, a computer, a Game Boy, and so forth. When asked if they're good parents, these moms and dads might tell you, "The kids won't starve." But there is no warmth, no physical touch, no emotional connection. The child's emotional needs go unmet.

Physical Abuse

We realize there's a fine line between a spanking and physical abuse. We're not talking about spanking. We *are* talking about clear-cut forms of physical abuse, those Linda experienced, for instance, which can be said to be "any nonaccidental physical injury, such as beating, punching, kicking, biting, burning, and poisoning."[7] This type of parental behavior devastates kids and makes it nearly impossible for a child to form healthy attachments.

Sexual Abuse and Incest

Sexual abuse is defined as sexual contact between any child from infant to midadolescence and another person who is at least *five* years old. And if the victimized child is an adolescent, the definition includes engaging in sexual activity with someone.[8] This contact may range from fondling to full intercourse.[9] We also add lewd looks and suggestive sexual talk to the list.

Individuals outside the nuclear family instigate the majority of sexual abuse incidents. However, when sexual abuse occurs within the family, it's called *incest*. It involves a parent or an older family member taking sexual liberties with a child—whether it is exhibitionism, fondling, mutual masturbation, or intercourse.

Exposure to Severe Marital Conflict

All couples argue from time to time. In fact, children learn how to manage conflict by observing their parents disagree, maybe even squabble, then work things out. But when the squabbles turn into a scream fest, physical struggles, or violence, a child's sense of security is threatened. The child worries, *What if the home breaks apart? What if one hurts the other?* Then, even though he worries about both parents, he may be compelled to side with one and hate the other. That alone produces anxiety. No child likes to hate a parent.

Addictive Behavior

Penny was in her mid-thirties and an alcoholic. She wasn't a fall-down drunk, but not a day went by when she wasn't under the influence. She drank to dull the pain of not liking herself very much. She had been seven when her father left, never to see her or her mother again. And because she had this need to be affirmed by men, she constantly found herself in emotionally abusive relationships. But that's not why she didn't like herself. She disliked herself because she dragged her six-year-old son, Bobbie, into those abusive relationships with her. They were doubly difficult on him. Bobbie had never known his father. In fact, Penny'd only known him for a couple of weeks when she got pregnant. Now Bobbie wanted a man in his life, and he gravitated to these guys she brought home, only to be manipulated and then rebuffed.

Penny saw it happening again and again, and she always felt awful about exposing her son to these guys, but she couldn't help herself. She needed whatever it was they gave her. So she drank to dull the pain and fawned all over Bobbie to make it up to him. In response to seeing his mother in pain, Bobbie tried to save her emotionally every opportunity he got. After all, he figured it was probably his fault in some way.

As this story shows, many types of abuse overlap. For example, psychological abuse and emotional neglect are frequently mixed together. Addictive behaviors, such as alcohol abuse, substance abuse, or Internet addictions, set the stage for the other types of abuse.[10] One expert described the addicted family as one of "chaos, inconsistency, unpredictability, unclear roles, arbitrariness, changing limits, arguments, repetitiousness and illogical thinking, and perhaps violence and incest. The family is dominated by the presence of the addiction and its denial."[11]

THE SINS OF THE FATHER

Scripture makes it clear, and psychological research confirms, that people are not islands unto themselves. The effects of sin pass from generation to generation, and attachment theory helps describe how this process unfolds.

First, we take in, or internalize, the way we've been treated. If we've been loved, we feel lovable. If we've been hated, we feel self-contempt. If we have been both loved and hated, we feel ambivalent about ourselves. Put simply, a "child comes to see himself modeled after the way his parents have loved him. A child's sense of self is shaped by the way others treat him or her."[12]

Recently during a radio talk show on childhood and attachment issues, Jeff, a young father, called to ask us how he could stop screaming at his children.

Men rarely call into a radio talk show to talk about their children, and most people who yell at their kids don't feel yelling is a problem. So it was quickly obvious that Jeff was different on both counts.

Cutting to the chase, Tim asked, "Jeff, were you screamed at as a kid?"

The answer? Of course it was yes.

The talk-radio format didn't allow us enough time to go into Jeff's entire experience, but we encouraged him to remember what life had been like for him as a child and then to empathize with his children. If he could put himself into his children's shoes as he yelled at them, if he could experience the same pain and fear he'd felt when his parents yelled at him, then perhaps he could use that role reversal to help stop himself from yelling at his own children.

VICTIMS OF UNTOLD STORIES: THE LEGACY OF AN UNRESOLVED PAST

When people are traumatized or when they bear significant losses, the emotional pain can be excruciating. Most people buckle under the intensity of such pain, and they bury the pain beneath a ton of forgetfulness. Then, in the same coffin, they bury everything that reminds them of it. Burying painful memories is the same thing as dissociation. We call these dissociated memories *untold stories.*

When memories of traumatic events are buried, they are literally stored in cerebral morgue-drawers in different parts of the brain. Researchers have used brain-imaging techniques to show that when trauma victims are reminded of their tragedy, the parts of the brain associated with intense emotions and visual images "turn on" and become active. Simultaneously, the part of the brain associated with speech "turns off."[13] The result is what Basal van der Kolk calls "speechless terror,"[14] the inability to tell the story of the horrific event.

Many traumatized individuals bury their stories quite well. Burying those memories lets these people function pretty effectively in their daily lives—at least on the surface. We've seen quite a few of them as successful professionals. They've completed college, taken on tremendous responsibilities at work, managed their time effectively, and made important decisions for their companies.

But the toxic effects of their tragic past, buried deeply in remote states of their minds, surface in situations usually involving intimacy, aggression,[15] abandonment, and fear.

The Power of Reflection

God made us in His image and blessed us with the profound ability to verbally describe the world around us. Then He extended the blessing so we can describe the world inside ourselves. This is the ability to describe our feelings, our thoughts, even our physical sensations. The more we understand that world inside, the better we understand the world at work within others. We *empathize* with them and see the world through their eyes. In other words, we learn to "walk in their shoes."

Developmental psychologists have found that this ability to label our internal experiences, a process called the power of reflection, and to empathize with others helps us bring some important elements to our lives:

- The ability to know and understand feelings helps us manage our intense emotions. We know what our emotions are, and we understand that they're only emotions; they don't have to take over our lives.
- It helps us manage our impulses. Our ability to reflect on what's going on inside ourselves helps us understand when we're acting on something unusual and unexpected. For example, you may want to tell your boss to pound sand, but the power of reflection keeps the thought locked up and harmless.
- The same intellectual and emotional process that allows empathy, the ability to see the world through another's eyes, also allows us to feel close and connected to the ones we love. It is the basis for caring and compassion.
- Finally, reflection lets us believe we can influence others with our words, not just our actions. This is the foundation and reason for prayer. We believe that God can understand our needs and that He is affected by our words.

The Grass Is Always Dead . . .

Trauma Destroys the Power of Reflection

Let's go back to the concept of *dissociation*. When children are traumatized, or are constantly threatened with trauma, their power of reflection goes undeveloped. The trauma is so painful it splits off, disconnects from the child's self-awareness. So instead of understanding the self, trauma forces children to step outside the self and leave the trauma behind—the very essence of dissociation. The abused child adapts this way, otherwise he or she would be overwhelmed by fear and anxiety.

Dissociation and reflection are incompatible. The more the brain dissociates, the more difficult it is to develop the power of reflection. Dante Cicchetti and colleagues found that abused children struggle with using words to describe what's going on inside them. Had this been the only problem and there had been no abuse, it wouldn't have been so bad, but without the power of reflection, a number of grave consequences may bubble to the surface as the untold stories fester within the child's inner world.

Revisiting Hannah and Darcy

Remember Hannah and Darcy from chapter 1? Hannah brought in Darcy, her rebellious seven-year-old, for counseling. He had an explosive temper and exhibited some pretty defiant behavior. Hannah's husband had left them awhile back, and it was just the two of them as she tried to do it all, be mom and dad both while she worked as an ER nurse. Whenever Hannah played with Darcy, even in our office's safe, structured environment, an abrasive power struggle erupted. When their playtime finally ended (never happily, by the way), Hannah felt powerless, so much so that she would frequently just go limp and stare off into space, as if her mind were a thousand miles away.

Over the next few weeks, we worked with Hannah, offering her support and suggesting ways to better handle Darcy's difficult behavior. But we also suspected there was more to this story than what we'd been told. We suspected Hannah had had some severe trauma in her past. To us, Hannah's long, cold stares were a subtle sign that Darcy's behavior had triggered something inside her that she didn't completely understand. When we got her to open up about her past, we discovered we were right.

Hannah talked to us about her past, but with some reluctance. Just as Darcy's dad had left her when Darcy was young, Hannah's dad had done the same thing. Instead of buckling down and doing the best she could, as Hannah had done, her mother was devastated and tumbled into a deep depression. Hannah described seeing her mother slumped at the kitchen table, smoking one cigarette after another and drinking cup after cup of coffee. "The look in her eyes was almost frightening. Looking into them was like peering into empty caves. Yet as empty as they were, there was something in them— like she wished she'd never been born. When she did talk to me, I was an interruption, a nuisance. And when she got mad . . ." She paused for maybe twenty seconds, her eyes narrow, looking past us. We were suddenly nowhere in the room. Then she came back, as did we. "She gets really, really mad. I'm so scared . . ." We noticed the tense of her story switched from past to present. She'd entered another state of mind and was experiencing emotions she had buried long ago, emotions she had desperately tried to keep buried. But as she remembered them, they worked themselves to the surface. As she began to relive them, she slipped back into her childhood again.

She paused again, this time longer, then said, "I don't know what to do . . . I can't do anything."

"What would happen, Hannah? What made you so scared?"

"I . . . I . . . I'd just run away. I have to . . . I have to hide from her." Her voice constricted to a whisper.

"Where'd you go?"

"Under my bed," she said as she drifted into another long pause, her eyes darkly hollow again as they stared at the floor on the left side of the room, which suggested to us she was accessing memories from the right side of her brain, the side of the brain responsible for intense emotional reactions.

She struggled mightily to tell us her untold story. And when it finally came out, it was broken and fragmented, a tale of her mother's rage and physical abuse. What she didn't realize was that her life, the life that this story comprised but a vague shadow of, intruded into her relationship with Darcy.

When she was with Darcy, his demands on her brought her face to face with her own childhood.

The Compulsion to Repeat the Past

Have you ever wondered why people with horrific pasts, instead of learning from them and living later lives of calm and order, tend to experience more catastrophes later on? When asked why, they might tell you they're convinced that tragedies stalk them, seeking to corrupt their lives like unholy phantoms. Of course, those unholy phantoms are usually themselves, and their misfortunes are a result of their own poor choices, or their I-don't-care attitudes. They don't see it, although everyone else does. They generally think they've just had bad luck, or others have had them in their cross hairs.

Basal van der Kolk powerfully describes how the wounded self continues to repeat this cycle throughout their lives:

> Some traumatized people remain preoccupied with the trauma at the expense of other life experiences and continue to recreate it in some form for themselves or for others. War veterans may enlist as mercenaries, victims of incest may become prostitutes, and victims of childhood physical abuse seemingly provoke subsequent abuse in foster families or become self-mutilators. Still others identify with the aggressor and do to others what was done to them.[16]

Van der Kolk then describes how traumatized victims may become addicted to trauma. Sounds crazy, doesn't it? But it's not. Whenever the brain is faced with extreme stress, it releases chemicals called *endogenous opiods,* what could be called the brain's equivalent to heroin. These chemicals are God-given painkillers. One study, for example, showed that after viewing a fifteen-minute violent movie, the brain released the equivalent of eight milligrams of morphine.[17] Imagine those fifteen minutes repeated over and over again in a stressful, even violent, situation. The brain could easily become addicted to the drug, and withdrawing from that drug can be as difficult as breaking a drug addiction. The withdrawal symptoms mirror the nightmare of the traumatized person: emptiness, tension, irritability, and an internal sense of unrest. To relieve these symptoms, the person must return to the trauma and its corresponding "morphine."

Fear of the unfamiliar is another way "addiction to trauma" can develop. Researchers see this when they place a rat in a "shock" box. They lock the rat in the box, then shock it, making the rat's life in that box painfully uncomfortable. But over time, the rat becomes familiar with the situation, and pain becomes a way of life for Mr. Rat. Now the researchers open the box so the rat can escape, and what happens? You'd expect Mr. Rat to hightail it out of there, to put as much distance between himself and that box as the researchers would allow. But it didn't happen that way at all. The rat did leave the box, but whenever it faced something unfamiliar, it returned to the box, even though returning was painful! Why? The box was a familiar place. The animal was used to its home and retreated there whenever it became anxious, no matter the cause, even when confronted by something unfamiliar.

A Need for Chaos and Turmoil

Pamela, a recent client, had been born and raised within the emotional uncertainty of an alcoholic home, but she was determined to make positive changes in her life. After months of counseling, she was beginning to identify her feelings, get in touch with the anger that had stalked her all those years, and set reasonable boundaries. Our hopes for Pamela ran high.

She eventually began to share with her husband those feelings she'd identified. Although he wasn't particularly abusive, he wasn't particularly sensitive either. One evening he was late getting home. Expecting a call if he was late, Pamela had started cooking dinner at the regular time. But when it was done, her husband wasn't there. He didn't answer his cell phone. She knew he needed a new battery for it, so she assumed it had run out of juice. Which meant he was probably on the road somewhere, probably stuck in traffic and unable to call from the car. She could have easily let the matter drop, particularly since he'd been working very hard lately and had been suffering a lot of frustration on the job. Instead she decided to confront him. She was angry, and she needed to express it to him. So the instant he walked through the door, before he'd even had time to put down his briefcase, she let him know how angry she was.

"*You're* angry?" he said. "I'm living through a private hell, working my tail off just so you can stay home and cook that stupid dinner of yours—and *you're* angry?!" Granted, his remarks were insensitive, but that was expected. What neither of us expected, although we have to admit we should have been, was that Pamela would explode at her husband the way she did. She told us she screamed at him, waved her arms, wagged her finger in his face, and finally stormed from the house, leaving him alone with the cold chicken and equally cold potatoes. The next day was her counseling appointment. Before she even sat down, she exploded at us as well. "I'm done with this program of yours. Finished. If he's going to be that way, then why should I even try?" Pamela had decided to return to the familiar.

Research tells us, and our experience confirms, that children who come from abusive and/or chaotic homes see those homes as familiar surroundings. It's not just the "devil they know." The fact is, their brains are addicted to the constant release of endogenous opioids because of those homes. So when they experience the unfamiliar, even the *positive* unfamiliar, like intimacy or deep friendships, they feel an overpowering urge to return to the familiar, which is chaos.

That's what Pamela was doing. She decided that instead of building a calmer, more stable environment, she needed the chaos that a turbulent environment brings. That's one of the reasons that adults fleeing an abusive relationship, even after they seem to have escaped it completely, will one day return to, or create for themselves, another turbulent setting in which to live, and often that setting will come complete with an abusive relationship.

Pamela's not the only one like this we've counseled. Repeatedly we've seen clients like Pamela start to make positive changes in themselves, like exercising, eating right, and committing to Bible study, prayer, and small-group work. Moving through this process, they face low levels of anxiety, which, for them, is uncharted territory, an unfamiliar domain, one that has no internal morphine connected with it. So they sabotage their progress and retreat to their old, well-worn, chaotic behavioral routines, just as Pamela did. She'd been pushing her husband's emotional buttons for years. She knew how he'd react if she confronted him the way she did. And she knew his reaction would give her the excuse she needed. Of course, we didn't allow her excuse to stand. When she told us about her confrontation with her husband, we calmly reframed her explosion as the fear of the unfamiliar. We told her she felt the need to be in a chronic state of conflict and turmoil, and when she was, although she was opening herself up for more emotional pain, she at least found comfort.

Passing on a New Story

Darcy's mother, Hannah, tried to keep her childhood walled off, severing all connections with it. But if those connections were all broken, how could there be any connection between her childhood and her adult life? The connection came when she repeated her past. It came when she married an angry, abusive man. It came when she became an ER nurse and surrounded herself with continuous trauma.

When it came to Darcy, she tried to keep her past buried, but it came out as she replayed her own mother's anger onto him. And why wouldn't she? In a way, her child was her new life. Just as he was starting fresh from the womb, she was *re*starting *re*freshed from her past's gravesite. But burying it, saying a prayer over it, playing "Taps" over it, packing dirt over it, and placing an ornate headstone over it just didn't work. It never does. The "untold story" remained very much alive, and just like water seeking its way in, it seeped back into her life in the form of irritability, impatience, and anger. She didn't tell us about her background early in her treatment; few parents do, because they feel uncomfortable about it and about being with us. But eventually, the truth came out. I just get so angry with him," she admitted tearfully. "He's so difficult when he's that way." Although she couldn't see it at the time, Hannah's behavior, influenced largely by her past, was passing on the legacy of her unresolved trauma to the next generation.

Our goal was to help her understand her whole story: what happened; how she felt; what she did to protect herself; how she handled her feelings; how she survived; how what happened to her influenced her selection of a husband; how her feelings about her childhood painted the picture she had of her son.

Was she seeing Darcy in the same way her mother had seen her? Was she afraid to get close to Darcy? Was she afraid to acknowledge his feelings of anger, abandonment, and fear because they reminded her of her own, buried feelings? Did she identify with her mother's aggression, her mother's despair and hopelessness? Was she reenacting the story of her own childhood with a role reversal in which she played the role of the aggressor and Darcy the victim? But there was a difference. Darcy was not willing to lie down and take the abuse as easily as Hannah had. He was fighting back. His temper tantrums reflected the same rage Hannah had felt as a child but had never expressed.

Only as Hannah came to trust us and believe we could bear witness to the tragedy she endured did she reveal her story, pasting it together, bit by bit. It took incredible courage to tell the devastating story of her upbringing. But as she did it, and as she acknowledged her fear, her anger, and her sense of betrayal, she was able to better understand what Darcy was going through. She wept bitterly when she finally came to see the situation through his eyes. She held him in her arms and cried.

Now she was no longer afraid to meet Darcy at his level. She came home from work looking forward to seeing him, hearing about his day, watching him play with his GI Joes before bedtime. She no longer avoided him emotionally.

She learned to set limits without becoming enraged. She learned, when confronted, how to stay calm and not be overwhelmed with memories and sensations from the past. Yes, Darcy was still a challenging little guy, but he was better able to deal with the loss of his father without worrying about whether his mom would slide away into a sea of despair or go off into a screaming fit of rage if he asserted his budding self.

Hannah's courage to tell her story—all of it—set the stage for her and Darcy to launch a new legacy. They would write a new story and pass it on to a new generation.

The Key to Breaking the Cycle

The research on disorganized attachment has produced some pretty straightforward data. Parents who have had significant trauma, emotional and/or physical abuse, or even the loss at an early age of one or both parents are likely to pass the toxic effects of that trauma on to their children. Often, the result will be as if the children have experienced the parent's trauma firsthand. The key to breaking this cycle is the victim's ability to get in touch with his or her particular story, the whole story. That means recalling incidents and patterns, all the facts and all the feelings related to the story, most of which have been stored away, deep in the parent's brain morgue, since the incidents occurred. When they are able to paste the story's components into a coherent narrative, the mere fact that they were able to do it buffers them from the toxic effects of their traumatic past.

On the other hand, when the story goes untold, the very act of keeping it bottled up forces it to gain pressure. It's like when you shake a Coke: The carbonation increases the pressure on the cap. Either it blows or, if it's in a porous container, it thrusts itself into the weaker surroundings. Hannah's untold story pressured itself into her relationship with her son. Linda, the victim of incest and the grocery store break-in, also had stories that went untold, traumatic experiences that seemed to catapult her into the next devastating story. We've already shared the evil perpetrated on her by her stepfather and the subsequent violence visited upon her by her mother. After all that, there were also several abusive marriages and multiple rapes in her early twenties; plus, five years before, she'd been the victim of a previous store robbery. Ironically, the robberies seemed like the least tragic events in what had happened to her. Yet it was the last robbery that brought her emotional boil to a head.[18]

How about you? Did you come from a tumultuous environment, yet today you see yourself constantly going back to it? Maybe not walking up the same exact steps to the same exact front door, but to places that might just as well be those same steps, that same door? If you do, you may have an addiction to turmoil. Later in the book, we'll take a thorough look at what you can do next to break this tragic addiction. For now, just be aware that there is hope. Pamela, Hannah, and Linda all managed to escape this vicious cycle. So can you or the ones you love.

The Grass Is Always Dead . . .

The Effects of the Disorganized Attachment Style (The Shattered Self)

As Hannah, Linda, and Pamela's experiences show, trauma can shatter the self. But maybe you're thinking, *So what? Okay, I have some emotional problems. Who doesn't? Is it worth making a big deal out of this? Is it worth turning my world upside down just to get a little peace of mind?*

The answer is yes. It is definitely worth your time and your emotional energy to make this change. And here's why. In the next few paragraphs we'll show you some of the core effects of the disorganized attachment style. Keep an eye out for them in yourself or your loved ones.

Identity Problems

A sense of identity and the personal strength that accompanies it allow us to form strong values and to commit ourselves to goals. It's the internal glue that helps us decide what we like and what we don't like. It also helps the "who I am now" to remain stable over time and across various situations. With a strong sense of identity, we can make and stick to our commitments, our relationships, jobs, goals, and even the precepts of our faith.

But when the self is shattered by trauma and turmoil, so is the sense of identity. As a result, the shattered self—the person with a disorganized attachment style—may commit to some goal during the fervor of an emotional high, but when the high fades, there is no internal sense of self-value to keep the commitment alive. Thus the commitment dies. To speak globally, those with the disorganized attachment style act on the emotions of the moment but have great difficulty staying on task when their emotions change—and they tend to shift rapidly. These persons can fall out of love as quickly as they engage it, so obviously any relationship is threatened, and chaos rules, reinforcing their attachment style.

Two more identity-related problems are common. First, the person with a disorganized attachment style has trouble learning from past experience. For example, this person may have financial problems that stem from unchecked shopping sprees. But he or she doesn't stop shopping, even though the problem is obvious. Because of the identity problems and the lack of self-reflection, the disorganized person is unable to recall the pain associated with past overspending and apply it to the present.

A second problem is the inability to consider future consequences. This person has difficulty seeing how current behavior will affect his or her future. For example, when faced with the stress of dealing with a difficult boss, he or she might go ahead and smart off to the boss, not even considering that the inappropriate remarks could lead to unemployment. These two problems are direct results of the identity difficulties of the disorganized attachment style.

Emotional Storms

The person with a disorganized attachment style also struggles with self-soothing and emotion regulation. What might trigger mere frustration or worry in healthier folks, people who are able to calm themselves down or gear their emotional response to the situation, might result in inappropriate fits of rage or full-blown panic attacks in these disorganized persons. Chronic feelings of depression, also known as *dysthymia,* are common. Those with dysthymia feel glum and emotionally hollow for no apparent reason. There is little pleasure in their day-to-day life and little joy in thinking about the future.

The disorganized attachment style also makes an individual prone to slip into deep depression. Because this person has been borderline depressed and anxious throughout life, when certain events occur—job loss, conflict with a friend, financial struggles—he or she can be rapidly plunged into serious depressions.

And then there are the flashbacks, emotional experiences that are similar to how the person felt in the past during the actual event. If we're talking about that first romantic kiss, a flashback can be rather pleasant, but when it involves being unreasonably beaten by an enraged parent, well, that's something entirely different. For the person with a disorganized attachment style, flashbacks create another emotional storm. What can be particularly disconcerting about emotional flashbacks—feeling those original extreme emotions—is that the emotions felt are totally out of proportion to the triggering event.

For example, one female client who at age nine had been sexually abused by her stepfather, avoided the gynecologist for many years, although she never made the conscious connection between her being abused and her reluctance to be examined. When she finally decided to go for a checkup, she experienced a full-blown panic attack while she sat in the doctor's waiting room. Angry with herself for being so frightened, she discussed the situation with us during her next visit. Over the next half-hour or so she came to realize that her time in the waiting room was like waiting at night for her stepdad to slip into her bedroom after her mother dozed off. She had experienced a flashback.

Physical Arousal

Hyperarousal is a state of physical alertness in which the body is ready to either fight or flee. The heart races, the pupils enlarge, hot or cold flashes spark, and the body is in a state of tension. Hyperarousal represents a central feature of the trauma response, no matter what the source of the trauma, and it leads to a number of problems. When faced with new stressors, usually completely unrelated to the original trauma, the person with a disorganized attachment style responds with panic, anxiety, and a sense of extreme helplessness rather than focusing on problem solving.

Identification with the Aggressor

Could there be anything more difficult for a child than dealing with the reality that the person he or she looks to for safe harbor is the very person who seems to be trying to sink the child's boat? Can there be a greater dilemma for a child than having no one to turn to for help? Than having nowhere to go for protection and comfort? For the child, these are basic needs, akin to food and air. The child can't exist for long without them. So he or she manufactures a new image of the parents. Instead of seeing them as bad and faulty, the child directs the blame for the situation inward, on the self. As Fredrick Firestone puts it:

Rather than suffer complete ego disintegration [caused by turning anger toward the parent], children make a strong identification with the same forces that produce the torment they are trying to escape. . . . The child's tendency is to split off from the identity of the powerless "victim," identify with the powerful parent or aggressor, and later act out parents' destructive attitudes against him or herself.[19]

In other words, if you can't turn against your sources of pain, it is easy to become like them.

The Stockholm syndrome is a similar phenomenon. Scientists have studied the unusual attachment bond that develops between hostage and captor. Hostages have gone to great measures to protect their assailants and identify with the sources of their terror. Bruno Bettelheim described this phenomenon with the "old prisoners" of the Nazi concentration camps, where they had been subjected to years of torment and deprivation: "Old prisoners who identified themselves with the SS did so not only in respect to aggressive behavior. They would try to acquire old pieces of SS uniforms. . . . [They] accepted Nazi goals and values, too, even when these seemed opposed to their own interests."[20] Under extreme duress, capitulation is common.

Faulty Assumptions

By identifying with the aggressor, the abused child can continue to view the parent as an attachment figure. The unfortunate outcome, however, is that the child is riddled with self-blame and guilt, which can lead to this kind of internal exchange: *The reason I'm being hurt is that there is something fundamentally wrong with me. I am a really bad person; nothing I do is right.*

A sense of "learned helplessness" also develops. Abused children often believe nothing can be done to change their situation. Even when beset by relatively small stressors, they can feel completely at the mercy of forces beyond their control. They think, *The world just happens to me and I can do little, if anything, to change it.*

At the other end of the scale, victims can overcontrol.[21] They become obsessed with every little detail of their lives and may spend hours scrubbing floors, dusting furniture, making beds, doing dishes, and straightening what-nots, rendering their houses immaculate. They may approach relationships the same way, trying to take complete control of others. Of course, in behaving this way they are reacting against a persistent sense of powerlessness. The obvious outcome is that they invariably alienate their loved ones by trying to control them, which results in more intense feelings of betrayal, abandonment, and hopelessness.

Distressed Relationships

Relationship distress is the hallmark of those with the disorganized attachment style, the shattered self. Their difficulties with trust, their fear of abandonment, their fear of intimacy, and their altered sexuality all doom relationships.

Two factors dwell at the core of these relationship problems. First is the constant tension between being a control freak on the one hand—and being a doormat on the other. Both extremes create problems. We've already mentioned how the control freak ends up driving loved ones away. The doormats have it no easier. They feel a mixture of anger and anxiety. They're angry that others walk over them, and fearful that their anger might push loved ones away.

Second is the compulsion to repeat the trauma and turmoil as described above. People become familiar with abuse, chaos, and even threats of abandonment. And their psychological systems are set up to repeat the past.[22] This happens in several ways.

Faulty Selection. The compulsion to repeat traumatic relationships can begin when the shattered self, the person with a disorganized attachment style, selects a partner. It's common for traumatized persons to select partners who treat them as their original abusers did; often they select partners who are prone to aggression, manipulation, and rejection. However, the disorganized person won't see or even acknowledge these faulty personality traits in the other person. So he or she proceeds with the relationship, even though everyone else can see the abuse coming.

Distortion. Even when their partners aren't behaving in abusive or rejecting ways, the shattered selves may read rejection or abandonment into the partners' behavior. Eddie, one of our clients, came from a chaotic, rage-filled home where both parents were unfaithful and eventually divorced. So we weren't all that surprised when Eddie said this about his wife: "I know she's having an affair; I can just tell by the way she looks at me."

"How can you tell that just by how she looks at you?"

"I can just tell . . . there is something different about her."

"Well," we said, "there may be something different about her, but why does that have to mean she's having an affair? Maybe something at work is bothering her, or maybe she worried about something."

But Eddie was not really open to an alternative explanation. In his mind, he was convinced that she was having an affair, and he treated her that way. He just couldn't see that he was distorting the situation to fit his past.

Provocation. In extreme cases, people with a disorganized attachment style may engage in behaviors that actually provoke others to abandon them or behave aggressively toward them. Thus, his or her life becomes a self-fulfilling prophecy. In Eddie's case, his angry distrust and constant bombardments of accusations eventually pushed his wife away, causing her to seek a temporary separation. This, of course, only fueled his feelings of betrayal and strengthened his belief that she was being unfaithful. He was seeing the past in the present, sure the past was repeating itself. Tragically, he just couldn't see how his behavior triggered the scenario unfolding before him.

An early, healing part of the journey to a new life is being able to see beyond and to live beyond present circumstances. Secure persons can do that. They're the ones we'll look at next.

TIME TO RECAP

Before we move on, let's take a moment for a quick recap of the attachment styles we've studied so far.

Individuals with an avoidant attachment style have negative views of others and a positive view of themselves, an emotional combination that turns them away from loved ones, especially during times of stress.

Those with an ambivalent attachment style, on the other hand, have a positive view of others but hold themselves in rather low esteem. When under stress, this dichotomy forces a determination to extract comfort and reassurance from those close to them. However, there's usually nothing subtle in the way they go about it. They pursue this refuge with an intensity that generally drives their loved ones to seek a refuge of their own—a refuge somewhere else. This leaves the ambivalent people upset as they deal with deep feelings of betrayal and abandonment.

And finally we've seen the devastating effects of the disorganized attachment style, the shattered self.

Now we'll turn our focus to the goal we all hope for: the secure attachment style that leads to rich, rewarding relationships. And in just a few more pages we'll get down to work and show you how you can overcome the damage that's been done to your past and achieve this wonderful way of connecting with those you love most.

7

EQUIPPED TO FACE CHALLENGES AND TAKE RISKS

To be loved, be lovable.
—OVID

W*here is he?* Ronnie Blaire wondered as she waited for her husband, Matt, to get home from work. He was late, and she was angry. So angry that she sat at the kitchen table staring out the window over the sink to the driveway beyond, tapping her fingers. Her nails, three of them broken by the day's events, clattered impatiently on the wood. Any second he'd turn into that driveway, walk through the side door, and the fight would be on. She could hardly wait.

It had been one of those days, and most of what went wrong did so because of him. It had even started badly because of him. He'd left for work at 6:30, an hour early, and the side door had slammed behind him. The crack of it woke up little Kevin, their four-year-old, who usually slept for another hour. For Ronnie, whose day consisted of rearing a boy who ricocheted off the walls all day, that last hour of sleep was precious. But not today. Today the tornado struck at 6:31 A.M. when it landed with an excited *whoop!* on the bed right on top of her.

About ten o'clock, when Kevin was in the backyard scrambling over the jungle gym Matt had built for him, the mail came, and in it was a note from the bank. Their account was overdrawn. Matt had written two emergency checks while he was out of town a week before and had forgotten to tell her about them. That meant an unplanned trip to the bank.

Oh, well, she'd thought, *Kevin needs new shoes; I'll combine the trips.* But when she'd got into the car, she found the gas tank empty. Matt's car had been in the shop the day before, and he'd used her car to drive all over town visiting

Comparison of Attachment Styles

Secure Attachment Style	Ambivalent Attachment Style
Self Dimension • I am worthy of love. • I am capable of getting the love and support I need. **Other Dimension** • Others are willing and able to love me.	**Self Dimension** • I am not worthy of love. • I am not capable of getting the love I need without being angry and clingy. **Other Dimension** • Others are capable of meeting my needs but might not do so because of my flaws. • Others are trustworthy and reliable but might abandon me because of my worthlessness.
Avoidant Attachment Style	**Disorganized Attachment Style**
Self Dimension • I am worthy of love. • I am capable of getting the love and support I need. **Other Dimension** • Others are either unwilling or incapable of loving me. • Others are not trustworthy; they are unreliable when it comes to meeting my needs.	**Self Dimension** • I am not worthy of love. • I am not capable of getting the love I need without being angry and clingy. **Other Dimension** • Others are unable to meet my needs. • Others are not trustworthy or reliable. • Others are abusive, and I deserve it.

clients and hadn't filled it back up. She had to take the chance and drive on fumes. And it wouldn't be exactly a short drive, because they lived a little way out of town, and the nearest gas station was several miles away. She'd made it, but only just. The car took more gas today than it ever had.

The last straw fell about four that afternoon when little Kevin, playing out back, leapt from the swing, a move he'd not quite perfected. Usually he made a three-point landing on the grass and stained a knee or his cheek. This time, though, he landed on Matt's hammer and tore a gash in his thigh on the claw. Matt had found an exposed nail in the jungle gym and had taken the hammer outside to deal with it. Then he'd started playing with Kevin and forgotten the tool. She was always after him for leaving his tools around, and now Kevin was injured because of it.

She hated when Kevin cried like that.

She'd cleaned his wound and put a bandage on it, fuming to herself that her day was too exhausting to have Matt's thoughtlessness adding to it. Now Kevin, his tears dried, wearing his bandage as a badge of honor, sat watching a *Winnie the Pooh* video while she waited to do battle.

Are you shocked? We expect you're probably asking, *Isn't this the chapter on the* secure *attachment style? So what sounds secure and good about Ronnie?*

Ah . . . our first point:

There's nothing superhuman about secure people. Like Ronnie, they're real people with real feelings and common, everyday tensions and problems, some of them devastating. It's how they deal with those feelings and problems that sets them apart.

Beliefs behind the Secure Self

When secure people run into problems, they can experience the whole spectrum of emotions from joy to depression, from confusion to peace, and even anxiety, sadness, guilt, and, yes, anger. But even though they experience the same emotions, some definite characteristics set them apart from other attachment styles.

Confidence about "Who I Am"

"Play the piano for Aunt Gertrude, dear," the mother of a secure child might tell her daughter. And that secure child will climb up on the stool and bang out her latest piece. But she won't do it to prove her worth to Mom or Auntie. She's already confident that she's a valuable kid whether or not she can play the piano perfectly.

Secure people don't feel the pressure to perform that other attachment styles do to earn their self-worth points. That pressure's off for them. They may drive themselves pretty hard, but that drive has nothing to do with proving themselves as worthy souls. That sense of value has been instilled in them since early childhood. And it continues into adult life.

This internal sense of security frees them from all the hidden and internal agendas present in other attachment styles so they're able to relate to others more genuinely and honestly. This, of course, is no surprise. People who feel fundamentally secure are able to express thoughts and opinions more confidently. They're not worried that they'll be harmed or emotionally bruised if others disapprove. That doesn't mean they go around saying whatever flashes into their minds. No, they practice restraint like any loving and thoughtful person would. But they're not threatened at their core by the fear that others will find fault with their opinions. And when others do find fault, they try not to take the disagreement personally. In fact, depending on the subject, they might find such disagreement a welcome opening for a lively discussion.

For example, a secure woman might say, "It sounds to me from the way you're talking that you don't like my hair style this way. That's okay. In fact, I've been trying to find a new style for months, and I just can't come up with one. Maybe you can help."

Ronnie was furious with her husband, Matt's, lack of dependability, a failing that had caused a nightmare of a day for her and Kevin. In fact, she didn't hesitate to express her disappointment to Matt. Had she not had a fundamental sense of self-worth, she might have felt threatened by her anger; she might have been afraid that if she really expressed what she felt internally, she might be rejected out of hand, with such rejection leading directly to emotional emptiness and a deep sense of loss. Anticipating all that, she might have suppressed her anger and swept it under the nearest emotional rug. Which, as any good counselor will tell you (and which you already know after reading this far in the book), leads to a whole host of emotional and psychological trouble later—such problems as panic attacks, debilitating guilt, deep depression, and self-contempt. Or, instead of burying her anger, Ronnie could have expressed her rage indirectly, in what are called passive-aggressive ways—giving Matt the cold-shoulder treatment or picking at him for tying his shoelaces wrong or leaving his toothbrush on the counter or watching football instead of cleaning up the oil stains in the driveway.

Instead, her willingness to enter the marital fray and do battle said she was comfortable with her feelings. Even her anger. She knew that anger is, essentially, a demand for change, and the changes she demanded were genuine, valid, and useful. She knew that anger can provide the energy and focus needed to set boundaries and express concerns. But she also knew that anger, unchecked, can become destructive. Instead of being the catalyst for positive change, it can become a tool of aggression, an emotional machete that can hack a relationship to bits.

So she regulates her anger—regulates all her feelings, actually. She's angry without criticizing. There's never any of this: "You're never there for me when I need you. You never take my needs into account. You only think about yourself. You're self-absorbed." Instead she makes specific, solvable complaints. "It makes me mad when you do stuff like that. You need to be quiet in the morning so you don't wake up Kevin. It's not that hard. Just take a little care."

Confidence about Effectiveness

To respect someone's feelings means you believe those feelings in the other person are valid, based on reality, and aren't there to manipulate you. For instance, if the person tells you he's angry, he may have a good reason for that anger. Secure people were shaped in an environment where other people respected their feelings and, as a result, they respected the feelings of others—or somehow, along the way, they learned this process.

Among other advantages, that kind of awareness taught them how to negotiate conflict. If both parties have valid feelings, and if both parties' feelings are based on reality, then both parties can make reasonable changes to accommodate the other. And since there are no destructive, manipulative hidden agendas at work, if both parties want only a vibrant, healthy relationship, then both should be willing to make the changes and accommodations that assure that kind of relationship.

That's why secure people are skilled at communicating their feelings and opinions. They're confident they can affect other people, that they can entice their loved ones to listen to their complaints and to respond favorably—without or with little need for manipulation or coercion. They are not conflict avoidant. They won't remain quiet just to keep the peace. They can turn up the heat when necessary. But simultaneously, they keep their feelings and the situation regulated.

In the secure person, anger has a different "flavor." It's not born out of fear, and it's not bubbling out of some newly aroused internal volcano. In the secure person, anger generally springs from *hope*.[1]

Ronnie was angry about Matt's thoughtlessness. But the anger came from Ronnie's knowing that Matt would respond to her complaints and suggestions. In other words, her anger came from her realistic hope for change. This hope was an integral part of her communication strategy. Granted, she probably didn't stop and deliberately think about becoming angry, but in a way she did think about it. Her anger came from a place inside her that was saying, *He needs to understand how strongly I feel when he does this.* She knew Matt would listen to her feelings, and she didn't have to damage the relationship in order to do so.

The anger that arises out of hope fuels adaptive conflict. Sounds like something sewn onto a silk pillow, doesn't it? Well, it should be. It says that these squabbles are a necessary part of a couple's growth together. In fact, as we'll see later in this chapter and throughout this book, *regulated conflict* is the building block of a healthy relationship. Just as kids go through growing pains on their way to maturity, so do loving couples, and those "growing pains" lead to a vibrant and thriving relationship.

Trust in Others

You've heard the old saying: Trust must be earned. Or, Lost trust is lost forever. Both statements are generally true. Trusting others is not easy. The reason is simple: Trust means you're trusting the other person with something—your money or your future. If you're a guy, you might be trusting your wife with your tickets to the Monster Truck Rally. What if she lets you down? The results may be devastating. Do you know how much those tickets cost?

All kidding aside, trust is often the only glue holding a marriage together. If a wife can't trust her husband when he goes out of town, or he can't trust her when he's away at work, what hope do they have to trust each other with their most intimate feelings? Secure people *tend* to trust others.

Now, that trust isn't a naive, immature, fantasy-based trust. It's a general belief that others, those they've carefully selected after seeing them in action during the dating process or in other ways, are capable of and willing to meet their emotional needs. Secure people don't expect perfection. In fact, they're generally more tolerant of others' mistakes because they don't see mistakes as signs of dishonesty or rejection.

Ronnie was angry with Matt, but she didn't question his love for her. She didn't see his thoughtlessness as rejection or abandonment of her. Matt's behavior was not construed as an attachment injury; he'd just been inconsiderate. His thoughtlessness wasn't the tip of a much larger iceberg, that iceberg being a global symptom of untrustworthiness that jeopardized the relationship.

Instead, her anger was launched and filled with hope that Matt would respond, that he would listen to and care about her feelings. And that he would take her expression of emotion as an opportunity to empathize with her and to make some behavioral adjustments. It might also give him the opportunity to understand just how difficult her day had been, which could bring them closer together.

The healthy expression of anger can actually be a healing experience.[2] Another monogram for a silk pillow. And certainly operative if the other person doesn't feel overly threatened by the anger and become defensive. In fact, anger is often the catalyst that leads to forgiveness and restoration, two prominent elements of just about all effective approaches to healing.

PATHWAYS TO THE SECURE ATTACHMENT STYLE

Sensitive parenting lays the steppingstones on the pathway leading to secure attachment. Now we'd like to look at this parenting style in greater detail and show you how it plays a central role in shaping our children into secure people.

Sensitive parenting is characterized by four main goals:

- *Regulation* to help children learn to self-soothe and calm down when they're upset. This is foundational to regulating emotions and allowing the children to develop an ability to focus attention outside themselves and onto other people and things.
- *Relationship warmth* to help children experience relationships as safe, warm, and interesting. Warmth instills the notion that relationships are where one turns when upset and in need of comfort.
- *Self-awareness* to help children learn how to express in words their internal experiences such as thoughts, feelings, intentions, and physical sensations. Self-awareness helps improve the regulation skills and becomes the basis of empathy.
- *Developmental focus* to help children meet the various developmental challenges of their lives: how to live within limits, how to become self-motivated, how to deal with separation, how to get along with peers, how to respect authority, how to develop spirituality, how to live morally, and so on. Basically, how to become good people within themselves and society.

Pretty easy to say all that, isn't it? But of course it's not all that easy to do. Sensitive parents have a lot on their plates. And around the edges of that plate is written in bold letters: *I am trying to construct an emotional foundation on which my children can experience healthy relationships for the rest of their lives.*

To make things even more complicated, a sensitive mother to a three-month-old infant is a lot different than the sensitive mother to a fifteen-year-old high-schooler. Each development stage requires a new face of sensitivity—new skills, new levels of patience, new elements of life's mosaic responses to stress. Later in this book we'll spend more time discussing those differences, but for now we'll highlight strategies and techniques sensitive parents should use in all stages to help their children develop secure attachment styles.

Finding the Zone: How Children Grow

God has set down some universal principles for how elements of His creation grow and mature. One particularly important principle is what developmental psychologists call the *zone of proximal development.*[3] Sounds impressive, doesn't it? And it is—although we prefer to think of it simply as "the zone." This principle says that anything that grows and matures does best when provided with the right mixture of two critical ingredients: support and challenge.

A personal example: Gary's wife has been encouraging him to get into better physical shape. If he wants his muscles to grow and develop, he needs to "challenge" them. That means when he's exercising them, he needs to use the right amount of weight, enough to cause them to work hard but not so much that they begin to break down. In addition, he has to support the development of his muscles by eating the right foods and getting proper rest. The right combination of these two factors, challenge and support, will create the proper conditions for muscle growth. (He'll get started first thing . . . tomorrow.)

Good coaches apply the right combination of support and challenge to each team member. For example, when Gary wrestled in college, his coach managed to always challenge him just beyond his capability. He never bulldozed over him by criticizing everything he did wrong, which would have been too much challenge and would've discouraged his growth. Rather, he supported Gary's efforts by highlighting what Gary did right and encouraging him to continue doing it. This combination of support and challenge caused Gary to improve exponentially, way beyond what he thought himself originally able to achieve.

Sensitive parents are good coaches. They find ways to boost their children into the zone to help them grow and develop new life-handling skills. When we evaluate a parent-child relationship, we often have them work on a puzzle together. In this way we can observe how the child uses the parent as a source of help and how the parent balances the delivery of support and challenge. Sensitive parents help children discover the solution. They don't just solve the problem for them (too much support, not enough challenge). Nor do they just sit back and say, "You've got a brain; you figure it out," so that the child gets overly frustrated (too much challenge, not enough support).

Emotion Coaching

Parents also must teach their children how to handle negative emotions, among them, sadness, anger, frustration, anxiety, jealousy. Although we've found many parents believe handling these strong feelings comes naturally to children, the fact is, it doesn't. Just like reading, writing, arithmetic, and base-ball, coping with strong emotions is a learned skill, one that requires parents and other connected adults to become good coaches. But how do you do that?

John Gottman, the eminent marriage and family researcher, and his col-leagues have studied families' emotional lives and identified four different parenting patterns, each pattern reflecting a philosophy of emotional life:

• *Dismissing pattern.* This parenting style ignores the children's feelings and views them as unimportant and, at best, a necessary nuisance. When their children display negative feelings, like anger or sadness, these parents ignore the feelings or brush them away. Usually the parents' goal is to not draw atten-tion to the negative feelings, believing that acknowledging them will reinforce the negativity. In this family, everyone is expected to always be happy; sadness is not tolerated. This approach doesn't offer the right mix of challenge or sup-port, which keeps kids from entering the zone.

• *Disapproving pattern.* This style of parenting disapproves of negative feel-ings. These parents use various coercive methods to stamp out negative emotions in their children. They'll put down the kids or use sarcasm and con-tempt to criticize them. They may even punish the kids for expressing negative feelings. This style also keeps the kids from "zone-dom." Disapproving parents may think they're challenging their children to deal with their emotions, but their "help" is too negative and derogatory to be a challenge. And they typi-cally offer far too little assistance in problem solving to be supportive.

• *Laissez-faire pattern.* Unlike the two previous patterns, this style can accept and empathize with children's negative feelings. But these parents have difficulty helping their children figure out what to do to solve the stress-creating problem. These parents also have difficulty setting firm limits with their children. They offer lots of support but not enough challenge.

• *Emotion-coaching pattern.* This pattern best helps children learn necessary skills to deal with negative emotion. It assumes that your children's negative feelings are an opportunity for you, the parent, to build a bridge of intimacy and to deepen your connection with your kids. It also includes these important characteristics:

1. Awareness of your children's negative feelings, even when they're at a low level of intensity.
2. Understanding and validating your children's feelings then communicating to them that you see why they feel the way they do (empathy).
3. Guiding your children in developing their own self-awareness by helping them find words to label feelings and thoughts.
4. Working with your children to find solutions to their problems, asking, "What can be done to make the situation better?" or "What might be a better way to look at this situation so it doesn't make you feel so bad?"
5. Setting limits on behavior. This is critical. Children must be taught that feeling intensely does not grant them a license to act out. Rather, it's an opportunity to examine their feelings and the situation prompting them, and then to govern their feelings and command that situation, just as Scripture indicates: "Be angry and do not sin" (Ephesians 4:26 NKJV). God understands our pain and suffering, but He still requires us to live obediently.[4]

Every day, parents face opportunities for emotion coaching. Let's say a five-year-old wants to go across the street to play with the neighbor but, for whatever reason, the answer is no. Suddenly there's an emotional outburst. Eyes fill with tears, little hands clench into fists, and a small voice becomes huge with indignation: "Nobody lets me do anything I want to! It's not fair. Everybody else gets to go over to a friend's house, and I don't get to."

At this point it would be a lot easier just to send the kid to a corner to calm down. And that's certainly an alternative. But it's also a time that can be more profitably used for emotion coaching. You might pick the child up and set her on the kitchen counter so she can look you in the eyes. Then you could have a conversation with her that goes something like this:

"Sweetie, you're really angry at Mommy and Daddy right now, aren't you?"

"You guys won't let me have any fun. There's nothing to do here."

Study her for a moment. Understand. For example, try to discern whether there are any other emotions you should be aware of besides the anger. What led up to the eruption? Is she bored? Or has an interaction with some other child gone badly?

"I know, sweetie," you say. "There's nothing to do, and you feel bored." (You're showing empathy and support.)

"Yes, Daddy, there's nothing to do," she whines, big, wet tears streaming down her face.

"I know. Daddy gets bored, and sometimes a little lonely when there's nothing to do and nobody to do anything with." (Now you're labeling the feelings while offering support and a little challenge.) She nods and then sinks her head into your neck, and you give her a big hug. You're connecting; she feels understood. Now you're ready for some problem solving.

"So," you begin, "let's think about what you can do about feeling so bored. Your idea to go across the road was a good one, but it just can't happen right now. So what else is there to do?" (You're presenting a challenge.)

"Nothing! There's nothing else to do!"

"I know you feel that way, honey, but let's think about some other things." (You're continuing your support while adding more challenge.)

"Like what?" she says, daring *you* to come up with something.

"Well, your brother and his friend Joel are down in the backyard playing on the jungle gym," you might say. Or, "Your sister and her friend are up in her room playing Barbies."

"Dad," she says with a bit of irritation in her voice, "you know Joel won't let me play with him, and I don't want to play on the jungle gym."

"But you do like sneaking up on your brother, don't you?" you say with a small dose of excitement in your voice.

Her eyes brighten. She's getting your drift.

"Dad, what if *we* snuck up on them?"

"Oh, I think that would be fun!" you say. "Why didn't you think of that before?"

"'Cause you was busy."

"Yes, and it was very respectful of you to not bug Daddy when he's busy. But, you know, Daddy likes to make a little time for fun. You just have to ask. Sometimes I can, and sometimes I can't. But it doesn't hurt to ask."

"Okay, Dad. Now let's go!"

That's a lot better than sending the kid to the corner, isn't it? And when such a situation unfolds for you, when it ends something like this one did, you'll be able to look back on it and see that you and your child got through a tense situation, that you connected with each other at a little deeper level, and that you were a good coach.

We believe Gottman's emotion-coaching style to be one of the best techniques sensitive parents can use to help their children deal with negative emotions. It offers the perfect combination of support and challenge while encouraging listening, validation, and empathy, and it helps children discover ways to cope with the negative feelings without acting out.

This parenting approach also creates fertile soil for the secure self to root, grow, and mature. It helps children develop the secure relationship rules we've previously mentioned, a healthy sense of attachment combined with a trust in others. The five-year-old in the conversation we just overheard learned her feelings were worth taking seriously, strengthening her sense of self-worth. She learned that those who love her were not threatened by her negative feelings and that she could approach them no matter how she feels—emotionally distraught, or just a little off balance. Or when she's just bored.

This approach also carries some important spiritual ramifications. When we see our children's negative emotions are opportunities to build intimacy, we also see that our emotions are steppingstones to greater intimacy with God. Ask yourself, when you get upset, do you feel God will meet you where you are, in the anger, in the sadness, in your fear? Or do you believe He requires you to calm down before coming to Him? Scripture teaches that God allows pain in our lives so that we seek Him and experience His goodness through His ability to be with us in our pain. Our emotion, our pain, and our sufferings pave the royal road to intimacy with God.

Emotion coaching is a model that teaches our children that God is not turned off or repulsed by our thoughts and feelings. Rather, He wants us to come to Him. He's not intimidated by the anguished cries of our soul. And as a loving father would be, He is there for us—helping to deliver us up with open arms. When we respond lovingly, supportively, and confidently to our children's emotion, we not only teach them how to better handle their feelings, we teach them that God is a God of comfort as they begin to see the Father in us.

THE LEGACY OF THE SECURE SELF

When we present this parenting model at conferences, we're frequently asked, "Doesn't this just teach our children they can get away with having a bad attitude? If all you focus on is emotion, how do kids learn discipline—how to behave and follow rules?"

These are both good questions, and we are finding the answers through ongoing research and through our experience. Gottman studied the effects of emotion coaching on preschoolers and followed them into middle childhood. He found that kids who received emotion coaching from their parents were

- doing better academically: They made better grades and enjoyed learning more.
- physically healthier: They got fewer colds and made fewer trips to the doctor.
- better equipped socially: They made and kept friends more easily.
- more emotionally stable: They displayed fewer negative emotions and more positive ones.
- better behaved: They had fewer problems with authorities and fewer fights with other children.[5]

CHARACTERISTICS OF THE SECURE SELF

So far we've discussed how sensitive parenting promotes secure attachment and how secure attachment leads to emotionally healthier children. Now we'd like to describe to you some of the important characteristics of that fortunate child who's reared by sensitive parents to become the secure self.

Emotional Strength

People with emotional strength aren't stonefaced stoics who display little or no emotion, as you might think. They're down-to-earth people, probably like you, who feel emotions pretty deeply. The thing that distinguishes them is that they're not afraid of emotions, neither their own nor others'. They don't consider negative feelings like anger, sadness, or even fear as signs of weakness or imbalance. Emotions, for them, are seen as indicators that they're people in touch with themselves and the world around them.

Because they accept their feelings, secure people—more often than not—face life head-on. They accept challenges and take necessary risks. They stand up for what they believe in with passion and fervor, and they invest in others because they're not haunted by the fear of loss.

A Willingness to Seek and Accept Comfort, Especially in Times of Trouble

We pointed out earlier that God programmed us to seek connection with and comfort from others. Those who study infant behavior call this *implicit relational knowing.*[6] Secure attachment is only an extension of our natural selves. Persons with secure attachment styles automatically seek their attachment figures when distressed, just as God programmed us to seek Him. Long before modern researchers identified this characteristic, John Calvin described it when he wrote, "A sense of deity is inscribed on every heart."

Do you seek comfort from others when you're distressed? Or do you turn inward and look only to yourself for comfort? Or do you look to others for comfort, but with a level of intensity that overwhelms those trying to provide you with support? Security is both seeking and finding comfort in the ones you love.

Turning to God in prayer is a powerful sign of security-seeking behavior. In fact, prayer, what Richard Foster calls "simple prayer,"[7] is turning to God for comfort even in the little situations of life. You don't have to wait for calamity to strike. Turning to God for even minor requests—that the kids have a good day, that your spouse makes it home safely, that you get today's jobs done—are all reflections of this principle.

Courage for Love and Intimacy

Best described in 1 Corinthians 13, known as the Bible's "love chapter," love is a total commitment to another person. And it's work! Intimacy requires tremendous trust and courage. Our culture, of course, paints a different picture: Love is easy, intimacy reaches fulfillment on the second date, and both are effortless. But we agree with M. Scott Peck, who says that anytime you see love without work, you don't have love. Instead, you're looking infatuation in the eye.[8] And infatuation is primarily a drug-induced state of elation produced by body chemicals called endorphins. When these drugs wear off, and they always do, if the relationship lasts, you're left with the real work of love and intimacy.

Secure people are willing to take the risk to love someone. And it's not surprising that the relationships in their pasts have been largely successful. As a natural outgrowth of their successful relationship track record, they freely seek wise counsel and comfort from those they love. In contrast, those with insecure attachment styles may also seek connection and comfort, but when they do they rarely experience a sense of peace from those relationships.

When Megan and Zach (Tim's children) were small, one of their favorite movies was *The Little Engine That Could.* Remember the story? "I *think* I can, I *think* I can . . ." All the little red engine wanted was to be able to pull the load of a big train, and when he put his mind to it, guess what: He did it! Now, that's a strong principle for kids and adults to live by.

The belief that attachment figures are nearby and accessible provides secure folks with an internal optimism. No matter what's coming, they're not going to face it alone. And they believe that together, they can face anything. That kind of attitude motivates secure people to face their lives boldly and with confidence. Bowlby puts it this way:

An individual who has been fortunate in having grown up in an ordinary good home with ordinarily affectionate parents has always known people from whom he can seek support, comfort, and protection, and where they are to be found. So deeply established are his expectations and so repeatedly have they been confirmed that, as an adult, he finds it difficult to imagine any other kind of world. This gives him an almost unconscious assurance that, whenever and wherever he might be in difficulty, there are always trustworthy figures available who will come to his aid. He will therefore approach the world with confidence and, when faced with potentially alarming situations, is likely to tackle them effectively or to seek help in doing so.[9]

Secure people realize there's safety in other people, and they manifest a sense of trust and look to others for help when needed. Ecclesiastes 4:9 says, "Two are better than one, because they have a good reward for their labor" (NKJV). Pessimistic people, on the other hand, have grown to expect their projects to crumble before their eyes. They're almost afraid to be happy when life goes well, because if they are, something bad is sure to happen. We call this "happy-phobia." If you are happy-phobic, you've probably never felt comfortable trusting or relying on anyone to come through for you in difficult times.

Secure people also know the truth of Ecclesiastes 7:14: "When times are good, be happy; but when times are bad, consider: God has made the one as well as the other." When parents and significant others live out this belief with us, what an incredible picture of God we get!

Optimistic people acknowledge that life is a thorny proposition and that the bumps in the road can be quite jarring. But optimism allows them to believe no bump is so bone-rattling it can't be overcome, and no thorn is so sharp it can't be dulled and dealt with. Eventually life will work out. For secure, optimistic people, Romans 8:28 is alive, well, and fully operative: "In all things God works for the good of those who love him." That doesn't mean they never hurt. But their optimism allows secure people to bounce back from adversity. They know God has a plan for their lives, and they trust Him that the suffering they're enduring today is merely preparation for triumph tomorrow. They believe every misstep is ultimately for their benefit.

Optimism is also realistic. Pain exists, and pain hurts, and pain can slow down even secure, optimistic people. It may even stop them for a while. But over time, pain eases a bit, and secure people see that as their cue to get up and get going again. After all, new life is waiting just around the next corner. The apostle Paul, speaking to Timothy, shared this type of confidence. In the midst of his trouble, Paul told Timothy, "For the . . . cause I also suffer these things: nevertheless I am not ashamed: for I know whom I have believed, and am persuaded that he is able to keep that which I have committed unto him against that day" (2 Timothy 1:12 KJV). That secure, optimistic Paul was the same one who, in his last days, wrote to Timothy, "Do thy diligence to come shortly unto me" (2 Timothy 4:9 KJV). In other words, Be with me. I need you.

Responsible for Themselves

Secure people feel totally responsible for who they are, for their lives, and for making the decisions that affect it. Psychologists call this *an internal locus of control.* While secure people can't keep all the bad situations from occurring to them—illness, loss of loved ones, and so forth—they *can* determine how they react to these events, and they take full responsibility for those reactions.

They generally don't feel like victims, even when they are. When beset by a problem not of their making, they usually assess the situation honestly and relatively dispassionately, and then set about to change their circumstances. Which means they engage in active problem solving, and when at first they don't succeed, they keep trying to solve the problem longer than insecure people do. And if they discover they can't improve things, they simply decide to cope. Generally, secure people concern themselves with how they interpret their suffering—they find meaning in their pain.

Viktor Frankl was a Jewish psychiatrist held in a German concentration camp during World War II. He found that those who were able to survive, both physically and psychologically, those who did not give up hope, those who persisted and even thrived in their captivity, were those who were able to find meaning in their suffering. He developed a whole form of psychotherapy based on the notion that people can find meaning even in the bleakest of circumstances.[10]

The New Testament Christians were like this. They were severely persecuted because they were followers of Christ. But when they were beaten and battered for their beliefs, they rejoiced for the opportunity to serve God and further His purposes. They lived "top-down," believing that God is in control and heaven is sure.[11]

In contrast, those with an external locus of control generally feel life just happens to them and they have little of control over it, including the way they feel when it happens and how they behave afterward. As you can easily imagine, when faced with trouble, those with this mind-set will expend little, if any, energy in problem-solving efforts. And when they do try to solve their problem, if at first they don't succeed, it's time for a latte. They give up more easily. They believe their feelings and thoughts are outside their control. If they should fall in love with bad persons, well, they'll just have to be with them. This mind-set allows them to take little responsibility for managing their lives. When they get themselves into trouble, they blame others, including God: "If God didn't want me to be with that person, why did He have me fall in love with him [or her]?"

Courage

Many define courage as the lack of fear. We consider the lack of fear as a sign of anything but courage. Indeed, we see fearlessness as the hallmark of someone who lacks good sense!

Fear informs us of what is dangerous or significant. Courage is to act in the face of fear when we determine that action is needed. For example, a woman who has been burned in a number of relationships acts courageously when she decides to try again. A father whose parents were very physically abusive when he was young has to try and appropriately apply discipline to his children, even though he is afraid he will misuse his power. Courage is daring to do right in the face of other emotions that would have you do less than right, or downright wrong.

THE SECURE ATTACHMENT STYLE:
AN EMOTIONAL IMMUNE SYSTEM

People who have healthy immune systems still get sick. They get colds, flu, sinus infections, and just about everything else, but they get sick less often and their illnesses aren't as severe as those with poor immune systems. And they get better faster.

In the same way, people with secure attachment styles get sad, angry, anxious, and just about anything else you can name, but they are more resilient. Not as much upsets them, and when they do get upset, they're not as severely upset as insecure people. Plus, the upset calms more rapidly. They get back to being their old selves more quickly. In fact, as we have already mentioned, they generally grow from their pain. It takes an awful lot to knock them off their feet. And even then, they eventually get back up and are usually much stronger for having endured the difficulty.[12]

In an interesting way, God has made us so that when we manage our stress levels well, our bodies' immune systems are strengthened. Health begets health. And secure attachment sets the foundation for health—spiritual, emotional, and even physical health.

Here's great news: You can develop a secure attachment style, no matter which style is governing your relationships now. Your life—your past—while powerful and influential, doesn't have to command your tomorrows. You can develop what researchers call an "earned, secure base"[13] for building and rebuilding your relationships. There is hope and help in the pages ahead.

II

Unlocking the Secrets to Loving and Lasting Relationships

8

GOD AND YOU

Embracing the Relationship That Transcends All Others

with George Ohlschlager

Relationship or bonding . . . is at the foundation of God's nature.
Since we are created in his likeness, relationship is our most fundamental need,
the very foundation of who we are. Without relationship, without attachment to
God and others, we can't be ourselves.
—DR. HENRY CLOUD

It took a long time for Rita, a thirty-nine-year-old mother of three, to realize that no man could fill the void that goes deep in a woman's soul. And also that she couldn't completely satisfy the longings of a man's heart.

One evening her husband, Frank, dropped the children off at the baby-sitter's and returned home to prepare a special meal for just the two of them. Rita, warming up to the evening, stepped out of the kitchen to light the fire-place's gas logs. Straightening, she took a quick step back toward the kitchen and, over the hiss of the gas and the warm crackle of the flames, she heard a thump in the kitchen. Knowing instinctively that something was wrong, she hesitated, then, her heart rock hard in her throat, she darted into the kitchen. Her worst fears were realized. Frank lay facedown on the kitchen floor. She managed a horrified gasp as she lay a tender, hesitant hand on his throat. Frank was dead. At age forty-three, he was killed by a massive heart attack.

Not long afterward, Rita came to us for help. It physically hurt to listen to her story. Frank had been her high-school sweetheart, they'd been married twenty-two years, and now he was gone and she was alone. Well, not completely alone. She had their three children, but now, instead of sharing and being even more connected to Frank because they were raising the children together, she faced the turmoil and joy of raising them alone. And he'd left her without so much as a good-bye.

We sat across from her in tears, wishing we could help her make sense of what happened. But in the end, we had no answers. Somehow, at that moment, the knowledge that God has a purpose in all things seemed irrelevant. Rita's pain was too raw to soothe.

GOD, THE ULTIMATE ATTACHMENT FIGURE

In times of trouble, God can seem far away, but He isn't. He's always near, and He wants us to know that. He wants us to feel His embrace and to feel secure in Him. But although He's always close to us, when trouble strikes we either move closer to Him or further away.

Before we discuss God and how our attachment model affects our relationship with Him, we want to remind you again of what an attachment relationship looks like. Imagine a mother sitting on a park bench with her eighteen-month-old son. Let's call him Junior and watch him as he explores the nearby world. As he does, both Junior and Mom are very aware of the distance between them, usually about eight to ten feet max. Junior keeps a wary eye on his mother, and if he confronts something he's unsure about, he looks back to Mom to see if it's okay to keep going. Developmental psychologists call this *social referencing*. It's a baby's way of saying (without words), *Hey, Mom, is it okay if I do this* (whatever *this* is)? *Or is it too dangerous?* If Mom gives a little smile or has a neutral expression, he will proceed. If she frowns or looks fearful, he hesitates.

Now imagine that a train roars down the tracks adjacent to the park, the explosion of sound frightening the little boy. He instantly makes a beeline to his mother's lap. She scoops him up and holds him close. She buries his head in her neck as she presses her hands over his ears. Shielded from the noise, Junior calms down. Then, after the train disappears, Junior's eyes come up to his mom's. She smiles down at him. "Boy, that was really loud and scary," she says, validating his fear. Then she gives him a reassuring kiss on the nose. She snuggles him even closer, loving the fact that he's come to her for comfort. A few moments pass, and Junior squirms to get down. His curiosity slowly returns, and he begins to explore the sandbox near Mom's bench.

This scene illustrates several of the core components of an attachment relationship (see the boxed list of attachment criteria). Junior keeps an eye on Mom to assure she's accessible and available. Then, when threatened, he seeks *proximity* to his mother. His mother provides a *safe haven,* which comforts Junior when he's distressed. And once he is comforted, he uses his mother as a *secure base* from which he launches himself on further exploration. We can only imagine that if he were suddenly separated from his mother, Junior would become anxious and upset. And if he lost her, he would grieve and experience deep sorrow.

Now think about our journey in this life. Our relationship with God satisfies all these conditions if we allow it to happen: We seek closeness to Him in times of trouble. He is our refuge, our place of safety, and we seek proximity to Him. We look to Him to provide us with a felt sense of security; He is our safe haven. He's also our "rock," our secure base, our foundation from which we can face the world with boldness, strength, and confidence. The thought of separation from Him produces significant anxiety—we find it scary. For us to give up on God or for us to feel that God has withdrawn from us produces grief and sorrow. Confusion can come, however, if we feel that God has let us down—that He somehow authored an evil fate for us—or could have prevented pain in our lives and didn't.

THE FIVE CRITERIA FOR AN ATTACHMENT RELATIONSHIP

1. Proximity (closeness) to the caregiver is sought, especially in times of trouble.
2. The caregiver provides a "safe haven," a felt sense of security.
3. The caregiver provides a secure base from which to explore the world.
4. Any threat of separation induces fear and anxiety.
5. Loss of the caregiver induces grief and sorrow.

A Refuge for the Wounded Soul

Before Frank's death, Rita walked closely with the Lord. She went to church, she prayed, she was involved in women's ministry, she talked to her children about the Lord. She behaved as any sincere Christian would. And her walk wasn't just a facade; her faith was real—a heartfelt experience. But, as she told us, she saw God as the One who prevented bad things from happening to her, while she looked to Frank for comfort.

We don't know why Frank died. We never will, not on this side of heaven. But Rita, in her state of brokenness, was forced into what psychiatrist Irvin Yalom calls *a boundary situation,* "an event, an urgent experience, that propels one into a confrontation with one's existential 'situation' in the world. [It] has the power to provide a massive shift in the way one lives in the world."[1] A wake-up call. One like the prodigal son had when he wasted all the money his dad had given him and ended up eating pig food. Scripture says, "He came to himself" (Luke 15:17 NKJV). In other words, he came to his senses and in essence said, "This is a crazy way to live."

Rita has been learning something that some of us may never really learn until heaven or until we are confronted with our own boundary situation: God is the ultimate attachment figure. He will always be there. He applauds our uniqueness, He cheers our joy, and He weeps with us in our sorrows. He will never die. His presence is eternal and His love is everlasting. He fills a place in our hearts that only He can fill. He'll work in every aspect of our lives—our brokenness, our rebellion, our beauty, and even in our plainness. And as He works, we too will work. After all, as the saying goes, It isn't what happens to a man; it's what he does with what happens to him.

Rita knew all this before her husband died. Had she heard it in a sermon, she would have nodded and given a strong "amen." But did she know it in her heart? She'd be the first to tell you she didn't. This boundary situation acted like an acid bath on her life: It stripped away everything she thought she knew about herself and God. She was forced to reconstruct her worldview so that God became the center of her emotional universe. Where before she had thought she loved God, she now hungered and thirsted for Him. That doesn't mean she wasn't angry with God or that she didn't grieve the loss of Frank. Her material world, her things and relationships, were undoubtedly God's blessings, and were good things in themselves. But they stood behind her like gray shadows, unable to help her in her time of crisis. Her utter vulnerability to the fickleness of this world was exposed, and she knew at a deep, bare-bones level that God was all that separated her from the abyss.

She felt so hurt, so bad, so alone, so vulnerable, and she was so poignantly aware of her need for God. She had known she needed God prior to Frank's death, but not in the same way as now. Before, Frank had been her primary caregiver. Whenever she was in trouble, she always turned to him first. Now she needed to turn to God first. She would look to Him for guidance, for direction, for security, for safety.

We're not saying God took Frank's life to teach Rita a lesson. We are saying, though, that as she dealt with her pain, which God had allowed into her life, Rita learned in her heart something she previously had known only in her head.

It's a hard lesson to learn. God knows just how hard our lives can be, not only because He's God but also because He experienced life on earth Himself. Christians believe that God and His Son, Jesus, as well as the Holy Spirit are all one Being, the Holy Trinity. So when God sent His Son, Jesus, to live on earth as a human being, He was actually sending Himself. While Jesus was here, He experienced the same joys and the same hardships we know in our lives today. For example, just as we mourn the loss of loved ones, Jesus wept outside the tomb of His friend Lazarus. But throughout his earthly lifetime, Jesus made His relationship with God His priority. And He expects the same of us today. Jesus said in Matthew 10:37, "Anyone who loves his father or mother more than me is not worthy of me; anyone who loves his son or daughter more than me is not worthy of me." Jesus wants to be the first link in the attachment chain. He wants us to turn first to Him, not to our parents or our spouses or anyone else. And when we do, our lives become properly ordered. In the words of C. S. Lewis, "Whenever we try to put second things into the first place position, we lose the joy of both God and whatever we are trying to replace Him with." Rita's loss was what Lewis called a "severe mercy." It became a "megaphone" calling her nearer to God.

To place God at the top of the attachment list doesn't mean we need God and no one else. Even though Rita has lost Frank, it doesn't mean God comes in and takes over the place in her heart where Frank lived. Nor does it mean she'll never long to see Frank again or that the break in her heart will automatically mend because her relationship with God has improved. Rita's heart will continue to ache; she will continue to groan inwardly and to experience pain and sadness as she grieves. But God will meet her and be with her within her pain. He will comfort her in the midst of her suffering. He will see her through, but will not remove, what hurts. Like a loving parent, God comforts His hurting child without healing the malady itself. He becomes a safe haven, a refuge for the wounded soul.

YOUR ATTACHMENT STYLE AND GOD: RESPONDING TO TRAGEDY

Rita's response to her dreadful loss was to seek increased security: She moved toward God, expecting He would not only provide security but comfort as well. Which He did. And because He did, her relationship with Him was actually strengthened through her affliction and anguish. But not everyone would respond the same. Your attachment style strongly influences how you will react to boundary situations. Let's look at some of the different responses.

Avoidant Attachment Style

Those with this style of attachment move away from God during times of distress and cling to possessions, success, or other addictions. They may angrily say, "Just as I expected, God can't be trusted. He gives you someone you can love and then just tears him away. Who needs a God like that?"

Others may fire off anger in God's direction by pursuing sinful habits as a way to self-medicate their pain. One husband whose wife was dying from ovarian cancer was consumed by guilt as he confessed to us that at night he would lie next to his ailing wife and fantasize about how, after her death, he would go to Las Vegas and sleep with a prostitute. Why did he think about doing this? Because he felt God deserved to be "repaid" for taking his wife.

Another gentleman who had lost his father to a sudden heart attack withdrew from his family and friends and buried himself in work. "God," he said, "is just like everyone else in this world. He's a stingy God. I really can't trust Him. Just when I do, just when I start to turn toward Him, something bad happens. I know it will. I'll just stick to what I know best—my work."

Ambivalent Attachment Style

Those with this type of attachment style are prone to vacillate. On the one hand they feel rage toward God, and on the other they are consumed by self-incrimination and excessive self-blame for their loss. Like those with the avoidant attachment style, ambivalent persons don't turn to God for comfort. However, instead of turning to things like success and addictive behavior, they may search frantically for a substitute attachment figure. Obsessed with having someone close, they may bounce from relationship to relationship. If none is discovered, their anger, sadness, and grief may deteriorate into a deep, morbid depression.

Disorganized Attachment Style

Those imbued with this attachment pattern view boundary situations as merely a continuation of their life story of loss. As seen through their eyes, God is malicious, like their early caregivers. And since there are a number of ways to respond to malicious people, these people respond with a mixed set of behaviors: addictions, self-protection, clinginess, anger, and even fiery rage. They may see God as seething with wrath and their personal tragedy as something they deserve. At the same time, they may actually bury other feelings of resentment, anger, and even rage.

They are, of course, terrified to express these feelings for fear that in savage response to them God may unleash even greater punishment. But these buried feelings probably won't stay covered for long. They may resurface as general anxiety, worry, and even panic attacks. Whatever happens, the results are the same: fear, anxiety, and pain.

ATTACHMENTS

Secure Attachment Style

Rita illustrates the secure attachment style. Of course she was devastated by her husband's death. She vacillated between anger and sadness. And she struggled with survivor's guilt, wondering, *Why him? Why not me?* She spent hours praying for God to show her the answer to all the *whys*. She felt lonely and afraid. She felt vulnerable. But ultimately she turned toward God and changed her *Why?* to *How?—How do I go on?*

She cried out to God and found Him waiting with open arms. And from that secure base she was able to view her tragedy through the lens of an all-powerful yet loving God and a waiting heaven. She faced the pain and grew with it. She was able to find meaning in the midst of crisis. She could see God's hand at work, how He was working things for good—though she would always and forever groan inwardly when she thought of Frank. She would always miss him. God may never remove her pain, but when it returns, she presses in closer to God and calls on Him to help her work through it.

ATTACHMENT AND SPIRITUALITY

Remember Junior and his mother, and the scene in the park we described earlier? This wasn't just a one-time event. In the lives of mothers and their children, these kinds of interactions occur many times a day and thousands of times during the first several years of life. Research shows, and our time in counseling confirms, that these stress-induced interactions lay the groundwork for how we respond in the future to God. They answer the questions, Is He present? Is He accessible? Will He welcome us into His lap for comfort, or will He trivialize the pain and send us with a bony, accusing finger from His throne room? They answer the question, Is God trustworthy and dependable?

First, an Awareness

We believe a core aspect of spirituality is an awareness of our vulnerability. As we become increasingly aware of our need and how truly vulnerable we are, our attachment system flips on. And when that "on" light begins to glow, we're motivated to seek His presence.

Think about the events of September 11, 2001, a horrific day by any standard. Terrorists intended to throw America—our beloved country, a country God gave us—into chaos and fear. But it had the opposite effect. The attack was a boundary event for the entire nation. It peeled away the veil of impenetrability and stripped away the robe of safety so many Americans wore with pride. But as we became aware of our susceptibility, our helplessness, and our apparent fragility, we sought refuge in God. In our distress we sought refuge and ultimately found comfort.

Attachment and the Fear of Death

Ask children about what scares them, and you'll get answers like monsters under the bed or in the closet, and answers like losing their parents—separation anxiety. The thought literally terrifies children. From the moment their lips touch the breast, their parents are a part of them, the part that comforts and satisfies them.

Megan and Zach (Tim's kids) both went through phases of obsessing about dying. Zach, at age six, said, "Dad, you're going to die, aren't you, and I'm the youngest—one day I'll be all alone." At age six! To children, the thought of losing a parent becomes tantamount to being totally annihilated themselves—and that's enough to scare anyone. Children's sudden awareness of this anxiety ignites attachment behavior, causing them to seek closeness and search for comfort. Separation anxiety confirms the children's helplessness without their parents—more reason to be anxious.

As children develop, separation anxiety turns into a fear of death—death anxiety. What are they afraid of? It has to be more than the sense that we're all going to die. We all have that sense. Anxiety about it means we're afraid of something on the other side of the divide. For example, we know a wonderful Christian woman who at age eighty-three is afraid of death. She wars against it. Why? Because she senses that she has lost her ability to control her life. She is coming to the end of self—her safety. And now she faces an unfamiliar future.

Christian philosopher Peter Kreft put it this way: "Life is always fatal, no one gets out alive." He goes on to quote Saint Augustine, "As doctors, when they examine the state of a patient and recognize that death is at hand, pronounce, 'He is dying, he will not recover,' so we must say from the moment a man is born: 'He will not recover.'"[2]

Many people try to defend against death anxiety by denying its existence. They rarely or never attend a funeral, never talk about loss and death. They press on in their Reeboks, looking for the fountain of youth. But the boundary situations of life, among them, illness, accidents, rejection, and tragedy, can cause death anxiety to seep to the surface. When it does, the various attachment styles activate as a defense against it:

• The *avoidant attachment style* avoids intimacy and dampens emotions in personal relationships. For these folks, closeness brings fear of rejection. So they remain on the periphery of intimacy and instead attach themselves to things and success. This defense ultimately destroys the true bond of love that can exist between two people.

• The *ambivalent attachment style* does the opposite. These people seek intimacy but grab for it too tightly. They may exchange "addictive attachments over genuine involvement, love, and concern."[3] They may deeply believe that if they can hold on tightly enough they can avoid separations and ultimately even death. Unfortunately, this defense can lead to the same outcome as the avoidant defense: feelings of alienation and aloneness. As Otto Rank powerfully points out, the fear of death is frequently translated into a fear of life: a fear of living and investing in relationships, in ministry, in meaningful existence.[4]

• The *disorganized attachment style* may use the avoidant or ambivalent response or even a mixture of both. These people also tend to go numb, feeling as if the world around them is not real.

• The *secure attachment style* can consciously and courageously invest in close relationships, but these persons "hold them with an open palm," realizing that while relationships provide comfort and safety, they can, and ultimately will, end. Death will always be the great separator.

Mankind's greatest fear is separation, with death being the ultimate form of it. If you have an insecure attachment style, this fear and an unwillingness to face it directly can deaden you to living life to its fullest. Crippled by this insecure attachment style, you shrink away from fully investing yourself in meaningful, intimate relationships and fail to be motivated to carry out God's purposes.

On the other hand, if you have a secure attachment style, you know it is this very fear that the Scriptures say Jesus came to conquer. Through His death and resurrection we are given the promise of everlasting life *with Him.* He promises we'll *never* be separated from Him. The writer of Hebrews said, "Since the children have flesh and blood, he too shared in their humanity so that by his death he might destroy him who holds the power of death, that is, the devil, and free those who all their lives were held in slavery by their fear of death" (Hebrew 2:14–15).

The apostle Paul echoed this fact when he wrote, "Where, O death, is your victory? Where, O death, is your sting? The sting of death is sin, and the power of sin is the law. But thanks be to God! He gives us the victory through our Lord Jesus Christ" (1 Corinthians 15:55–57). In the next verse Paul said that because the fear of death has been doused, we can experience what amounts to a secure base, a solid foundation from which to boldly and fully invest in life, in ministry, in relationships. And we can know it is all meaningful: "Therefore, my dear brothers, stand firm. Let nothing move you. Always give yourselves fully to the work of the Lord, because you know that your labor in the Lord is not in vain" (v. 58).

Those with secure attachment patterns also know that though they'll be separated from current earthly relationships, death *unites* them with the supreme heavenly Father—eternally.

BUILDING A SECURE BASE WITH GOD

God is our principal attachment figure. But we still need others. In fact, we know that God has brought those relationships into our lives to provide, in an earthly setting, what God wants us to have. But when we're in trouble, we know to turn to God first. He is the One "who sticks closer than a brother" (Proverbs 18:24)—One who will never leave nor forsake us (see Hebrews 13:5).

As God's children, we also know we're most motivated to find God when we become aware of our earthly helplessness and vulnerability. We understand from our earliest childhood experiences that our greatest fear is separation— being left alone, at the mercy of the surrounding, hostile elements. As we mature and become more self-reliant, that ever-present fear of being left alone morphs into the fear of death—death anxiety. No one escapes death. "It is appointed unto men once to die," says Hebrews 9:27 (KJV). One of Jesus' chief resurrection goals is to free us from the fear of death and provide us with a place of refuge. He hands us the keys to heaven, an eternal place in God's throne room, the place where we realize our birthright, to serve Him forever in the halls of His love. God and His heaven are our ultimate secure base.

This perspective frees us to live boldly and to relish our sense of meaning and direction. Paul lived in this newfound freedom. Romans 8 echoes his confidence. Here are just a few of the powerful verses found there (from the New King James Version unless noted):

There is therefore now no condemnation to those who are in Christ Jesus, who do not walk according to the flesh, but according to the Spirit. (v. 1)

For ye have not received the spirit of bondage again to fear; but ye have received the Spirit of adoption whereby we cry, Abba, Father. (v. 15 KJV)

. . . and if children, then heirs; heirs of God and joint heirs with Christ, if indeed we suffer with Him, that we may also be glorified together. (v. 17)

Not only that, but we also who have the firstfruits of the Spirit , even we ourselves groan within ourselves, eagerly waiting for the adoption, the redemption of our body. (v. 23)

And we know that all things work together for good to those who love God, to those who are the called according to His purpose. (v. 28)

He who did not spare His own Son, but delivered Him up for us all, how shall He not with Him also freely give us all things? (v. 32)

Who shall separate us from the love of Christ? Shall tribulation, or distress, or persecution, or famine, or nakedness, or peril, or sword? As it is written: "For Your sake we are killed all day long; we are accounted as sheep for the slaughter." Yet in all these things we are more than conquerors through Him who loved us. For I am persuaded that neither death nor life, nor angels nor principalities nor powers, nor things present nor things to come, nor height nor depth, nor any other created thing, shall be able to separate us from the love of God which is in Christ Jesus our Lord. (v. 35–39)

As we embrace our relationship with God in Christ, we seek intimacy with others, knowing that in the end we will ultimately be with both God and the ones we love who know and love Him. As Peter Kreft so aptly points out, God's "love is stronger than death."

How to Experience God's Presence and Peace

The heavenly kingdom provides refuge for our souls in times of trouble. But do we have to wait for death to experience it? The Pharisees asked Jesus this question, to which He replied, "The kingdom of God does not come with your careful observation, nor will people say, 'Here it is,' or 'There it is,' because the kingdom of God is *within* you" (Luke 17:20–21, italics added).

Jesus told the Pharisees, and He tells us today, we don't have to wait until we reach heaven to experience its peace. It resides within us right now! (See also Acts 1:8; John 14:16–18.) So the burning question becomes, How do we embrace it? How can we experience God's presence and peace in our everyday lives? Do we have to go through the kind of suffering that Rita endured? Do we have to lose someone we love to gain access, to realize God's place in our lives?

God is eternally present; there's no question about that. But that doesn't mean we're as aware of His presence as we should be, even in times of severe crisis. But how do we become aware? How do we know when we look up, look to the right and left, look before and behind us, we'll always sense Him there? Experiencing God's presence is a skill that must be developed and then sharpened, just like carpentry or sewing. And it's a skill we can use anytime, anywhere. We don't have to wait for tragedy to find Him. In fact, in the midst of such exceeding pain, we may not find God as quickly as we'd like. Not because He's unwilling, but because at those times we're often tangled up in confusion. The time to hone our awareness is in our day-to-day journeys, the times when we're confronted by small challenges—difficulties at work, troubles with your parents or children, results of your own sins. If we haven't learned to find Him in the small episodes of our lives, it may be painfully difficult to find Him when we're thrown into deep troubles.

So how do you do it? We're glad you asked! As it turns out, we have a pathway of steps you can walk that will help heighten your awareness of God's presence throughout your daily life. And as a side benefit, this pathway will lead you to become more secure in your attachment style with both God and your loved ones.

THE PATHWAY TO SPIRITUAL GROWTH AND AWARENESS

We know that probably the last thing you expect to hear about right now is Little League, but that's a great place to learn the first steppingstones to spiritual awareness. If you wander out to your local field, you'll see two kinds of coaches. One assumes kids just inherently know how to play baseball; he sees his job as coaxing that ability out from beneath their skin and into their shoes, their gloves, and their bats. He sees himself as a motivator. If a child makes a mistake, then the kid's obviously not motivated enough. He might say, "Johnny, what are you doing? You know better than that! Now, get your act together and catch that ball. Do you really want to win on Saturday or not? You know we can't win if you don't catch those easy balls. Now come on. Make it happen."

A second type of coach assumes kids don't know a baseball from their elbow and need to be taught. Mistakes mean a lack of skill. And correcting mistakes means teaching new skills. This type of coach might say something like, "Okay, Johnny, you went after the ball, but you didn't stay down on it. Remember to get in front of the ball like this." Then he slaps a knee to the grass as though a grounder is coming full speed. If Johnny makes the same mistake again, the coach pulls the kid aside again and in a tone that has nothing to do with motivation, focuses more specifically on the skill needed to make the play. If the boy blunders anew, he might even create a drill for the kid to practice at home. Of course, whether the child practices at home or not is largely based on motivation.

The difficulty with the first coach is that he doesn't understand the fundamental nature of growth. When his players don't perform, he chides them for not "wanting it bad enough."

Think of this kind of coach in high-school football. Gary remembers, "Before each game Coach would give us a big motivational speech. Then he'd play adrenaline-popping rock-'n'-roll songs and talk about the 'will to win.' When we were all pumped up—when our eyes blazed and we were ready to 'kick some football butt'—we'd prance out onto the field and get slaughtered. It was grueling for our fans, but even more so for us.

"The problem with that football coach was that he wasn't enough like the second coach. He certainly cared about winning, maybe even too much, but he didn't teach us any skills." The friend continued, "It wasn't until I got into high-school wrestling that I had a coach who understood this difference. If we lost a match, he'd pore over the films with us. He'd identify our weaknesses then help us find a drill that would cultivate the skill we needed. He even held match-specific drills to target specific deficits in our techniques. The results were astonishing."

In his classic book *The Spirit of the Disciplines: Understanding How God Changes Lives,* Dallas Willard shows that spiritual growth is governed by the same principles that regulate growth in other areas of our lives, like those experienced by the Little League players or by Gary during his football and wrestling days. Willard zeros in on Paul's first letter to Timothy, where he instructs his young friend, "Have nothing to do with godless myths and old wives' tales; rather, train yourself to be godly. For physical training is of some value, but godliness has value for all things, holding promise for both the present life and the life to come" (1 Timothy 4:7–8).

Willard tells us, as Paul told Timothy, that to lead God's people effectively, we've got to train in the "spiritual gymnasium." Just as with physical exercise, Willard says, "there is a specific round of activities we must do to establish, maintain, and enhance our spiritual powers. One must train as well as try. An athlete may have all the enthusiasm in the world; he may 'talk a good game.' But talk will not win the race. Zeal without knowledge or without appropriate practice is never enough. Plus, one must train wisely as well as intensely for spiritual attainment."[5]

Spiritual growth occurs by the same principles as other important aspects of our lives, any of those strengthened by exercise. Yet many Christian leaders still talk about spiritual growth as that first coach talked about baseball, implying that growth is all about having the pure willpower or motivation to behave in a Christlike manner. Or, in lieu of motivation, they talk as if God will strike us with a bolt of Holy Spirit (inspired lightning and instantly make us into godly men and women. So we just sit back and wait to hear that perfect motivational sermon or to get hit by that perfect bolt of lightning, believing either one is fine, because either one will finally inspire us to change our ways and walk as Jesus walked.

But What Would Jesus Do?

Think about the movement that began a few years ago symbolized by jewelry and license plates and bumper stickers with the acronym WWJD—what would Jesus do? The movement was based on Charles Sheldon's novel *In His Steps*. This powerful movement has inspired and challenged millions of people around the world. But in one sense, it assumes that motivation alone forces the change described above, that if we want to be like Jesus we'll just be on the prowl to take the action He would take in the circumstance at hand. If we can just figure out what Jesus would do, we'll "just do it." (This is the Nike approach to change.) However, as Dallas Willard points out, the premise of Sheldon's book and its approach to spiritual growth can spring from an inadequate view of how humans change:

The book is entirely focused upon trying to do what Jesus supposedly would do in response to specific choices. . . . There is no suggestion that he ever did anything but make right choices from moment to moment. And . . . there is no suggestion that his power to choose rightly was rooted in the kind of over-all life he had adopted in order to maintain his inner balance and his connection with his Father. The book does not state that to follow in his steps is to adopt the total manner of life he did. So the idea conveyed is an absolutely fatal one—that to follow him simply means to try to behave as he did "on the spot." . . . There is no realization that what he did in such cases was, in large and essential measure, the natural outflow of the life he lived when not "on the spot."[6]

Practicing the Spiritual Disciplines to Strengthen Your Attachment

What is required to cultivate a more secure attachment with God, one in which we look to Him first for comfort and security? How do we enhance our awareness of God and see Him in the inner workings of our daily lives?

Well, just as we learn that effortlessly fielding an eighty-mile-an-hour ground ball doesn't come naturally, so we learn that turning to God during times of distress doesn't just emerge out of a simple desire to make Him first. Both require training. And training starts with discipline. As Dallas Willard puts it, "A discipline is . . . nothing but an activity undertaken to bring us into more effective cooperation with Christ and His Kingdom."[7] A discipline helps us learn to rely on Him so that in times of crisis we've already developed the habit and we find Him much more easily. A little later, we'll offer some specific examples of disciplines you might practice to develop a keener spiritual awareness. But for now, let us give you a broad overview of the impact they can have on your life.

Besides cultivating a more secure attachment with God, there are two more goals to these disciplines: First, they help us break free from addictions. In this case, we use the word *addiction* broadly, referring to anything that repeatedly replaces our need for an intimate relationship with God. Second, the disciplines help us find God as our *safe haven* and learn to use Him as our *secure base.*

As a safe haven, God is our comfort in times of trouble, and we carry within us a sense of security, a knowledge that He is always there and He is more than sufficient to meet all our needs. Armed with this security, we can approach the world with boldness and confidence, and our obedience follows more easily and naturally.

In the same way, when we work with defiant children, we begin by enhancing the parent-child relationship. When we do this, discipline problems begin to evaporate once the children become more certain about their attachment relationship with their parents. Of course, we know that the relationship doesn't change everything, but it's a critical step toward more cooperative child. Rules without relationship lead to rebellion. Rules with strong relationship lead to willful obedience.

It doesn't take much thought to realize how easily we allow material possessions, other relationships, business, success, or even ministry to replace what we see as our need for God. Too often we find our "rest" in them, not in Him. We feel self-sufficient, perhaps like Adam and Eve felt in the Garden. When they ate the forbidden fruit they were in essence telling God, "We don't really need You." Which, of course, is what we're saying when we turn toward our possessions, positions, or other people for the comfort and security that only God can provide.

The disciplines are also hard work. What makes them hard? They may produce uncomfortable feelings like anxiety, depression, irritability, and intrusive memories about bad past events, particularly for those who have a history of abuse and other trauma. Those with such a history may want to practice the disciplines at first under the watchful eye of a trained pastor or counselor. But remember, no pain, no gain. Just because the disciplines may cause some discomfort don't avoid them. The turmoil they trigger is often necessary, like the muscular discomfort experienced when lifting weights or in the agony of childbirth.

Because pain may be involved, practicing the disciplines requires courage, the willingness to endure the necessary cost to achieve something far better. When we avoid necessary pain, we only invite unnecessary anguish later. As Carl Jung counseled, all neurotic suffering, or unnecessary pain, is caused by the avoidance of legitimate pain.

What disciplines are we talking about? Well, for starters there is corporate worship, Bible reading, prayer, and fasting. You probably know about and hopefully practice some of these disciplines already (whether or not you have *thought* of them as spiritual disciplines). Here we'd like to discuss a few others you might not have considered.

Searching the Scriptures

People who come to God must first believe that He is a rewarder of those who diligently seek Him (see Hebrews 11:6). Where can we learn about God? Where can we find truth? One of the most fascinating elements of the Christian life is how God has given to us the Bible (the sixty-six books of the Old and New Testaments). It is God's special revelation to us about Him, how we should live and, most importantly, how we can know Him. In the Bible He reveals Himself more fully than He does through any other mode of knowing Him (nature, reasoning, science). He does so because He wants us to know Him—not just know about Him, but to know Him personally, as a dear and intimate friend, as Savior and Lord, as Redeemer, as Spirit, as Father to His children.

Second Timothy 3:16 tells us that "all scripture is given by inspiration of God and is profitable for doctrine, for reproof, for correction, for instruction in righteousness" (KJV). Steeping ourselves in God's Word prepares us for everything life can throw at us, and it speaks volumes about children, health, safety, and security in this life when faced with temptation and challenges. Even Jesus quoted Scripture: "It is written, Man shall not live by bread alone, but by every word that proceedeth out of the mouth of God" (Matthew 4:4 KJV). Psalm 1:1–2 reminds us, "Blessed is the man that walketh not in the counsel of the ungodly, nor standeth in the way of sinners, nor sitteth in the seat of the scornful. But his delight is in the law of the LORD; and in his law doth he meditate both day and night" (KJV).

No wonder the psalmist wrote, "Thy word is a lamp unto my feet, and a light unto my path" (Psalm 119:105 KJV).

Joshua faced a pretty difficult task when he was to take over for Moses in leading the Israelites to the Promised Land. Where would his courage and strength come from? You guessed it. God told Joshua, "This book of the law shall not depart out of thy mouth; but thou shalt meditate therein day and night, . . . thou shalt make thy way prosperous, and then thou shalt have good success" (Joshua 1:8 KJV). When the Word of God intersects with human need, healing takes place; a soothing occurs. The Holy Spirit teaches and guides us in all things. The bottom line is this: God's Word is true. And in truth we are free. Searching the Scriptures prepares us for other disciplines.

Solitude

Solitude is the missing link in our everyday lives. Everyone needs at least ten to fifteen minutes of personal quiet time every day. But as a spiritual discipline, solitude is far more than just a few moments we manage to set aside for ourselves each day. It usually involves a retreat, maybe to a secluded cabin in the mountains. Wherever you go for solitude, put some distance between yourself and other bipeds. You might even head for the seashore and find yourself a very large rubber seahorse complete with a built-in writing table for holding a Bible, a pen, and a journal, all essential. What are *not* essential for solitude— in fact, they are forbidden—are radios, televisions, cell phones, and pagers. *Definitely* cell phones and pagers!

When we seek solitude our goal is to disconnect from life's distracting, normal routines, those activities and elements that superimpose themselves between ourselves and a closer relationship with God. In solitude that relationship is strengthened as we hear His quiet, still voice that directs and shapes our vision of reality—the appropriate blend of the physical and spiritual. How amazing to think that we can discern in our lives today God's same "still small voice" that Elijah heard thousands of years ago (see 1 Kings 19:12).

Solitude helps us strip away the almost unconscious defenses we use to soften the experience of aloneness and our fear of death. When we get away from others and from our typical daily routine, we're thrown into the reality of being completely dependent on God for existence. This can provoke some pretty stiff anxiety. But remember, it's this anxiety, this helplessness and vulnerability, that expose our need and heighten our thirst for God, our desire to seek refuge in His peaceful sanctuary. In contrast, those who constantly have the gas pedal to the floor are doomed to be godless.

Solitude can be especially powerful for those with ambivalent and disorganized attachment styles.

Ambivalent persons separate from those they look to for guidance and direction. They become anxious and fearful, bedeviled by thoughts like, *I can't do this; I'm too anxious. I can't stand to be alone. I have to have somebody with me, or I can't do this.* They may also struggle with feelings of guilt, thinking, *This just proves what a bad Christian I am. I try being alone with God and look how upset I get. I'm miserable.* Such thoughts come from insecure attachment patterns. If you experience them, endure them. They result from your past, not from today's reality. As you practice the discipline of solitude, the power of God takes over. Eventually the Word of God and the leading of the Holy Spirit will give you a true sense of security—of safety. God will also show you just how powerful He is at bringing you peace.

We've seen a variety of responses among our clients when we suggest they practice the discipline of solitude. For example, Edward's eyes popped open in terror. He was a very dependent person, and during the next three sessions he literally experienced several partial panic attacks in our office as we tried to convince him of the discipline's merit. Gradually we convinced him there was no other way to develop a true dependency on God if he continued to replace God with other people and his business. Reluctantly, he agreed to try it.

As we asked, upon arrival at his retreat he began to keep a journal of his thoughts and experiences. After three hours he wrote comments like these: "I feel so inadequate. I really don't think I can do this for four whole days. . . . I've never felt so lonely in all my life. . . . It feels like I'm going to die. I can't stand it. . . . I want to go home."

However, he stuck it out, and as the time melted away, so did his anxiety and his feelings of aloneness. His journal entries became: "The Lord is good. . . . He has seen me through my fear, my aloneness. I know the Lord is near. He will meet me in my darkest hour, if only I will let Him into my heart."

What about you? How long has it been since you were alone with the Father?

When he returned from his retreat, Edward was ecstatic about his encounter with God. We encouraged him to practice this discipline on a routine basis for six months. We also added other disciplines, such as fasting, Bible study, and simple prayer.

Interestingly, the more Ed practiced solitude, the more secure he became in his attachment with others, especially his girlfriend. She'd found him too clingy and controlling and had previously thought about leaving him. But as he became more dependent on God, he was able to relate to her on a more mature and secure level.

The same paradox can work for you. The more dependent you become on God, the more independent you become in life.

Ed also became less dependent on his parents, which, predictably, caused *them* some anxiety. Ed was approaching the point where he could honestly and boldly set appropriate boundaries with his parents—not an easy move for him. Previously he would have worried that they'd be angry with him or that he wouldn't survive without their constant guidance and support.

In persons with *disorganized attachment styles,* solitude can produce many of the same results, but it should be practiced carefully. If this is your attachment style and you have a significant history of trauma, we recommend that you practice the discipline of solitude only under the guidance of someone experienced and trained in working with trauma victims. Why? Because solitude literally dismantles defenses, which can allow flashbacks and other intrusive recollections to come rushing back. Under the right person's care, however, there is a time when solitude is quite appropriate.

Silence

Surrounding oneself with silence and experiencing solitude go hand in hand. Silence occurs when we remove ourselves from all the noise that fills our lives: radio, TV, people, cars, and other human activity. Obviously, it's nearly impossible to completely isolate yourself from sound, but by drastically reducing it, you will become aware of just how often sound drowns out the Lord's voice.

Silence is the essential ingredient of solitude; without silence the impact of solitude is greatly minimized. Willard notes that silence is frightening because it strips us as nothing else does, throwing us upon the stark realities of our life. It reminds us of death, which will cut us off from this world and leave only us and God. And in that total quietness, what if there turns out to be very little to just "us and God"? Think what it says about the inward emptiness of our lives if we must always turn on the tape player or radio to make sure something is happening around us.[8]

As you can see, silence, when combined with solitude, dissolves our normal defenses that keep the feelings of aloneness, vulnerability, and death anxiety at bay. When we're silent and alone, we may actually feel naked before a very large universe. It is here, without all the distractions, that we can seek God's face, rest in His comfort, and respond to His invitation as recorded in Matthew 11:28 (NKJV): "Come to Me, all you who labor and are heavy laden, and I will give you rest."

Like solitude, silence addresses the fear of abandonment in both the ambivalent and the disorganized attachment styles. It can also be an effective discipline for those with the avoidant attachment style, especially narcissists with an inflated sense of self-love (see chapter 4) who seek the company of people who offer frequent praise and adoration. They also love to listen to music, watch television, and hear people prattling around them.

The discipline of silence can help neutralize all these defense mechanisms when you lay them at the foot of the cross.

On a practical note, we sometimes recommend two other versions of solitude and silence. The first is a scaled-down version of solitude in which you wake up in the middle of the night to meet God alone in the silence of your home. This form of solitude has many of the same effects for all the attachment styles, but it is most suitable for those with the disorganized attachment style because it provides the safety net of the home, just in case emotions begin running too strongly.

A second version of the discipline of silence involves silencing the tongue.

This discipline can be practiced within our everyday lives at home, work, or church. It doesn't involve being rudely silent to people, but it changes the emphasis from talking to listening—of being deeply, intently aware of subtleties you may normally overlook.

This form of silence can help the various attachment types make some important changes. It helps the avoidant person engage others on a different level. This was a powerful discipline for Arnold, a client with the avoidant attachment style who we introduced in chapter 4. Arnold was a guy who did a lot of talking. And if he wasn't talking, he was ignoring people. Practicing the silence of the tongue forced him to tune in to his wife and children and to ease into their worlds. Not only did this practice improve his relationships with his family members, as he learned to bridle his tongue he also became more sensitive to God's gentle urgings.

This silence of the tongue helps those with the disorganized attachment style by slowing them down and letting them listen to and label their own thoughts and feelings, rather than just blurting them out. Thus, it helps increase the power of self-reflection (see chapter 6).

Simplicity

When you practice the spiritual discipline of simplicity, you stop complicating your life with your pace and your possessions. You put the brakes on your usual rush of activities.

Keep life simple for a while: Kill the TV for a couple of weeks, put the credit cards away, stay out of the mall, and buy only essential food, toiletries, and other basics. Slow down, declutter your calendar of activities, and, in short, stop doing anything that complicates your life. Then see what happens.

Simplicity's target, much like that of the other disciplines, is to help us seek God first. It's so easy to lose sight of how strongly our material possessions control us and how much we actually look to our possessions as sources of emotional comfort. It's an incredibly strong bond, but you may not even be able to see it.

When we asked our client Jennifer to simplify things, to abandon her devotion to accumulating valuables, she reacted as if we were asking her to give up a trusted friend. She balked. What good could such a discipline bring? she demanded. The mere suggestion nearly sent her into a tumultuous depression.

We pointed out to her that simplicity also involves slowing down. We live at a frantic pace. We drive our kids to ball practice, ballet, school plays, movies, and concerts. We attend church meetings, church socials, extracurricular activities related to work and school, and so much more. Our lives are time starved. So where's our time for God? During coffee breaks, if we take them, or as we snatch a moment to listen to Chuck Swindoll or Charles Stanley in the car on our way home from work?

It has been said that if the devil can't make you sin, he'll make you busy instead. Slowing down means reducing the number of activities we get involved in. Maybe not permanently, but for a season. The idea of the discipline of simplicity is to give yourself the time to rebuild your relationship with God. Chaos and a frenzied pace create the illusion of a full and productive life while they are distracting us from our need to be in connection with the Creator. God doesn't want what you do—He wants you! Remember, if we never slow down, sooner or later we'll *be* slowed. And then it will be difficult to move closer to God. Simplicity helps us identify and break our addictions before they break us.

You might be like Jennifer. Before we suggested simplicity, she would never have dreamed she was addicted to money and possessions or that she relied on them for her sense of safety and comfort. But as she began practicing simplicity, it only took a short time for her to realize just how attached she was to her belongings. You may find the same or a similar addiction within yourself.

"I can't be addicted to money," you might say, "because I don't have any to be addicted to." But it's been said that those who want money the most are the ones without it.

The discipline of simplicity focuses us inward, but when it's practiced, it may force radical external life changes in how you spend your time and your money, and how you use your talents. As you change inwardly, the perspective you have on external things will be transformed. Jesus challenged us to make this change, saying, "If you want to be perfect, go, sell your possessions and give to the poor, and you will have treasure in heaven. Then come, follow me" (Matthew 19:21).

Secrecy

You may not be addicted to material goods. But you may be addicted to your reputation, your success, or your prestige. Not that they're bad things. They aren't. In fact, Scripture encourages us to have good reputations so as to advance the cause of Christ.

In the discipline of secrecy, however, we keep our successes, our accomplishments, and our good qualities secret. We not only abstain from self-aggrandizement, but we actively work to prevent some of our achievements from getting out, as Jesus advised in Matthew 6:3–4: "But when you do a charitable deed, do not let your left hand know what your right hand is doing, that your charitable deed may be in secret; and your Father who sees in secret will Himself reward you openly" (NKJV).

Of course, keeping our accomplishments secret doesn't mean we lie about anything, but our goal is to be understood by others through our actions—and only those actions that are absolutely necessary. The rationale for this discipline is to help us "lose or tame the hunger for fame, justification, or just the mere attention of others."[9] As we practice this discipline, we learn to focus on what's above, not the adoration of man, and even to accept misunderstanding without the loss of the peace, joy, and purpose we get solely from God, through Jesus.

Simple Prayer

We started this chapter with a look at Junior and his mom's attachment relationship. An important element in that relationship was Junior's ability to receive silent messages from his mom: a cock of her head, an arch of her brow, a subtle nod that told him it was okay for him to proceed with whatever he was doing. This is called *social referencing*. The spiritual equivalent to social referencing is simple prayer.[10]

As Paul told the Thessalonians, "Pray continually" (1 Thessalonians 5:17).

The idea is not to live on your knees beside your bed or flat on your face before a chapel altar. The admonition refers to a state of mind where we constantly talk with God about our ideas, thoughts, feelings, and concerns. And if we're not talking to Him, we're consciously including Him in every element of our daily walk. We filter everything through His perspective—maintaining fidelity to the Word of God, remaining sensitive to the leading of the Holy Spirit, and seeking wise counsel from spiritual friends.

Another dimension to the discipline of simple prayer is that we turn to God, we look for His presence, His comfort, and His security in the nooks and crannies of our lives. And as we talk to Him and include Him constantly in our consciousness, we come to Him as we are, not as we think we should be, believing that He can, and will, meet us where we are. Richard Foster states, "To believe that God can reach us and bless us in the ordinary junctures of daily life is the stuff of prayer. But we want to throw this away [because it is] so hard . . . for us to believe that God would enter our space. . . . We must never believe the lie that says that the details of our lives are not the proper content of prayer. Share your hurts, share your sorrows, share your joys— freely and openly. God listens in compassion and love, just like we do when our children come to us. He delights in our presence."[11]

Through the lens of attachment, when we turn to God for guidance, direction, and comfort in the "ordinary junctures of daily life," God is our secure base. He's the foundation from which we confidently explore our world. Again, remember Junior. He used social referencing, constantly looking to Mom as a way to make himself more secure, reassuring himself that Mom was nearby and accessible. In the same way, we use simple prayer to cultivate God's presence, His availability, and His accessibility. Prayer opens heaven's door, where, because of the work of Christ, we can enter boldly into the throne of grace. Just as Junior became willing to explore the park when he assured himself that Mom was there for him, so our readiness to boldly face this world and endure its hardships, love others deeply and intimately, and live with a sense of purpose and meaning is grounded in our unshakable belief that "the Lord is near" (Philippians 4:5).

As Paul exhorted his Philippian brothers and sisters, "Do not be anxious about anything, but in everything, by prayer and petition, with thanksgiving, present your requests to God. And the peace of God, which transcends all understanding, will guard your hearts and your minds in Christ Jesus" (Philippians 4:6–7).

Let's look at things another way: Prayer is to our attachment relationship with God the same as the act of crying is to the attachment relationship between mothers and their babies. Even though tiny babies can't express their needs in words—they can't say, "Hey, Mom, I'm famished!" or, "Mom, I'm sitting in a lake, here. It's definitely time for a change"—sensitive moms know and do whatever is required to bring their infants comfort and security. Likewise, God understands our prayers, our inward groaning, and responds to our needs in the same way. The Bible says, "The Spirit helps us in our weakness. We do not know what we ought to pray for, but the Spirit himself intercedes for us with groans that words cannot express. . . . And we know that in all things God works for the good of those who love him, who have been called according to his purpose" (Romans 8:26, 28).

Meditation

In the same way that talking and listening are two sides of the same conversational coin, prayer and meditation are two inseparable dimensions of our relationship with God. When we pray, we bring our requests, our concerns, our worries, our frustrations, our hopes, and our dreams and present them to God with thanksgiving for all He's done for us so far.

But there's more to prayer than that. As Søren Kierkegaard observed, "A man prayed, and at first he thought that prayer was talking. But he became more and more quiet until in the end he realized that prayer is listening."[12] When we meditate we learn to listen to God, to discern that still, small voice that directs us and comforts our souls. As Richard Foster points out, "Christian meditation, very simply, is the ability to hear God's voice and obey his word. It's that simple." Paul guides us on this journey of meditation in Philippians 4:8 (NKJV): "Finally, brethren, whatever things are true, whatever things are noble, whatever things are just, whatever things are pure, whatever things are lovely, whatever things are of good report, if there is any virtue and if there is anything praiseworthy, meditate on these things."

We encourage you to practice prayer and mediation together. They're both equally important elements of our ongoing conversation with God. As we practice them, they amplify our awareness, our absolute conviction, that He's present and active in our lives. If we ignore these disciplines, it'll be tough to trust that He's close. We'll eventually lose sight of Him; it will become as if He's left. But, of course, He hasn't. Instead we have, in a sense, left Him. Then when we face tragedy, our instincts will take over and we'll end up enduring the tragedy essentially alone. In contrast, when we are anchored in truth and fill our hearts and our minds constantly with Him, we are promised the peace of God that passes all understanding (see Philippians 4:7).

First Things First

As Saint Augustine once noted, "Man was made for God, and he'll never find rest until he finds it in the One who made him." God is the ultimate attachment figure. He created us first to be in relationship with Him—and then with those who share our lives. When our relationship with God is secure, our other relationships become richer, easier, and more rewarding. Thus, our first priority is enhancing our attachment to God through worship and through the spiritual disciplines—including those we've discussed here as well as others such as fasting, confession, Bible reading, submission, and celebration. All play important roles in transforming our attachment relationship with God.

Again and again in our practice we have seen that when clients work on strengthening and, as needed, healing, their relationship with their Creator they soon begin to see noticeable changes in their attachment relationships with others. The result is akin to a whole new start on life and the joys it offers. Jesus said, "I am the true vine, and My Father is the vinedresser. Every branch in Me that does not bear fruit He takes away, and every branch that bears fruit He prunes, that it may bear more fruit" (John 15:1–2 NKJV).

Do you want new life? Strengthen your relationship with the One who created you. Start today!

9

Taming Emotional Storms

Conquering Depression, Anxiety, Anger, and Grief

---

*Love can be angry . . . with a kind of anger in which there is no
gall, like the dove's and not the raven's.*
—Saint Augustine

Joe was at the pinnacle of his career. Just one year ago, at age fifty-five, he had
become the CEO of a prestigious insurance company. His children were
grown and married, and he and his wife had five beautiful grandchildren who
loved to come and spend the night on weekends. His wife was a lovely, gracious woman who loved him and supported his every effort. They owned a
stately colonial home near his work and also had a glorious lake house in the
mountains where they retreated with family and friends every month or so. Joe
had always walked closely to the Lord and was very active in a local
Presbyterian church. But recently Joe sat in a miserable, nervous heap on our
floral sofa, barely able to make eye contact with either of us.

About a year after landing his new job, Joe became riddled with panic
attacks. He had tried a number of medications but was overly sensitive to the
side effects. His wife had urged him (in fact, she had insisted) that he see a
therapist.

Joe's story was a tragic one. He had grown up on a dairy farm in Indiana.
He remembers his dad as a hardworking man, devoted to his family and the
farm, always putting in no less than fifteen-hour days every day of the week,
even Sundays. But he always made some time for his kids too. Then when Joe
was nine years old, his dad had died of a heart attack right in front of Joe while
stacking hay in the barn. He was fifty-five years old.

Joe was left feeling helpless and was never able to grieve because he inherited much of the responsibility of the farm. He spent the rest of his life trying to forget what had happened. But he lived in the spirit of his father's footsteps: hard work, devotion to a cause, and love of the family.

Five years ago, Joe's mother had also died of a heart attack. He remembers being in the hospital room with her, alone, waiting for the rest of the family to arrive. She had undergone relatively minor surgery, and the doctors expected her to recover rapidly and return home in a couple of days. She was a bit drowsy from the pain medication but was able to talk. Then suddenly she became sick to her stomach and started to vomit. Joe called for a nurse, and within a few minutes his mother was unconscious. The nurses asked him to leave, and while he was in the waiting room he could hear on the overhead speaker, "Code blue, post-op recovery. Code blue, post-op recovery."

"I just remember standing there in that little waiting room," he told us. "My head was spinning with confusion. It felt like I wasn't there, like I was standing outside myself, looking at myself and the room around me."

"Were you having a panic attack?" we asked.

"Yes. I think I really was in a state of panic. My heart felt like it was going to leap right out of my chest, and I was having a hard time breathing. I was breaking into a cold sweat. Then I started getting that weird feeling that I was on the outside looking in . . . I thought I had died and was looking at myself from the other side."

After that horrible day, Joe was able to pull himself out of subsequent panic attacks when they occurred. But he did so by completely numbing himself to all his feelings. He remembers that he couldn't cry at his mother's funeral. He became very focused on his work, and his family supported his efforts to succeed.

And this brings us full circle. When Joe reached his peak, that place in his career when he had accomplished what he had always dreamed, he felt numb and empty on the inside. And within a few months of starting his new position, he became intolerably grumpy and irritable at home and at work.

His anger continued to escalate. Soon Joe was going off at everyone: his wife, his children, and his co-workers. It got so out of hand that about six months ago, his company's board of directors recommended that he get some help to deal with his anger. His wife, Sarah, also told him that he needed to get some help or she was going to leave with the kids until he did. Joe didn't seek help; that would be out of character for him. Instead, he stuffed his anger— just like he had learned to do when he was a kid. In his family, anger had not been allowed, especially after his father died.

It wasn't long after Joe got the ultimatum from his wife and his job that he started having the paralyzing panic attacks.

Attachment Styles and Regulating Emotion

Attachment theory isn't just a theory of relationship; it's also a theory of emotion. The idea is that how you approach relationships reflects how you "do" emotion.

For example, those with *secure attachment* are more comfortable with relationships. They have a fairly positive view of themselves, and they expect that others are available and trustworthy. So they don't avoid deep, satisfying relationships, and they are willing to accept the risks involved in loving another person. They handle their feelings in a similar way. They aren't afraid to feel even powerful feelings like fear and anger. They use their feelings judiciously to help them make decisions and to motivate behavior, but they aren't ruled by their feelings. They live according to Dallas Willard's dictum: "Feelings are . . . good servants. But they are disastrous masters."

As we have seen in previous chapters, those with insecure attachment styles handle relationships differently. Not surprisingly, they handle their feelings differently as well. Persons with *avoidant attachment* tend to keep people at a distance, avoid true intimacy, and value success and power over relationships. They are also quite prone to addictive behaviors, which serve as a substitute for intimacy, and they tend to keep feelings at a distance and work to deny or repress any negative feelings. They are more prone to feeling empty and hollow on the inside (the consequence of avoiding intimacy), and they use addictive behaviors (like pornography, substances, or workaholism) to help them feel alive.

Those with *ambivalent attachment* become entangled in relationships, with lots of ups and downs and excessive concerns about rejection and abandonment. They have difficulty setting boundaries with others and may often confuse themselves (i.e., their goals, desires, wants, needs, etc.) with those of others. Likewise, they are often consumed with a whirlwind of emotions. Whereas the person with avoidant attachment style overregulates feelings, the ambivalent attachment style underregulates emotion, allowing normal, healthy emotions to mutate to more intense, destructive, and self-defeating outbursts. For example, instead of getting perturbed at his or her spouse for being late, an ambivalent person might go off into a full-fledged temper tantrum. Or a normal concern about his or her child's safety might lead to a panic attack.

Those with disorganized attachment bounce back and forth among the insecure styles. At times they might be like the avoidant person, keeping people at a distance and overregulating emotion. On other occasions, they might shift into an ambivalent style, becoming more clingy and entangled in relationships and underregulating emotions. Also, those with disorganized attachment might be overwhelmed with feelings from the past. Especially when trauma is part of that past, this person might be consumed with flashbacks and intrusive recollections about past losses and terrifying experiences, and not just remembering those times but reliving them. Every detail of the terrifying events like they were happening all over again—now.

Have you ever considered how you feel about your feelings? Some people feel that emotions, especially emotions like anger, sadness, and fear, are dangerous and should be avoided. Others believe that feelings are inconvenient and troublesome. These folks take a more logical approach to life and tend to put their feelings on the periphery. When they experience such feelings, they either stuff them, like Joe did, or they become very critical of themselves for having such feelings. Perhaps they have heard sermons about how our feelings get in the way of spiritual growth. Or they may have been taught to just "stop feeling that way and move on." Still others consider their feelings to be valid expressions of their internal world, and they allow them to come and go without becoming overly consumed with them.

When God created us, He gave us emotions. The Bible is replete with examples of emotion. A quick look at your concordance reveals that the word *anger* appears literally hundreds of times in Scripture. In 1 and 2 Kings, the word *anger* is used about two dozen times, and the psalmists used it at least thirty times. In the majority of the cases where it is used, *anger* describes God's feelings toward man when man turned away from God. Other emotions, such as fear, sorrow, joy, and peace are also mentioned throughout the Scriptures.

Primary and Secondary Emotions

Emotions shade the world and add color to our experiences. But more importantly, emotions motivate us to take action in an organized, goal-directed way. Emotions prepare us for action. Each emotion is like gasoline with a purpose; it provides the energy for us to act.

Emotions also help organize our behaviors into patterns that can be quite helpful. For example, if someone were trying to harm one of your children, the emotion of anger would move you to a state of preparedness to take action in a productive way. You really wouldn't have to think about it. There would be no mulling over in your mind, *Gee, I wonder why that person is trying to take my child (or hurt my child). Would it be a good idea if I said something to him? What would be the possible outcome? . . . What are my alternatives?* None of that would be going on inside your head. Instead, you would probably act and act quickly. You might control yourself and try not to hurt the person, but he or she would get the picture, loudly and clearly: *Keep your hands off my child.*

Emotions help you make important life decisions. Those who totally restrict their emotions can't just choose from the gut; they get caught up in endless cycles of pondering the pros and cons: *Should I do this? Should I do that?* They never really feel like they *know* what is the best course of action. So they get stuck, often obsessing endlessly about what they should do. Many people with avoidant attachment styles have this difficulty. They've cut themselves off from their emotions, and since how they feel is a valid input to the decision-making process, they now have difficulty in making decisions. They get stuck on, and obsess about, upcoming decisions because they never arrive at a point where they emotionally know a particular direction is the right way to go. Those with ambivalent attachment might also have difficulty making decisions, but for the opposite reason. Their emotions are constantly changing. One moment they might feel an action is right, and in the next they change their minds.

As we have mentioned throughout this book, attachment theory views our emotions as built-in responses that help us achieve a sense of closeness to our attachment figures (see the table on page 184). So a child who is frightened will seek closeness to his or her parents. If an attachment figure fails the child in some way, the emotion of anger is designed to send a specific message: *You'd better not do that again.* It's an anger of hope because the intention is to bring the person back into a state where he or she is again available and accessible.

If an attachment figure is permanently lost, the emotion of sadness informs you of just how important that person was to you. If experienced fully, and if you don't become flooded with a sense of hopelessness (e.g., *I can never heal from this wound; nothing will ever work out for me),* the sadness will "run its course"[1] and you will ultimately be able to return to normal functioning. But a return to "normal" doesn't mean the lost attachment figure is ever forgotten or that he or she can be replaced by someone else. In this way, a sense of sadness remains, but it doesn't prevent you from living life with a sense of purpose, meaning, and direction. It doesn't stop you from loving again.

Primary emotional experiences are clearly adaptive because they give us the energy and focus to accomplish important goals. It's critical to see that these emotions are not "wrong" or "bad." They are God-given "action potentials" that drive adaptive, productive behavior. Think of Jesus' anger when He came into the temple and found merchants buying and selling their goods—a literal Wal-Mart set up right there in God's house (see John 2:14–16). Jesus set a clear boundary, taking a whip and driving away the merchants and their animals. His anger drove and organized His behavior to accomplish a specific goal: protecting His Father's house. This was a primary emotional reaction.

Secondary emotional reactions are different. They usually involve trying to deny or repress the primary emotions. For example, a friend of ours, Ashley, recently complained of feeling very anxious and nervous. She could not figure out why she felt that way and was beginning to feel self-critical and guilty about not being able to control her emotions. Because she was our friend, we could see what was happening. Her new boss was placing entirely too much pressure on her. He wanted her to stay after hours and would frequently ask her to take work home with her. It was really getting in the way of her family life; both her husband and kids were becoming perturbed.

Ashley was angry with her boss, but she had an underlying assumption that blocked her from experiencing that anger. She believed anger was always bad, and she thought if she let herself feel it she would "lose control" of herself. She had learned to fear anger, especially toward authority figures. So she "stuffed" her primary emotion, which led to a secondary emotional reaction: fear and anxiety. Because she also believed that fear, and now worry, were anxiety signs of weakness, she started to feel guilty and depressed. This led to a vicious cycle in which her negative, secondary emotional reactions were covering up her more primary adaptive feelings.

You might be thinking that what Ashley needed to do was set a boundary with her boss and tell him that she was only able to work normal hours. We agree. But before she would be able to do it successfully and stick with her decision, she would have to access—or get in touch with—her primary emotion of anger. She soon learned how to access these feelings without being overwhelmed. She learned that anger, if used correctly, was not a bad thing and could work to her advantage. When she did this, she was motivated to take action. Of course she was nervous about having to set the boundary and feared that she would get fired, but she realized that it was worth the risk.

She told us later, "I was not going to let a job come between me and my family." Her boss actually responded quite favorably to her assertiveness and backed off. He said he had no idea that she was being stressed out by his demands. Her eagerness to please had been perceived by him as a sign that she did not mind doing more than "normal." So, of course, he piled it on even higher. There are still times when he starts to press over the line, but she is more willing to quickly nip it in the bud before it gets out of hand.

A Tale of Frozen Grief

Another primary emotional reaction that people often stuff is grief. When we do that, the emotional consequences are similar to those that occurred in Joe. Grief and sadness are common emotions we experience when we lose someone

Attachment Themes

Attachment Themes	Primary Emotions	Adaptive Behavior	Secondary Emotions	Destructive Thoughts
Separation or threat to the relationship	Anxiety Anger of hope	Seeks closeness Rebukes attachment figure	Worry or panic anxiety Irritability or rage (anger of despair) Worthlessness Guilt/Shame Helplessness	"What if?" thinking "I'm losing control." "The world is not fair." "I must be a horrible person." "Nothing I do ever works out."
Loss of relationship	Sadness and grief	Appreciating and re-membering the lost loved one	Anger of despair Panic anxiety Worthlessness Guilt/Shame Hopelessness and helplessness	"The world and God are against me." "Nothing I do is right." "God is punishing me for be-ing such an awful person." "Why should I try anymore?" "Nothing really matters."
Closeness/ Intimacy	Joy, peace, love, and security	Acts of kindness Gentleness Sensitivity	Anxiety Anger Despair and hopelessness	"What if I get abandoned?" "You are trying to control me." "You are trying to smother me." "I can never love anyone." "No one can really love me."

very special. We may also feel these emotions when we lose an important dream or when we realize that we never got to experience something very important—like the warm, tender love of a mother or the precious time and attention of a father.

Joe was in that position. He lost his father, and his hardworking farm family took no time to grieve. Instead, they had to reorganize their lives. Joe became the new "man of the house." His mother tried to keep the family in "good spirits" by telling them, "We have to move on; your father would want us to do it that way."

Joe was able to get by. The frozen grief and the anger he felt toward his dad for "abandoning" them was turned into productive energy. By the time he came to us he had obviously become a successful man. But his mother's unexpected death five years earlier and his recent promotion had caused the buried emotions to resurface. When they did, Joe was overwhelmed.

Instead of accessing and working through the feelings, however, Joe stuffed them. To him, these feelings were a sign of weakness. The result was irritability, depression, and explosive episodes of anger. When his work and marriage were jeopardized by this anger, he tried to stuff that too. The end result was panic anxiety and more depression. He was simply miserable. Our ability to help Joe required that we help him get in touch with, validate, and heal these primary feelings. Ultimately we wanted him to grow closer to his loved ones and to experience God in a new and very different way.

We believe that when primary emotions are experienced and processed they lead to a transformation of our souls and our behavior. For example, the apostle Paul spoke of "godly sorrow" in his second letter to the Corinthians. But he also saw that the Corinthians' pain (i.e., their sorrow) had created the impetus for change: "See what this godly sorrow has produced in you: what earnestness, what eagerness to clear yourselves, what indignation, what alarm, what longing, what concern, what readiness to see justice done" (2 Corinthians 7:11).

Up to this point, Joe's sorrow had not been completely processed. He had been frozen in time, trapped in the past for too long. He realized he had everything he ever wanted (wife, family, friends, success), but there was a deep wound in his heart that had never been healed. Now he was ready to let God heal that wound. In the end, the process of healing would help him more deeply appreciate the loss of his father and help him reconnect with his family. God wouldn't take away the grief, the heaviness in his heart, because to do so would diminish the importance of his father and mother. But He would help Joe live with it in a different, more courageous way.

THE FIVE TRIGGERS OF EMOTIONAL STORMS

Now that we've explained the difference between primary and secondary emotional reactions, we want to help you see the five triggers that can lead to emotional upheaval in your life.[2] Any one trigger is sufficiently powerful to stir up emotional distress. However, people often experience a combination of the five.

Trigger One: Relationship Disputes

A relationship dispute involves you and at least one significant person in your life (spouse, parents, other family members, close friends, boss, co-worker, etc.) in an unresolved conflict. Such disputes can involve different levels of conflict: renegotiation, impasse, or dissolution.

> Examples of Relationship Disputes
> - Marital conflict
> - Conflict with friends
> - Conflicts with church
> - Conflicts with co-workers
> - Conflict with boss

Level one (renegotiation) is usually the most florid, where you can be very angry with one another and actively argue and bicker about your differences. A number of poor communication skills may be involved that keep you locked in chronic conflict. Examples of these poor communication skills include excessive criticism, defensiveness, contempt and put-downs, and stonewalling (refusing to talk about the problem any longer).[3] At this stage the anger is the anger of hope, the desire that things might be worked out or resolved.

Level two (impasse) begins when you are "argued out" and begin to emotionally disengage from one another. At this stage, you may still talk with each other, but not about the problem. Your relationship has changed such that you no longer confide in or trust one another. The anger here steps up a level to resentment (anger with a history) and even bitterness.

Level three (dissolution) involves complete emotional cutoff. There is little, if any, communication, and you may treat one another as complete strangers. The resentment builds, and you may attempt to live in denial of your anger and grief that comes with losing an important relationship.

At some point in your life, you have probably experienced some type of relationship dispute. Or you may be in one now. It takes only a little reflection to see how upsetting these conflicts can be. Level one disputes involve a lot of observable emotional turmoil, usually a mixture of fear or anger. The fear is about whether the relationship is in danger. The anger is about being wronged (whether in reality or perceived) or about the other person's not being accessible, trustworthy, or reliable.

If these disputes are resolved within a few days, the emotions usually evaporate fairly quickly. However, if they persist, the conflict usually advances to levels two and three. Here the primary emotions of fear and anger are buried, leading to a host of secondary emotions. Take Ashley's situation with the boss who overloaded her with work. When Ashley denied her anger, it quickly turned to worry (negative thinking), panic anxiety, and eventually depression and feelings of hopelessness.

Trigger Two: Transitions

Every year we see college freshmen who have become depressed. Most people think of this as just homesickness, and in some ways it is. That was the case for Scott, a nineteen-year-old college freshman who was sent to us by the on-campus physician. Scott had become mildly depressed about two months after arriving at school. A farm boy from Wisconsin, he had really loved high school, where everything came easy. He'd been a celebrated sports hero—his team had won the state championship—and he'd had a girlfriend, lots of friends, a close family, and loving parents. Plus, he had been heavily recruited by several big colleges for baseball but chose to accept a smaller Christian school's athletic scholarship offer instead.

For Scott, leaving home was like leaving his whole identity behind. It was like starting over. In college no one knew him, no one treated him like he was someone special, no one really appreciated his talents and gifts. He was getting "rocked" a little on the baseball field. His sense of "specialness" was gone, and his identity was shaken.

Scott was going through a role transition. Although it was a step forward developmentally—that is, he was going to college, he was leaving home, he was playing baseball at a higher level of competitiveness—he felt like he was moving backward. The pillars on which he had built his sense of self-worth were shaken; his self-esteem was floundering.

Even when we make positive transitions in life, it can rattle our sense of self. The things we come to trust for safety and security are often taken away. For example, consider a family who moves from one state to the next because Dad gets a job promotion. While this is a positive occupational change for Dad, it can uproot the family from their normal sources of security: The kids have to go to a new school and make new friends. Mom has to find new

> ### EXAMPLES OF TRANSITIONS
>
> **Positive Transitions**
> - Graduation
> - Starting new relationships
> - Marriage
> - Parenthood
> - Parenting teenagers
> - Launching children out of the home
> - Job promotions
>
> **Negative Transitions**
> - Dropping out of school
> - Ending relationships
> - Demotions, layoffs, getting fired
> - Health problems
> - Changing churches

friends, new support systems. And the family as a whole has to search for a new church. That's why moves can be extremely stressful on families. We always caution parents about making frivolous moves, especially when they have children who are older than five or six.

Scott was easy to work with. It only took five or six sessions to help get him back on track. This was in part due to his underlying sense of security. He knew he was loved; his parents were extremely supportive, even though they stayed back home in Wisconsin. In part, we were able to help him shake the depression by drawing on his internal resources. We helped him challenge the negative, self-critical thinking that so frequently accompanies depression. He started to do what he already knew how to do well. He made new friends, buckled down on his studies, and got back into the groove in baseball practice. He was also challenged to reexamine his relationship with the Lord.

Like so many successful people can easily do, Scott had confused the blessings with the "Blesser." He knew how to talk about God's goodness, but he was not used to really turning to God for comfort. This transition was ultimately seen as a good thing by Scott because it challenged him to reorganize and strengthen his relationship with God.

Scott's transition was clearly a new developmental challenge: being able to leave the quiet, comfortable, safe nest of his home and transitioning to adulthood, where he had to take even more responsibility for his life. A similar transition occurs for the so-called "tweenagers," those kids moving between childhood and the teenage years. In school, they move from having one primary teacher to having five or six. Physical changes begin, and their child bodies begin to change into adult bodies.

Relationships, especially with the opposite sex, become more complex, especially as hormones are added to the mix of feelings and bodily sensations. They are also introduced to the challenge of developing a sense of individual identity apart from their parents. This can be stressful not only for the children but for the parents as well. A secure attachment style helps make this transition easier, but it challenges both children and parents to reorganize their relationships.

During such developmental transitions, the insecure attachment styles discussed in the previous chapters only add jet fuel to an already heated situation. Without an inner sense of security and a fairly healthy sense of self-esteem, children are extremely susceptible to a host of negative emotions.

For women, another important developmental transition occurs when they enter their early forties. Not only are they encountering a sea of hormonal changes that come with premenopause, but also they and their families are facing a number of serious role transitions. Their children are preparing to leave the nest and launch out on their own. Some are becoming mother-in-laws and grandmothers; others may be dealing with the pregnancy of their unmarried daughter. With the children leaving home, mothers may be faced with reorganizing their relationships with their husbands, whom they may have lost contact with while the children were growing up. To complicate matters, they also may be faced with taking care of their own parents or in-laws, who are now moving into their senior years when their health may be deteriorating. They may also be considering career changes or even entering the work force for the first time. Or they may be advancing into more senior-level positions. All these changes, while they can be positive, can also challenge women's inner sense of security. Such shifts can trigger changes in biology and in mood, as well.

Men are faced with their own set of transitions, which begin in their early to mid-forties. By this time they have usually reached the apex of their careers and often find the top to be a very lonely place. They have sacrificed time with their wives and children and now that they are ready to plug in to family life, their family members may be angry and resentful, unwilling to reconnect with Dad.

Other men may find that while they are successful in their careers, they derive very little meaning and satisfaction from their occupations. We know of one individual who worked very hard to become a successful engineer, but at age forty he wanted to give it all up and go into missions work. Other men may start having health problems like high blood pressure and cholesterol problems during these years. These diseases, combined with the deterioration of their own parents' health, can put a chink in the armor of what Ernest Becker calls "the denial of death."[4] Many men walk around believing a personal fable: *I am invincible. Death only happens to other people; it will never happen to me.* To deal with this reality, men may enter into what is classically called the midlife crisis, which begins with more basic emotions, like anxiety about death and sadness and grief about a past that may have been lost.

One forty-two-year-old truck driver who came to see us a few years ago had been mildly depressed for several years. His mood had begun to change not long after he was diagnosed with severe rheumatoid arthritis, an illness that creates a sense of loss. He had lost his physical abilities, something he had prided himself on his whole life. He was a hard worker. When he wasn't at work, he loved to tinker around the house, work on cars, mow the lawn, plant the garden, or chop firewood. But he couldn't work like that anymore. This transition caused him to rethink his definition of self. Plus, he had to reexamine his view of God. Up to this point, he had believed God would always protect him from getting sick. Yet, as we have discussed throughout this book,

God doesn't always deliver us from our infirmities, but He helps us draw closer to Him in the midst of our suffering.

If you reflect back on your own transitions, you might see how they may have originally triggered sadness, anxiety, or even a full-fledged depression. However, you might also see how God's hand was involved and how you were able to grow from the challenge. While unpleasant transitions are not in themselves good, they can lead to incredible growth on many levels: spiritual, emotional, and relational.

Trigger Three: Unresolved Grief

When we looked at Joe's situation, described earlier, we saw a man frozen in grief. Like many families who lose a parent, there is little time to come to terms with the incredible sense of loss and sadness that accompanies such a tragedy. When Joe lost his father as a boy, he learned to "stiffen his upper lip" and continue life in his new role as "the man of the house." For a while this seemed to work. He learned to replace grief and anger with a drive for success.

Likewise, when his mother died five years prior to his promotion to CEO, Joe responded in a similar way. He "sucked it up" and became even more focused and driven. But role transitions, even those that include promotions, can peel back the layers of denial and repression used to block out grief and other painful feelings of loss. When Joe reached the pinnacle of his career, he expected to feel differently. He expected to feel alive and complete. Instead he only felt a gnawing emptiness, a feeling far too close to the grief and sadness he had locked away many years ago. He replaced his sadness with anger, an emotion that often accompanies grief; but when it is directed toward others and oneself, it only creates more problems. It almost cost Joe his career and his marriage. For the first time, he was faced with feeling helpless. This triggered the immobilizing panic attacks.

Surprisingly, many people who have developed a case of clinical depression do not see the relationship between their mood problems and their unresolved grief. In some cases, the loss occurs within six months to a year before the onset of depressive symptoms. In other cases, like Joe's, the onset is more subtle, and the unresolved grief is not so easily identified. Joe's feelings of loss were uncovered by what appeared to be a positive role transition. Important transitions, whether positive or negative (for example, graduating college, getting married, birth of a first child, retirement, demotions, unexpected moves, layoffs, etc.), cause us to reflect on the ones we love, those who have stood behind us, those who have hurt us, or those who have betrayed us. They also cause us to confront the past. When the past has been checkered with loss, especially unresolved loss, it can send us spiraling into a depression. Or we may try to avoid these feelings by intensifying addictive behavior.

Trigger Four: Loneliness

We all need support figures, people we can count on to be there for us. In some cases, though, we may have friends and loved ones but still feel lonely on the inside. This loneliness may be a chronic sense of being disconnected, or it may have a relatively recent onset. When loneliness is chronic, it can be linked to different forms of insecure attachment. When loneliness has a recent onset, it is usually linked to one of the other three triggers: a relationship dispute, a transition, or a loss. Whatever the source, it is critically important that you make strong relationship connections. Without them, you are excessively vulnerable to negative feelings, including depression, anxiety, hopelessness, and worthlessness.

Trigger Five: Negative Thinking

While some people consider our emotions and our thinking to be separate functions, many experts believe they are two sides of the same coin. How we think can affect the way we feel, and the way we feel can affect the way we think.

For example, if you came from a family that placed a very high value on success rather than on relationships, you might hold a basic, core belief such as, *To feel good about myself, I must be successful at everything I do.* If so, the next time you encounter failure, you are likely to experience feelings of worthlessness. In that emotional state, you might say things to yourself such as, *I can never do anything right* (overgeneralization). *Why should I ever try again? Nothing will ever work out the way I want it to* (negative fortune-telling). *I've never done anything worthwhile* (selective recall of the past). *I'm a nobody* (negative labeling).

All these thoughts will exacerbate your negative feelings. Plus, as you get more emotionally distraught, your negative feelings will direct your thinking to focus on negative things about yourself, about others, and about the future while selectively ignoring anything positive in your life. And, of course, the more you think about how much you have failed at life, the worse you will feel, thus perpetuating a vicious cycle of painful emotion and negative thinking.

To make matters worse, destructive thinking patterns can lead to behaviors that cause others to act in ways that confirm your negative beliefs and heighten your toxic emotions.

For example, when people get depressed they often feel like no one really likes them. So they can be defensive and irritable when they get around the ones they love. They can also complain a lot and be quite pessimistic. Not surprisingly, others are turned off by this kind of behavior, which leads to their disapproval and withdrawal, which confirms the depressed person's pessimistic, negative mind-set.

Anger and anxiety have similar, self-defeating patterns. When you are angry, your focus is on how you have been wronged. Think about it. When you get mad at someone, you may think of the person in all-or-nothing, black-and-white terms: *He always thinks about himself first. He always treats me like scum. Come to think of it, I've never really liked him because he's so self-centered.*

When you are angry with someone, you selectively attend to that person's faults and systematically ignore his or her strengths. This only intensifies your anger and leads you to be even more critical and negative. As a result, your negativism will be reacted to negatively by the other person, which confirms your negative view of him or her.

With anxiety, the tendency is to focus on the signs of danger and rejection and to ignore any signs of safety and security. In relationships, you might take the smallest sign of disapproval as a sign of total rejection. This might lead to clinginess or angry attacks, both of which lead the other person to become more rejecting and disapproving. And the cycle continues.

To help clarify, let's consider two of the most common types of negative thinking: all or nothing, and jumping to conclusions.

The first type, all-or-nothing thinking, occurs when you see things in either-or, black-and-white categories. Take Katie, for example. She seems to always have a foot just inside a panic attack, especially since she's started dating Jimmy. Her attachment style leans more toward the ambivalent category, so she is especially sensitive to signs of rejection. Any sign of disinterest from Jimmy, even a yawn at midnight, is perceived as a sign of rejection. Of course, once anxiety and anger kick in, Katie's thinking becomes more rigid. She starts pressuring Jimmy for more attention, which may lead him to become irritated and to withdraw. This only intensifies Katie's fears, so she turns up the heat. And the cycle continues.

Jumping to conclusions happens when we act like we can read other people's minds. (David Burns calls this mind-reading.[5]) For example, listen as Susan talks about her very close friend, Mandy:

"I know Mandy hates me. She never wants to talk to me again. And you know what? I think she's crossed the line this time. She's really hurt me badly."

"What happened?"

"I just had an argument with my sister on the phone. Mandy was at my place visiting me and was getting ready to leave. I hung up the phone on my sister; I was really steamed—she drives me crazy! Then Mandy says, 'What's up with her?' I told her, 'I don't want to talk about it right now.' She shot back, 'Fine! I have to go anyway.'"

"Susan," we asked, "help us understand what it was about this conversation that upset you so much that you feel like Mandy has 'crossed the line.'"

"She was basically saying, 'I hate your guts. I never want to talk to you again. You're stupid, and I don't want to hear about your problems ever again.'"

"What do you mean she basically said 'I hate your guts, and I never want to talk to you again'? Did she actually say this?"

"No, but she might as well have. It hurt all the same."

Susan was mind-reading. Why? Partly because her past is checkered with rejection and disappointment; people have treated her like they didn't care, like they really didn't want to hear about her problems. Plus, she had just broken off an emotional conversation with her sister; she was already feeling rejected. Seeing Mandy as mean-spirited and rejecting fit her mood at the moment. Notice how Susan concluded that Mandy didn't care about her problems, even though Mandy asked what was upsetting her. Susan selectively ignored this, writing it off as, "She didn't really care. She was just trying to make me feel like she cared."

Burns identified another type of jumping to conclusions called fortune-telling. This happens when we assume the worst and make negative forecasts about how people will behave. This creates a sense of relational paralysis, where we stop trying to work on relationships because we are convinced they will never work out.

As we worked with Susan, we helped her see that perhaps Mandy didn't really mean anything negative by her terse comment, "Fine. I have to go anyway." She may, in fact, have been a little angry because *she* felt her helping hand was being rejected. We tried to get Susan to go back to Mandy and patch things up, but this was no easy task. Susan was convinced that Mandy would criticize and reject her. "There is no use in trying. She'll just throw it back in my face that I'm too sensitive. She's written me off now that I haven't talked with her for a couple of weeks."

Susan's fortune-telling was keeping her frozen in a state of turmoil. Based on past experiences, she was convinced that the future would repeat itself. Unfortunately, she was playing an important role in repeating her past experiences of rejection. In her mind, she was convinced that Mandy had completely rejected her. But her belief was based on faulty perception, not reality. And because she had convinced herself that the conflict couldn't be worked out, she wouldn't try to reconcile with Mandy. Nor would she agree to consider new information about relationships that might disprove her old set of relationship rules (*I can't count on others. They believe I'm fundamentally flawed. They will always let me down*). Thus she had painted an exact replica of the past in her present friendship. And in the future she will undoubtedly use her memory of Mandy as just another example of how people have let her down.

META-EMOTION—EMOTIONAL ATTITUDES

There is another type of thinking that can intensify negative emotions. It is rooted in the basic assumptions we have about our feelings. John Gottman calls this thinking *meta-emotion* (meaning emotion about emotions). We prefer to call it the *emotional attitude.*

As we noted earlier, some people have very negative attitudes about negative feelings. Remember Joe's situation? He held a number of negative emotional attitudes about his feelings. He considered sadness, for example, as a sign of weakness. So when he felt sad, he would become self-critical: *What's wrong with me? I need to toughen up. If I let myself get down, I'll never get back up. People shouldn't wallow in their problems; they need to pull themselves up by their bootstraps.* While this reaction worked temporarily, it finally caught up with him. And when it did, the consequences were disastrous: He criticized himself for feeling sad, which led him to feel secondary anger and irritability. When he almost lost his job and his marriage, he tried burying the anger, which led to panic attacks. And for a man like Joe, anxiety was the ultimate sign of weakness, so next he heaped on the guilt and shame. Then depression set in. Joe's emotional attitudes were getting him into deep trouble.

You may have some of these attitudes yourself. A sure way to find out is to ask yourself how you feel about your feelings. Do you think negative emotions in yourself or in others are unacceptable? To what degree? Since emotions, especially the primary ones we discussed earlier, are as basic to our existence as hunger, thirst, and the need for air, it would be calamitous for us to deny them, or worse, to flog ourselves for having them. It's not unlike the difficulties people with anorexia get into. They criticize themselves for getting hungry and tell themselves they are weak if they give in and eat what others consider to be a normal meal. For them, the result is physical deterioration. Likewise, to cut yourself off from your primary emotions will lead you to develop an emaciated emotional and spiritual self.

Others, however, may confuse their secondary emotional reactions with primary ones. These secondary emotions are the ones we want to help you target and eliminate. However, in a paradoxical way, the best way to rid yourself of the secondary emotions is to face your primary ones. As Carl Jung pointed out, the source of all unnecessary emotional pain is the avoidance of legitimate emotional pain. People who are trapped in emotional storms fail to see that the way out begins by identifying, accessing, and working through their primary emotions.

Six Steps toward Calming Your Emotional Storms

Changing your emotions from unhealthy to healthy requires hard work. As you are probably well aware, your feelings are not easily changed, and brute force and pure will power will get you nowhere. We believe four elements are needed to transform your emotions: a desire to change them (Dallas Willard calls this *vision*), a commitment to see the process through *(intentionality)*, a healthy investment of time, determination, and effort (the *means*)—and finally, *courage*. The experiences that have been deeply engrained in you won't give up their hold on you willingly. But God will supply the grace and the way for the process to unfold.[6]

Below we will describe a six-step process we teach our clients to help them learn to calm their emotional storms. But before we begin, we need to tell you: It's not really a process; it's more of a journey. The goal of the journey is not only to teach you to calm your intense, out-of-control, destructive feelings, but to help you transform the way you *look* at your feelings. Instead of making them your enemy, or instead of having them as your master, we want to help you make them your servants.

Step One: Identify the Primary Feeling

As we discussed above, primary feelings are adaptive because they are designed to help you resolve problems. For example, one mother, Phyllis, came to see us because she was feeling so much anger when she was around her children. She was always irritable and grumpy when her kids were playing and having fun. As we talked about this more, we found that she was filled with fear. About a year before, her son had been happily riding his bike—and wrecked it right in front of her. He'd had a helmet on, but he'd still required several stitches in his mouth. Since then, Phyllis had been on edge, always on guard, afraid that one of her kids would get hurt.

A key first step for Phyllis was to see that her anger was a secondary emotion and that her fear was primary. Her son's accident shattered her assumption that being a careful, watchful mother could *always* prevent bad things from happening to her children. She was now afraid that something else would or could happen and that she would have to stand by helplessly and watch it happen— just like the bike accident. This fear was understandable, given her circumstance. But she had resisted this emotion and replaced it with anger, which made her feel more powerful. Unfortunately, the anger was placing a wedge between her and her children, and she was feeling increasingly guilty and depressed.

"No matter how hard I try," she said, "nothing I do is right. My kids can't stand to be around me. But I can't help it. I don't know what's wrong with me."

We helped her access the more primary fear she had of one of her children being seriously hurt or killed. We also helped her realize that this fear was based on a very healthy longing or desire: that her children be safe from harm's way. Any good mother desires this. It is a part of the attachment/caregiver system. It was a sign that she really cared about her kids and their safety. By focusing on this, Phyllis was about to validate her more primary emotion of fear.

Step Two: Connect Primary Emotion to a Triggering Situation

Earlier we discussed how the advent of strong emotions can be tied to specific types of situations. When you experience strong feelings—rage, fear, and anxiety, among others—first, to keep from beating yourself up about them, label them appropriately. Then identify what triggered them. Were you cut off on the highway? Did your spouse try to mother you? What happened? Here are some clues to look for with each of these specific primary emotions.

• *Anger* springs from situations where you've been wronged or mistreated. You're not being treated fairly, and you focus incessantly on that, replaying the event in your mind repeatedly.

• *Fear* surfaces when you or someone you love is in danger. The danger can be physical—fear of getting killed in a car accident, having a heart attack—or emotional—being criticized, ridiculed, or abandoned.

• *Sadness* is connected to the loss of some*one*—a loved one or a close friend—or some*thing*—like a dream or an important expectation or, in the case of failure, the loss of a part of the self.

If you experience chronic negative emotions such as a clinical depression or prolonged, serious anxiety, or if you believe you have a disorder, look within yourself for one of the five triggers described previously.

Step Three: Target Negative Thinking

We've discussed ways that negative thinking can intensify negative moods. Philippians 4:8 reminds us it's important to tell ourselves the truth. Paul said, "Finally, brothers, whatever is true, whatever is noble, whatever is right, whatever is pure, whatever is lovely, whatever is admirable—if anything is excellent or praiseworthy—think about such things."

Take Paul's advice to heart. Whenever you catch yourself in the act of negative self-talk, you've taken the first step to repairing your destructive thinking pattern. The process usually involves three more steps.

1. Now that you've caught yourself, identify the pattern associated with your negative thinking. Ask yourself, *What am I telling myself about my situation that is not true or accurate?* Remember: Be brutally honest. Blaming someone else for your own inability to do what needs to be done does you no good.

2. Search for a new way to look at the situation, a way based more on truth than on emotion. Ask yourself, *Is there a more honest way to look at this situation?*

3. Practice looking at the world from the new perspective. Test the new belief.

For example, Susan could've told herself, *Okay, maybe Mandy doesn't hate me. It is possible that I read something into the situation.* But to solidify this new perspective, Susan would have to test it. She'd have to visit Mandy. "I'm sorry about the other day," she might say. "I just felt like you weren't interested in me." Mandy would then have the opportunity to clarify herself and help Susan see how she had injected past experiences into the present, much to her own dismay.

Another possibility for Susan would be that she could step outside of her own feelings and put herself in Mandy's shoes for a moment. Perhaps Mandy had also felt rejected, as we suggested before. Susan could go to her and say, "I want to apologize. I'd just gotten off a difficult call with my sister. I was angry, and I think I took some of it out on you. Talk to me."

Step Four: Behave Differently

Although many counselors believe lasting change only comes by working from the inside out, we're suggesting what we consider to be a complementary method—changing from the outside in. Let's explore this method for a moment.

People who fear criticism often avoid social situations. To facilitate change in these persons, we suggest they practice going into social situations, for example, the company picnic or a friend's party. Each time the person takes another social risk—says hello to someone, asks a question, strikes up a conversation—the anxiety will diminish just that much more.

The same is true for other change. Whatever triggers your unwanted behavior, seek it out. Act the opposite of how you feel. Sure, doing so takes courage. But change never was for the fainthearted. Each time you assault your fears, your anxiety, or your sadness, your action generates new information that can revise your negative thinking patterns. If you're afraid of social situations, then by throwing yourself into them, by challenging yourself to open up and take part, you help yourself see what others see, that people are warmer and more supportive than you expect. And if you do happen to meet a cold fish, the world keeps turning and you survive unscathed. So consider the cold fish the cold fish's problem, not yours, and keep going.

Another example concerns depression. Here's a surefire way to launch yourself out of depression: Get busy. Get your head and body moving. Why does that help? When we plunge into depressions depths, we generally don't feel much like doing anything. We sit. We stare at the tube. We raise procrastination to new levels of nonactivity. We disengage. We may not ever get dressed, brush our teeth, shave, or put on makeup. The more we do nothing, the more time we have to stew about whatever threw us into the hole in the first place. As we often say, the sofa is the greenhouse of depression. Trying to change negative thinking while wallowing on the sofa watching Jerry Springer is as close to a lost cause as we'll find anywhere.

But when we get up and get going, the adrenaline starts pumping, our brains start looking around for better ways to do whatever we're doing, and our depression fades. It may happen slowly at first, but when we're persistent, it'll eventually fade away.

And as we get up and get going, if our activities lead us to cross paths with others, and those others get us to laughing and enjoying life again, all the better. And if you just happen to do something good for yourself while you're out and about, it also helps change your negative, self-defeating thoughts. Finally, if while you're doing something good for yourself you manage to extend that kindness to others—well, nothing attacks depression better than a thank-you from someone. Now you see you have real value.

Maybe you see why, when we work with folks who are depressed, we begin by getting them active.[7] We help them plan small activities for every day of the week. Things like taking a fifteen-minute walk, putting the dishes into the dishwasher, vacuuming the living room, etc. The more they do, the more positive they feel and the more positively they see themselves. And the emotional stairway spirals upward. The better they feel, the more they feel like working, and the work we have them do helps them identify and deal with some of their fundamental relationship issues, which may have triggered the depression in the first place. And the more they feel positive about the work they've accomplished, the more good feelings that have resulted from that work, the more work they want to do. Depression soon becomes an unwanted memory.

Step Five: Use Problem-Solving Techniques

Our negative moods can cause us to feel helpless, make us feel like there's nothing we can do to change the bad situation we're mired in. Then the more passive we become, the more hopeless we feel about it all. Nothing gives us a greater sense of being able to deal with our environment or our situations than working to solve the problem. But sometimes our attachment styles get in the way of that.

Those with avoidant attachment styles often just want to detour around their problems, especially those involving close relationships. As a result, their problems only mount. Those with ambivalent attachment styles, however, become so overwhelmed with emotion they believe problem-solving techniques just won't help. In fact, they usually frame problems as global chaos, and who can possibly take on global chaos? So they become absolutely passive.

The trick for people in both these groups is to look at the situation they're in, possibly define a problem that's a workable chunk, and then build a problem-solving scenario—a set of steps that, when taken, will solve the problem, or at least make the situation more manageable.

When we come up with such a plan, we put depression and hopelessness on notice: *We're taking control, God willing, and step by step, we're going to climb out of this hole.*

Let's take a look at how one of our clients, Amy, might take this proverbial bull by the horns. Amy's attachment style is ambivalent, so instinctively she fears rejection and clings to those close to her whom she thinks might be getting ready to bolt on her. Her husband doesn't like being smothered, so when she does cling to him, he withdraws into a project at work. The deeper he buries himself, the angrier she feels because of his rejection. She feels abandoned and helpless to do anything about it, which makes her feel even angrier. She cries out, "I know he loves work more than me. He always has. And there's nothing I can do about it."

Really? Let's take a look.

First, she can stop saying there's nothing she can do about it. There *is* something, but to keep from being rejected again, she's afraid to attempt anything.

So we suggested that her first step should be to go to the Lord and ask for courage. Pray for it, we said. Beseech God the Father, through the work of His Holy Spirit, using Jesus' courage on the cross for you as a model, to help you take a deep breath and tell yourself, *Amy, you have power in this situation.* Then we suggested that she ask God for wisdom in dealing with it.

The next step for Amy was identifying the problem. We told her to ask herself, *What is really bothering me? How is it a problem?* This step seemed easy for Amy. She quickly answered, "He works all the time." But this problem was too large. We could tell that because it included the words *all the time.* Other giveaway terms might include *he/she never . . . ,* etc. Those with ambivalent attachment styles like to use phrases like that to get themselves off the hook. You see, those phrases make the problem unsolvable.

So we asked Amy to restate the problem more honestly in a way that might even be a little riskier for her. "He doesn't want to spend any time with me," she said. That was better.

Now we suggested that she come up with some possible solutions. Be creative here, we nudged. Amy's first response was that she had already tried everything. But she hadn't. In fact, there was a whole set of responses she'd avoided. And for good reason. She was afraid to try them. All her previous responses had come from that fearful side of her, that side that wanted to grab on to her husband and not let him leave, that part that approached him with angry negatives and with sharp criticism, a common strategy for ambivalents.

Now Amy had to explore that side of herself she'd just prayed to be strengthened and made more courageous, that part that needed to assume her husband did love her, that part of her that said, *Build a pleasant environment, and he will come home.* Well, Amy *did* gather up her courage, and we were proud of her. She asked hubby for a date. And he said yes! She lined up the baby-sitter and planned the entire evening. She also put all her irritation about his work schedule behind her and committed to just having a good time with him.

But she also took another important step. Even though it had become an enemy, that project at work was important to her husband. Getting it done right and on schedule would mean kudos at work, maybe a raise later, and certainly a more agreeable and satisfied husband at home. Amy decided to support him in his effort. During their evening out, she told him, "I know I haven't supported your work on the project as strongly as I could. In fact, I know I've been more hindrance than help. I want you to know you can take all the time you want to make sure you get it done on time. And if I can arrange things at home to make working there easier and more pleasant for you, I'll do it."

Her husband was openly appreciative. Then, over the next few weeks of the project's duration, Amy followed through. She knew her husband loved sun-brewed tea, so she made sure he had a good supply of it as he worked in his home office, and she made sure his area was clean and quiet. And to her delight, before the project was over, he was working in the living room with her. Occasionally he even stopped work and made Amy the hot herbal tea *she* liked.

Next came one of the most important steps in any problem-solving process: checking the results. We instructed Amy to ask herself these questions: Did your plan work at all? Could it work better? What should I change? When she assessed the results she could make changes and work the new plan.

Amy was overjoyed with the results. Her hubby seemed more willing to spend time with her and was actually behaving more warmly. She loved it when he made her tea. But there were still times when her negative instincts took over and she felt herself reverting.

What should she do when that happened? Set about solving the new problem. Starting with prayer, she worked her way through the steps again and came to a solution, one that worked.

She brought her husband in on the process. She told him about the emotional work she was doing and why she was doing it. Then she told him that if she ever reverted back to her old habits, he was to call her on it, maybe saying something like, "Honey, I don't like the criticism. I think you're getting angry and there's no reason to."

Something wonderful happened when Amy did this. Her husband began to search his own behavior and how his busyness had bothered his wife, how it had stirred up her negative feelings. He saw that her lashing out had come about because she was angry about his distance. So he moved toward her, not away. He learned to slow down and listen to her. Now they would both work together to make their marriage stronger.

Taming Emotional Storms

Step Six: Plug In to Healthy Relationships

For us to truly deal with our heart-level emotions, we have to seek out close, supportive relationships—relationships that allow us to take risks and grow. The previous five steps are necessary for taming emotional storms, but they don't take you all the way without healthy relationships.

As we stated earlier, four elements are needed for successful change: vision, intentionality, means, and courage. A new vision of yourself is needed to calm your emotional storms, a vision that you're someone who has strong, reliable, healthy, trustworthy relationships. God will help supply the courage and grace to help you make personal changes that will improve your current relationships. But you need to be *intentional* about making this transition happen.

Amy needed to change herself so that she could make her important relationships better and so that, if she ever does walk alone in the future, she'll know how to seek out new relationships with eyes of health.

Relationships can be, in part, the means through which you will ultimately find healing and transformation. That's why you've just *gotta* muster the courage to risk "plugging in" to healthy relationships. And this may include relationships you're already plugged in to. You fathers may need to plug in to relationships with your children. You wives may need to plug in to relationships with your husbands.

It's time to break free of what we've come to call the acceptable level of pain in attachments that may cause more grief than joy. It's time to choose a different way of relating, even though it may be a little frightening. It's time to have loving, lasting relationships with those we hold dearest. It's time for a new way to live.

10

LOVE, SEX, AND MARRIAGE

Working Out Our Most Intimate Relationship
with Sharon Hart Morris, Ph.D.

Therefore shall a man leave his father and his mother,
and shall cleave unto his wife, and they shall be one flesh.
—GENESIS 2:24 KJV

As a graduate student, one of my (Tim's) first counseling sessions wasn't going all that well. Tom and Cindy, a couple in their twenties, sat on the sofa opposite me talking over some pretty weighty relational matters, and they were getting tenser by the second. Jaws were tightening, eyes were narrowing, phrases were getting shorter and penetrating like bullets. Suddenly Cindy reached her limit; she sprang from her chair and screamed at Tom, "All I've ever wanted is for someone to love me. Is there anything wrong with that?" Then she ran from the room.

Tom immediately eyed me—and I eyed him. In Grinch-like fashion, his eyes grew wide and, for the first time, he *heard* her; he could see what was happening.

"If you love her," I said, "go get her."

MADE FOR CONNECTION

We opened the first chapter of this book with God's creation of Adam, then Eve, how God saw that it was not good for Adam to be alone and created Eve from Adam's flesh and bone to be his companion and helper. God designed us for intimacy. In fact, He created us for the most intimate of intimacy, to be united as one flesh. That intimacy is to be shared with our spouses—free, close, together.

Since we were created for such a relationship, God lodged the longing for it in our hearts. So when we are free of the external and internal influences clouding our true desires that drive us to become islands, we truly crave to be seen, known, understood, and valued, to have someone kiss our faces, hold us close, make us feel cared for and, in a word, *loved* by our mates. Just as that was Cindy's dream, it's the dream of every bride and the hope of every groom.

But I Don't Feel Connected

As you read this, and if you're honest with yourself, you're probably saying, "That's nice, but you're not talking about *my* marriage. It doesn't always feel close and connected."

This reaction isn't surprising; most married couples don't. And every marriage, to a degree, will go through periods of disaffection—times when we don't always feel respected or cared for by our spouses. Being only human, and each of us having our own share of human frailties, we're prone to intentionally, and more often, unintentionally, cause each other pain. And this happens whether or not we're secure in our attachment styles.

On your wedding day, when all the world seemed caught in the unfathomable vortex of your love for one another and you gazed into your new husband or wife's eyes, both of you undoubtedly saw love and acceptance for who you are gazing back at you. Neither of you wanted, even contemplated, a marriage of strife and emptiness. You wouldn't have said "I do" if you did. But if you are like most people, over the years your marriage hasn't been everything you'd hoped. You've discovered that you two are very different in many ways, ways that often irritate. And your spouse hasn't always been thoughtful or emotionally accessible, and when he or she was, it was less than satisfying.

You probably haven't been all that emotionally accessible either. When you've responded to your spouse, sometimes you haven't been as kind and considerate as you could have been. It may not have been your intention, but at times over the years you've hurt each other. You've disappointed each other, let each other down, stepped on each other's feelings, and occasionally, when trying to protect your heart, you've lashed out and said things you later regretted.

Maybe for years you've tried to get your mate to understand you and all those hurts you've felt. But there's never time to talk, and when you do talk, you end up criticizing one another and defending yourselves. When the dust clears and the voices die, you know your spouse just doesn't "understand," and you leave the room feeling judged and overwhelmed. And when you *do* leave that room, both your hearts carry feelings of painful resentment and fear that all that love and acceptance you felt so many years ago have met the same fate as the *Titanic*.

So—what causes all this trouble and friction in marriage? Some blame it on one or a combination of issues—crowded schedules, money pressures, communication problems, midlife crises, or all those differences we just discussed. It *is* easy to target the differences. She might be gregarious, he might be thoughtful; he might be plagued by fears, she might live on the edge. They might have differing political opinions or want to emphasize different elements of God's Word—she wants to be embraced by God's love, and he wants the order of His law. Every one of these differences can become the center of an argument, and maybe has. And, of course, before the battle ends, you're told how your way is "wrong" or somehow inferior, and you're given unwanted advice that leaves you feeling totally unknown. Which, of course, only pumps on more flammables.

Difficulties in marriage also arise out of unresolved relational hurts—past and present—arguments and misunderstandings that flare up, then die, but never deal with the issues that caused all the flames. And as the battles boil around them, the battles and the scars from them become issues in themselves. As those scars build, they eventually become emotional attachment injuries and seriously mar the marital landscape. This happens particularly when you feel hurt and your feelings go unnoticed, which causes your wounds, many of which probably started out as paper cuts, to become deep and raw and produce pain that just doesn't go away.

People can't live like that for long. Look around you.

As emotional pain becomes unbearable, both spouses will try various fixes, various salves. A wife might try to repair the hurts by pointing out all that's wrong with her husband. Her intentions are pure; she hopes hubby will see his faults and change. A husband generally defends himself and goes on to point out the faults in his wife, hoping, as the wife did, to promote change. Usually it's a vain hope. In fact, these failed attempts to draw each other closer usually cause the spouses to push each other even further away, the wife becoming hurt and angry, the husband frustrated and resentful.

Eventually, when unresolved pain becomes absolutely unbearable and hope of reconciliation dies, each spouse emotionally disconnects and is left empty, exhausted, and feeling far apart. Husband and wife are left saying, "He/she just doesn't know me. We just can't talk about the deep emotional stuff. He's/she's not capable of understanding me. He/she hasn't for a long time. No matter what I do, it doesn't make a difference. I'm always walking on eggshells. It's best just not to care."

THE KEY TO A LOVING, LASTING MARRIAGE: STAYING EMOTIONALLY CONNECTED

In marriage, when spouses no longer feel safe, secure, or significant, or—even worse—when they become emotionally bruised, even bloodied, and see nothing but a future of more wounds, they do what any thinking human being would do: They distance themselves from the threat. It's a "reasonable response" to an unreasonable situation. Faced with persistent nagging, rejection, rage—you fill in the pain—the mantra becomes, *You go your way, and I'll go mine. Take all the shots you want. They'll never hurt me again* (but they do). *I'm far away. They'll all fall short of their mark.*

Now emotionally disconnected, each spouse unites with the other only around chores or family tasks. They may live side by side, sleep side by side, face problems side by side, but they're really individuals, each seeing the other as part of whatever problem they're setting out to solve. But they don't *want* to be disconnected. They want to be again as they were in the beginning. They protest the disconnect: "You used to be so understanding, so tender. Now you want nothing to do with me." But their protests fall on deaf ears.

As their emotional separation evolves, one spouse usually repeatedly expresses anger while the other often just shuts down on the inside. Both stay guarded and protective. Before long, desire dies. After a while, each concludes that staying married is no longer an emotionally safe option.

Interestingly, studies show that it is not *what* couples fight about or the fact that they *do* fight that threatens the marriage. Actually, what couples argue about at the beginning of their marriage they usually argue about for the rest of it.[1] And they often disagree about issues that can't be changed and can't be resolved, like differences in lifestyle—she's a night person; he shines in the morning. So if differences between spouses or the battles themselves don't necessarily destroy marriages, what does the fatal damage?

The key to the success and longevity of marriages is not *if* but *how* couples fight. The crucial factor is that they're able to remain emotionally connected through and after their fights. And what's essential to staying emotionally connected? A healthy, secure attachment bond. In fact, a recent study showed that couples who perceived their spouses to be emotionally available, accessible, and responsive reported having happier and healthier marriages.[2]

Worth fighting for . . .

Before we write another word, may we say that your marriage, no matter how difficult it's been, is *not* beyond the reach of God. But maybe you're not so sure. Maybe you're at a relationship crossroads. Could it be that the two of you just got lost in all the stress—the pain, the past—and are responding to each other out of the hurt and rejection? No wonder you're asking yourself, *Do I want to risk my heart one more time—turn it back toward my spouse and try to heal our marriage? Or should I just disconnect altogether?* Or maybe you want desperately to try to reconnect again, but you just don't know how. Stay close. You *can* turn your marriage around.

Or maybe your marriage isn't on life support; maybe it's just time for a marriage tune-up. We believe you can strengthen your love by applying the principles we'll explain in this chapter.

In any case, we encourage you to step back from—not out of—your marriage and work to rebuild your relationship on a different, much firmer, foundation. As we've already said, no marriage is beyond God's healing hand. And what can God's healing bring? A marriage in which both of you are seen, understood, and loved by each other within a nurturing, secure attachment bond, a bond that allows your hearts to turn passionately toward each other as your marriage finds new life—as it heals its wounds and creates a relationship structure that offers comfort for all future wounds as they come. Fostering such a close, deep secure bond with one's spouse is a process that can take a lifetime—too long for couples who quit before the end. So hang in there. Don't lose heart. Some of the healthiest marriages we know are ones that have weathered some pretty severe storms.

THE ATTACHMENT STYLE'S IMPACT ON THE MARITAL RELATIONSHIP

A marriage filled with warm, earnest promises and held together by an all-consuming love is really about attachments and, as such, it is governed by a curiously strict set of relationship rules. These rules sprout from our relationship experiences with parents, caregivers, and those closest to us as we grow, and in their entirety, the rules shape how we view ourselves and our own worth and whether or not we see relationships as being safe. This web of rules and ways of being that arises from our past relationships forms an attachment style. This style is strongly formed as we're nurtured, or not nurtured, by our caregivers and shaped by our relationships over the course of our lifetimes.

These ways of being in a relationship—how you view yourself, the ability of others to love you, and the safety of the world around you—are what you bring into your marital relationship. You each enter your marriage with a relationship belief (which we described in chapters 3 and 7) that informs you how safe it is to trust your partner with yourself. This style, developed when you were young, comes to life each day as you relate to your spouse. Seeing your marital relationship through an attachment lens can help make sense of your own reactions along the way as well as the reactions of your spouse. It can even help you realize that your partner is not out to get you, is not weird, or is not just too bizarre to be understood.

Love, Sex, and Marriage

Five Key Aspects of the Marital Attachment Bond

What is it about the marriage relationship that accentuates the impact of the attachment style? To help answer that question, let's take a look at what sets marriage apart from other close relationships.

First, spouses *seek out* their partners for comfort and closeness. Their hearts ask each other, *Will you be there for me when I reach for you? Can you be found emotionally as well as physically accessible when I need you?*

Second, when our partners respond with sensitivity and care, they become *safe havens* to which we can turn for comfort and love.

Third, the relationship then becomes a *secure base* that launches the spouses into the world with assurance and confidence. Spouses talk about going out into the world and battling the dragon of the day's tasks while feeling secure in the knowledge that their mates are safe havens they can return to at sundown. They know that when they return they'll be understood and cared for.

The fourth aspect of attachment bonds in marriages is that *when the bond is threatened or when spouses perceive that their partners are not there for them, then fear and anxiety is triggered, and the fighting begins.* These behaviors, even the arguing, are aimed at restoring the bond, retrieving the spouses' attention, repairing the disconnection, and restoring closeness.

Fifth, after failed attempts to restore or reestablish the bond, *the loss of the connection causes grief, sorrow, and finally an emotional disconnection.* It's not a peaceful or joyous disconnection but rather one that guards the spouses' deep emotional beings. All the while, the spouses are yearning for reconnection—"someone to love me."

The Secure Attachment Style in Marriage

In relationships based on a secure attachment bond, spouses have a reasonably confident deep assurance that the other spouse will be there for them, no matter what. Their relationship is a safe haven. They ascribe the best motives to each other and are able to place any misunderstandings, forgetfulness, and disappointments in a positive, or at least neutral, context as they interpret their mates' intentions in the greater, more positive context of who those persons are. They shake off sarcasm, even hurtful remarks made to one another, and are honest and open when disappointed. After a hurt, they might say to themselves, *Oh, he's just tired and has had a long day. Sure, he's grumpy, but I know he doesn't mean it. I'll let him know that his mood is hurtful, but I have a deep assurance that he has my best interest at heart.*

Sometimes there are real hurts, of course. But couples with secure attachments are better able to tolerate them, and after a fight, they bounce back and emotionally reconnect. Often they catch themselves midfight and admit, "I really don't want to be doing this. You know, what I said was unkind. I'm sorry; it's just that my day was the pits." Then, instead of turning on their heels and leaving the room with the hurt still alive and well, they usually take their apology to the next level. They wrap their arms around each other and restore the intimacy to their relationship.

The Ambivalent and Disorganized Attachment Styles in Marriage

Persons with an *ambivalent attachment style* live their lives vacillating between being drawn to and fearing being hurt by relationships. They perceive themselves as not all that lovable and find it hard to believe their spouses will love them as they want. It's not that they think their spouses are incapable of love. They have every confidence that if presented with someone worthy of being loved, their spouses would gladly oblige. They just don't perceive *themselves* as being lovable. They believe they're unworthy.

These partners fear that if their spouses really knew them, they would just up and leave. Terrified of being found unworthy and even more terrified of the abandonment that would result, these spouses cling ferociously to their partners and accommodate their partners' wishes. As outlined in chapter 5, spouses with ambivalent attachment styles have low self-confidence and shy away from making decisions and from speaking their own minds. They desperately aim to please their spouses. So they cling in hopes of obtaining their spouses' assurance and support. But no matter how much they work at the relationship, they usually end up feeling that they've fallen short and can't obtain their spouses' love and attention. In fights they say things like, "I don't know why you married me. I'm just not a good wife to you. I can't do anything right. I wouldn't blame you if you left me for someone else."

In a similar vein, those with the *disorganized attachment style* believe that even if their spouses did love them, the spouses would still be incapable of meeting their needs. They fear their partners will eventually hurt, disappoint, and/or let them down. They desperately long for closeness, and so they cling to and pursue their spouses. But fearing that those spouses will be unable to love them, they suddenly retreat and turn inward to themselves for comfort.

When all seems well between them and their partners, they come across as warm, understanding, and trusting. But if an incident happens that threatens the bond, then the alarms go off, warning them that the relationship is dangerous. They cling for closeness, but just when closeness looks possible they pull away in fear and protection. *Come close, please* is the message they seem to send their spouses, but when those spouses draw in, the message changes to *Get away! You'll hurt me.* For them there seems to be no safe haven, no place to go to feel loved and emotionally safe. Trouble in these marriages elicits an array of emotions ranging from fits of rage to a sense of empty hollowness.

Spouses with disorganized and ambivalent attachment styles are anxiously attached and experience greater stress and anxiety during marital fights. Arguments and disagreements stoke up greater anger and hostility toward their partners. After fights, these anxiously attached spouses view their partners less favorably. Disagreements sour their perception of love, commitment, respect, openness, and the supportiveness of their spouses.

Since anxiously attached spouses feel unworthy of love, they don't expect emotional support from their partners. Their relationship belief states that their partners will not respond to them the way they hope for. They fear they won't have the close connectedness they long for, which, in turn, makes it difficult to trust their spouses to provide comfort and support.

For example, Gregory has the ambivalent attachment style and feels and thinks this way. His mother died when he was ten, and afterward his dad was so overcome and preoccupied with grief that he was unable to give Gregory the comfort and support the lad needed. Now, as a husband, Greg longs for a deep, sustained connection with his wife. To that end, he argues for time together but fears she won't really be there for him when they *are* together. He believes his fears are confirmed when her attention wanders away from him toward her hobbies and family.

For instance, when she calls him while he's away on a business trip, before she has said two words, he'll ask if she has called her mother yet. If she says, "Yes, just before I called you," he goes ballistic. "If you really loved me," he crows, "if I was really important to you, you'd have called me first. No matter what I do, your mother will always come first."

Gregory sees his wife's actions and reactions through the lens of this belief: *You will eventually not be there for me.* He scans the horizon for incidents that prove she's redirected her attention and interests elsewhere and that she is failing to love him the way he needs. He always questions her intentions and doubts her honesty when she tries to explain. No matter what she says or does, he believes she will eventually fall short and not be there for him.

The Avoidant Attachment Style in Marriage

Spouses who are avoidant, who are fearful of being hurt by others, make absolutely sure they remain self-sufficient and in control. Staying aloof, they avoid intense emotions and dodge any conversation that may elicit strong emotions or emotional closeness. Their relationship belief is simple: *Nearness means getting disappointed and hurt. It's best to stay disconnected, distant, and disengaged from emotional involvement. Loneliness is better than agony.*

With this belief guiding their thoughts and actions, they keep their hearts in neutral—aimed right down the middle of the emotional road. At night they rest their worries on comforting sofa cushions and scan the channels just to keep their minds occupied and their hearts unavailable to pain. In an argument, they tend to be more avoidant, colder, and less supportive. Afterward, they don't feel much anger and don't necessarily see their partners less positively. Usually, avoidants marry anxiously attached people who frequently search for and cling to their mates to experience closeness and affirmation. Not knowing what else to do, the avoidant spouses respond by remaining self-contained and regulating their partners' high emotional level.

PURSUE-WITHDRAW:

A RELATIONSHIP PATTERN THAT KEEPS YOU DISCONNECTED

As couples attempt to love each other, their attachment styles and way of dealing with closeness and disconnections can cause some powerful negative relational patterns to be set in motion. Typically, the interactional pattern that is found between hurting couples is "pursue-withdraw." One spouse, reacting to a disconnection in the relationship, pursues the partner. In response, the partner withdraws. This withdrawal keeps the hurt alive and causes the pursuing spouse to pursue further, which causes the withdrawing partner to withdraw further.

Does any of this pattern allow either spouse to understand and empathize with the other? Not hardly!

Here's an example: Remember the bad day Ronnie Blaire had back in chapter 7 because of her husband? As she strummed anxious fingers on the kitchen table while waiting for her husband to come home from work, her neighbor, Emily, knocked on the back door and then, seconds later, burst through it. Red-faced, fists clenched, she blurted out, "I just can't believe that man!"

Eyes wide, Ronnie asked, "Who? Your husband? Have a seat. I'm waiting for Matt. You'll enjoy the fireworks. I'm one mad lady."

"You don't know what mad is," said Emily angrily as her nostrils flared. "I'm fuming!" she continued. "Tom's really in for it this time. He's definitely going to hear how I feel—loudly and clearly. If you happen to feel a local earthquake, it's us. He won't get away with it this time. Why'd I married him, anyway? We're just too different. And he's clueless. He just doesn't care. That's it, really. He just doesn't care."

Ronnie's fingers went silent. "I'm not quite that mad," she said doubtfully. "I mean, I'm mad, but I'm not going to explode or anything. I just want Matt to understand what happened today so he knows how I feel."

"So he can ignore you once more?"

"He won't ignore me. That's the neat thing about him. I mean, if *he* were mad, I'd want to know what I did. When I'm mad he wants to know what he did. We each have our perspective on things. He'll think about what's happened. And I bet when all the dust settles we'll both work to make things better—make our lives run more smoothly."

"Is the sky blue in that fairyland you live in?" Emily grunted. "How can you even think everything's going to work out? Eventually it all comes crashing down around your ears. And why? Because men just don't have the emotional capacity to understand us women—understand with their hearts. Boy, are you ripe for getting slaughtered. Naive, that's what you are, Ronnie. You're going to end up getting hurt. Hurt bad."

Before she could say another word, Tom's SUV growled to a stop in the next-door driveway. Emily's ears perked, and her eyes narrowed. Storming out the back door, she gave out a blistering oath. "I'm not going to let him get away with this, Ronnie. I'm through compromising. This worm has turned!"

Emily greeted her husband with a glacial glare. Tom knew the look. Also knew the next one—the one when her brows made sharp cliffs over those narrow eyes and her cheeks flushed and her lips puckered and stiffen. Folding her arms defiantly, her whole body went rigid.

Tom knew he was in deep trouble, and if history had taught him anything, he also knew nothing he could say would make any difference. But it wasn't in him to just fold. So he tried to defend himself. He made excuses in an attempt to justify why he had done what he did. Emily let him get a few words out, but only a few. Then she attacked. Her accusations became louder, harsher.

Tom, knowing Emily was about to start hammering him with her big guns—with a seemingly limitless lung capacity—pulled back and retreated into his shell. Over the years he'd found this was his best strategy—to shut down until she cooled off. They both knew the cycle: She pursues him, he withdraws, then they skulk around the house in silence for several days. Then something happens that requires that they discuss something—the dishwasher explodes or a children's event brings them together. They talk. But nothing's resolved. It's just swept under the rug. Neither feels safe.

Emily and Tom have developed an interactional pattern of pursue and withdraw. As Emily comes at Tom with her intense emotions and disappointment, Tom defends himself. But when that fails to convince Emily of his honesty and good intentions, he pulls back to protect himself—which means his heart cranks up the drawbridge, fills the moat with water and alligators, and places another layer of protection between him and his wife.

Emily always has her "connection" antenna up and, of course, senses Tom's protective shield going up. Consequently, she pursues Tom even harder, assuring herself that he won't even have the opportunity to leave her out in the cold. She's sure he'll respond and stay close if he only sees her broken heart and her longing to be connected. So, armed with anger, criticism, and contempt, she charges over the hill to decimate what she sees as Tom's indifference. But her effort ends without a gentle reunion of hearts. Instead both of them stay hurt, resentful, and emotionally disconnected. Why? Instead of becoming vulnerable and sharing their hearts' longings and fears, they bludgeon each other with their frustration, misdirected anger, and resentfulness. Instead, had they confronted each other with controlled, purposeful anger and solvable complaints, had those complaints been aimed at creating an environment in which they felt comfortable sharing their hopes and feelings, their hearts and their empathy, they would have fostered change and emotional connection.

The Emotions That Fuel the Pursue-Withdraw Cycle

As it turns out, anger is a natural response to finding one's attachment figure unavailable. When couples have secure attachment patterns, their anger is laced with the hope of restoration. As we discussed in chapter 7, anger that springs from hope can be constructive and bring healthy change to a relationship. This anger signals the partner that hurt has occurred, and it is communicated with the hope that change will strengthen the marital bond.

Spouses with secure attachment styles not only *recognize* but also *regulate* their thoughts and emotions, controlling, for example, what they say and how they say it. They also recognize their secondary emotions, such as anger and resentfulness. They are able to experience their full array of emotions and to dig past their secondary emotions to access their deeper primary emotions, such as sadness, hurt, and fear. Judiciously expressing the softer primary emotions usually draws the spouses to each other and elicits empathy; expressing these primary emotions helps connect the partners even more closely. Part of expressing their anger, hurt, and frustration is an admission of their longing and their need to be understood and accommodated. As listeners, secure spouses accurately hear their partners' emotions and generally don't take the complaints personally. And since they don't, they're usually able to face the conflict assured that resolution will result from it.

On the other hand, couples with ambivalent, disorganized, or avoidant attachment styles are often caught in, and can't extricate themselves from, the pursue-withdraw cycle when dealing with emotional conflict with their mates. They express anger and frustration explosively then defend and criticize contemptuously. Their secondary emotions, anger and frustration, are vaulted to the primary position and are volleyed back and forth, increasing in volume and temperature each time they fly over the net. These volleys are usually harsh and accusatory, and instead of enticing their mates to listen to them, understand them, and empathize with their complaints, they do just the opposite; they shield, bury, and drive their partners away from the gentler primary emotions. The emotions underpinning these secondary emotions often are fear of being abandoned, left alone, or disrespected, or they may be fears of being found unworthy or unlovable. Fighting with only harsh secondary emotions keeps defenses and heart protectors up.

Anger, disappointment, frustration, and resentfulness are often the only emotions insecure couples share with one another. These emotions cut, rather than establish, healthy emotional connections, and couples who deal with one another this way usually develop a negative cycle of relating. Most frequently, it's pursue and withdraw.

The Stories behind the Reactions

As we shared earlier, primary emotions often can be found tightly connected to the stories behind the strongest reactions and feelings. Overreaction to a relatively minor incident is the signal. Whenever it occurs, pause to look past the reaction and attempt to discern your spouse's true motivation. Is something more profound going on? Is the attachment system being triggered? What is the story behind the pain that's driving the overreaction? If the reaction is unusually harsh and critical, what primary emotions might be boiling underneath?

Those are the kinds of questions Henry used to figure out the primary emotions behind his wife, Tracy's, overreaction. Henry came home from work and tossed his sports coat over the back of a chair. Loosening his tie, he gave Tracy a quick peck on the forehead and shared a joke he'd heard at lunch. But Tracy didn't laugh at the punch line; in fact, her lips remained ruler straight and tight. She didn't care that Henry was making an effort to reach out and connect. Instead, her abandonment antenna went up. "So, was that pretty little secretary of yours at lunch with you? Was that *her* joke?"

Henry rolled his eyes and sighed wearily. Anyone with any sensitivity at all could see his heart roll up and take in the welcome mat for the evening. But Tracy didn't care a whit about his welcome mat. In her mind it was welcoming the wrong people, so she kept pushing and probing for evidence that would confirm her fear that Henry would eventually leave her—an eventuality she was sure was just over the horizon. Had he been flirting with that secretary? Was that going to finally be a clear reason for her concern?

Tracy had overreacted, a signal that something bigger was going on. That was Henry's clue to step back and look for the story behind her overreaction. When he did, he discovered that Tracy was deeply bothered by his friendships with other women because, when she was growing up, her father had cheated repeatedly on her mother. Her father's infidelity had devastated her mother and ruined many special times between Tracy and her mother, times that began happily but ended in tears when her mother was reminded of her husband's betrayal. Too consumed with his affairs, Tracy's father often stood her up when they were scheduled for father-daughter times. These betrayals also left Tracy, like her mother, distrustful to the core.

Realizing her sensitivity, Henry now monitors his behavior. Whenever he can, he avoids even the appearance that he might be straying. And when a situation inadvertently occurs that might be so construed, he lays himself open for any questions she might have and proves his innocence without protest.

For her part, Tracy recognizes and takes responsibility for her own insecurity. She realizes these feelings aren't Henry's fault. So she downplays them and puts the best, most trusting face on every situation. And when she just can't do that, she's open and honest, and she asks questions without being accusatory. Because Henry answers her questions openly, she has, over time, convinced that place within her that reacts instinctively that she's really *not* in emotional danger.

Tracy also reaches out for her husband by sharing her heart with core primary emotions rather than criticizing his behavior with anger and contempt. She "owns" her sensitivities and makes an effort to absorb his words of assurance. As she begins to trust him, he becomes even more willing to express empathy and change his behavior even further. In this way the relationship begins to feel safer, more respectful and trustworthy.

Tracy's attachment pattern begins to shift toward the secure style as she becomes more certain that Henry will be there for her and respond to her needs in a caring way. In response to Tracy's more secure attachment style, Henry no longer hides from his emotions or needs to be self-sufficient. As Tracy proves to be increasingly trustworthy with the feelings Henry shares with her, he allows himself to be more vulnerable, carefully letting her know when she has hurt him. Eventually, instead of recoiling or attacking each other when they are in conflict, they listen, understand, and respond tenderly toward one another. Slowly Henry and Tracy are building their marriage into a safe haven.

That's Your Problem, Not Mine

"Okay," you might say, "you're making my point. My spouse's problem started long before I married him. Which makes it *not my problem*. So why doesn't he just get over it on his own?"

In one sense, you're speaking truth. Perhaps the problems in your marriage are primarily your husband's or your wife's. They spring from relationships that may actually have ended long ago, or relationships that are beyond repair—relationships that have nothing to do with you. How her parents treated her, for instance, has nothing to do with how you treat her now.

As hard as a personal change can be, why should you have to do it when you're not the one with the problem? Why can't your spouse be the one who does the changing?

The answer is that as wives or husbands, we need to consider our mates' lives and their ability to relate healthily with those who are important to them. In fact, Scripture tells us we need to live *for* them (see Ephesians 5:21–33), which makes their problems our problems. And, if we truly are one flesh, how can our spouses have issues reverberating so deeply within them and we *not* consider that we have those same issues?

Your job as a Christian partner is to consider your mate in a way, whenever humanly possible, that brings understanding and healing to your relationship. Which means you're to hold each other in your hearts and listen attentively and gently to the stories that undergird the hurts and pains.

That's attentively and gently—got it? No statements like, "That's ridiculous! How can you think that? I can't believe you said that" or "Oh, just get over it." We need to be sensitive to the heartfelt stories of our spouses' journeys. In the safety of our acceptance and empathy, our mates can more aptly correct the misconceptions built into their attachment patterns that produce their fears.

Now, we know you may be asking, What about God? And you're right; *you* can't fill what only *He* can fill. But the truth is, God wants to work *through you* to make your spouse more like Him! That's your role, and it's a big responsibility. When your spouse repeatedly experiences your understanding and your caring responses, both of you will find your attachment styles gravitating toward more secure patterns. And as they approach these secure realms, a trusting and caring relationship atmosphere will be created in which both of you can experience emotionally corrective experiences and learn to trust and reciprocate love in a meaningful way.

How to Begin Fostering a Close Connection

So how do you foster a close connection between you and your spouse? How do you get started, and what should you expect as the process continues?

We're so glad you asked!

Step One: Be the First to Change

"Why should I change first?" we hear you ask. "I'm tired of giving and never getting anything back."

These are words we often hear from husbands and wives the instant we suggest this course of action. They ask this question because they know that *change* equals *vulnerability,* and *vulnerability* equals *risk.* And taking risks is what got them hurt in the first place. We know that. We understand that the last time you put your heart out there, it was stomped on. And now you're thinking that doing it again, loving again, can be downright scary.[3] You might say, "Never again will I hold my heart out to her so she can slap it down again, so she can disappoint me or criticize me again. It's best that I just keep my distance, stay one step removed, protected, and on guard."

Or maybe your particular protest goes like this: "I won't open up and share my feelings with him again. Why should I? He won't be there for me. He won't even listen. No matter how much I tell him he's wrong and needs to change, it makes no difference, none whatsoever."

Why *should* you risk change? Because *you* are the only one *you* have control over. And your relationship is too important to simply abandon. The marital commitment you made before God is too binding to let anything, least of all pride, resentfulness, and fear, prevent you from making every effort you can to fulfill it. What's more, your own emotional health and, as much as our emotional health influences us physically, maybe even your physical health, depends on it. But as important as all these reasons are, if your changing first wouldn't help your relationship, the reasons wouldn't matter. But your taking the first steps usually *does* work. And if yours is one of those rare relationships where it doesn't, at least you'll be able to look the Lord right in the eye and tell Him you did your best. So let's look at some of those initial changes you can make that we believe will bring you a closer bond with your spouse.

Step Two: Pack Away Your Radar System

We all have radar systems. Just like countries use radar to protect their coastlines, we use it to protect our hearts. And it's always on, always scanning the horizon for signs that our spouses are about to let us down, about to not be there for us. And whenever a blip appears on the screen, when we find any indication at all that illustrates they really just don't care—if our spouses aren't listening, aren't being considerate, if they give out one of those telltale sighs—we then complain bitterly, criticize their intentions, and go on the attack. Or we just withdraw.

Those with avoidant attachment styles may nervously scan the horizon for signs of relational "warmth" heading their way—such things as "touchy-feely" talks, a warm hand on the shoulder, or dinner by candlelight. "If the electricity's working, why candles? And what's that smell, bug spray?"

"It's my perfume, dear."

"It'd make a good bug spray." Avoidants instantly become defensive or busy. "Which reminds me, I gotta spray for termites in my great-grandfather's wooden leg. It got him through the Civil War. I don't want it to not survive our attic."

Or the avoidants scan the horizon for any behavior that confirms their mates' unreliability. "I can't find the termite spray. I've told you repeatedly to keep that sort of thing on hand. Are you trying to sabotage my inheritance?" Or, to be a little more realistic, "Did you do what I asked you to and mail those bills?"

Those with the ambivalent attachment style scan the horizon for proof that their spouses will abandon them and they'll be left alone. Instead of manufacturing wedges between them and their spouses as the avoidant person does, though, the person with an ambivalent attachment style looks for the evidence that wedges have already snuck in: *He doesn't call on time. She talks with friends more than she talks with me.* The blips appear, and in the mind of the ambivalent perceiver, they grow until there's no doubt they represent incoming missiles intent on doing grave harm.

Shut down the radar. Pull the plug, and the instant you find your instincts telling you something you just don't want to hear (*The missile's on its way!*) . . .

- Back off.
- Quieten your heart.
- Allow your intellect to override your instincts and do what you think someone with a secure attachment pattern would do. If you're avoidant and a warm fuzzy is "incoming," accept it. Enjoy it. If you're an ambivalent and you sense abandonment on the way, assume the

opposite; move in and be the mate your mate wants you to be. Assume that the best, whatever it is, is about to occur, and react to it positively.

- Disorganized persons drink from both of those cups periodically, so they need to be sure and open their hearts, not retreat, especially in the face of intense emotions. They must remember that their feelings, especially their anger or fear of rejection, are temporary states. The feelings may seem like they're ingrained, but they're not. They may feel like they'll last an eternity, but they're temporary.

No matter what's going on, ask yourself, *Are my fears based on fact or what I think might just possibly be going on?* More often than not, it'll be the latter: elements of your past that have caused those elements to be associated with the realization of your worst fears. And when you find that you're just reacting to a radar blip, choose to react like someone who's secure in his or her relationships.

But now, having made this change, so what? As an avoidant person, do you feel you're just destined to endure unwanted closeness for the rest of your natural life? Or, if you've always had an ambivalent or disorganized attachment style are you thinking you'll still end up abandoned, but this time, as a surprise to your spouse, you're ignoring all the signs of approaching disaster?

Nope. Won't happen.

Your spouse knows when you are on radar watch, and to guard against the coming accusations he or she becomes defensive or withdraws. So your watchfulness is always rewarded. You always find something—incidents, attitudes, tones of voice, omitted information—all or any of them confirming your attachment fears and bringing your spouse the confrontation he or she had prepared for. Maybe, as the avoidant, you merely glance over to the stack of bills you had asked your mate to mail, and before you can say anything, your spouse fires a salvo. Instead of saying in a calm, matter-of-fact voice, "I was busy today. The bills aren't due until Friday. I'll make sure I send them out tomorrow," your spouse tightens up and lets you have it with, "Oh, give it a rest. Don't start that with me. You just don't trust me, do you? Fine! Then *you* do it."

Now that you're trying to change, though, you don't blast each other. Instead of hovering over the unmailed envelopes threateningly, daring your spouse to respond, you might just pick them up. "I'll mail these on my way to work tomorrow," you could say. "You're working so hard, let me take a little of the load." And you mail them on the way to work tomorrow without another word.

There. Wasn't that better?

Step Three: "I Grace You"

How do you make this sudden transformation? Right now, just contemplating it, thinking ahead to actually doing it, you might think such a change is impossible. But it's not.

The secret to making the change is simple: See your spouse as God's son or daughter—someone Jesus loved enough to hang on a Roman cross for. Remember that your mate is one of God's people, a part of His work in His kingdom, so he or she is worthy of your respect. Also realize that you too are one of God's people and that you have been given to your spouse by God so He can work through you to accomplish a number of goals. Not the least of which is to help influence your mate to become more like Jesus. Which means you need to be like Jesus too. And to do that, your behavior needs to exemplify all that is meant by a single word: *grace.*

Grace *heals.* No, we're not forgetting that you might have all the reason in the world to blame your spouse for all your hurts. Okay, so he wasn't there for you. Or she's always critical. We know you have repeatedly been wronged. We understand that you have every right, in a worldly sense, to retaliate or just emotionally shut down. But that's not living a relationship in grace. The hallmark of grace is forgiveness, and one aspect of forgiveness is the attitude, *I'm giving up my right to retaliation—my right to hurt you back.* Think about it. Your spouse has given you every justification for withdrawing, pursuing, and fighting. And you're going to just let it go. You're going to cancel that debt.

But forgiveness is more than just canceling debts. You can cancel your spouse's debt but still just turn around and walk away. Real forgiveness also includes reestablishing an appropriate relationship. We're not talking about being foolish and opening yourself up so wide that you invite more hurt, but about having enough courage to take risks, to be vulnerable. Let your spouse in again. Share those parts of yourself you've been keeping locked up—secret feelings, risky opinions, times when you risk rejection but share an idea anyway.

Be willing to say, "I forgive you. I *grace* you." Say it often. Say it at every meal; include it in your prayer of thanks for your food as an act of obedience to God's command that will nourish your relationship. And when your spouse responds by becoming more vulnerable too, say,

"Sweetheart, I choose to give up my right to hurt you back."

"I forgive you."

"I risk to reach out to you and trust you with my heart."

"I will hold your heart in safekeeping."

Step Four: Accept Offers for Connection from Your Spouse

One researcher found that couples who were happy and stayed happily married were able to accept each other's "bids for connection."[4] We see this when both spouses are going about their business of living and one of them tosses out a comment, tells a joke, asks a question, or shares an interesting point, and the other responds in a caring way, taking the opportunity to move closer. Distressed couples didn't pick up on these bids from their spouses and missed those opportunities to connect.

So when your spouse cracks a joke or tells you an anecdote or just brushes your cheek, respond as if it came from your best friend. When you do, you'll see more bids for connection coming your way. Often, being intentional about small ways of connecting can revitalize your marriage and foster a sense of closeness. Relationship rituals, those things you do every day or every week, create rhythms in your relationship that create a sense of connectedness and safety. You know what they are, but often you get too busy or tired to do them regularly. They are such gestures as

- kissing your spouse before you leave for your day
- seeking out your spouse when you come home from work to give him or her a warm smile, a stroke on the cheek
- sharing a joke of the day

- connecting for a fifteen-minute recap of the day over dinner each night
- holding and kissing each other close for five minutes before falling asleep
- scheduling regular date nights

Step Five: Pray Together

Remember what we discussed about God and you in chapter 8? It would be good to review that information now as we near the close of this chapter on creating a closer, more loving connection in your marital relationship. Now we want to place an added emphasis on prayer.

Prayer demands vulnerability. That's why it is so hard to pray together. But do it anyway—not only because it's a meaningful discipline but also because it has a powerful impact on a couple's attachment bond. It softens your hearts, turns your focus toward God, and makes each of you vulnerable and willing to be shaped and refined by God's gracious touch. It produces a powerful inner spiritual life with Christ and brings that life into the marital relationship. And that is truly bond-strengthening.

CLAIM THE CONNECTION YOU WERE CREATED FOR

Couples too often call it quits when difficulties arise and they become emotionally disconnected. The disconnection causes them to become despondent, fearing they will never be able to blend again—never be able to emotionally reconnect—and so they divorce. In so many cases, we look at the situation and think, *Oh, if only they had stuck with it a little longer!*

All marriages have seasons, times where spouses blend, and times when they separate then emotionally reconnect. Holding on to your commitment and being dedicated to growing and working through the disconnected times can result in a marriage that is rich and sweet, a marriage that lasts a lifetime. Retracing your attachment history and your marital story and responding out of a heart of empathy, then building safety and learning to accept love from one another will set your feet on a new path of loving and being loved. That's what God has always wanted for you.

11

ATTACHMENT-BASED PARENTING

How to Be a Sensitive, Secure Parent to Your Children

---

*Deep down inside a child's inner world are a multitude of needs, questions, hurts,
and longings. . . . The busy insensitive, preoccupied parent, steamrolling through
the day, misses many a cue and sails right past choice moments never to be
repeated or retrieved.*
—PAUL TOURNIER

Cody, a Little League centerfielder, stood in the grueling afternoon sun
while the batter, nearly two hundred feet away, waited anxiously for the next
pitch. It came, and a line drive exploded high over the pitcher's head, a line
drive that had Cody's name written all over it. But Cody just wasn't ready for
it. Everyone—coach, team, and a stand crowded with gasping parents—
watched in horror as he not only missed the ball but stumbled around,
confused and disoriented, as if he didn't even know where the ball was. Later,
in the dugout, his coach asked him what'd happened. Sheepishly, eyes locked
on his shuffling shoes, Cody admitted that he just hadn't been paying attention. "I was looking in the stands for my dad. He promised he'd be here."

HERE'S LOOKIN' FOR YOU, DAD AND MOM

Like this little outfielder, all kids want to see their parents in the stands. In fact,
they need their parents to be there. Not just for baseball games, soccer tourna-
ments, spelling bees, and Christmas plays, but for evening meals, bedtime
books, scrapes on the knees, and to provide warm, comforting arms after bad
dreams. Kids want their parents there for the good and bad, the highs and
lows, and every moment and every level in-between.

When parents are there for their kids, they create within their children an
important, attachment-based sense about themselves. The kids will grow up

knowing they're loved. And they'll believe others are available and trustworthy, not rejecting and unreliable. Finally, and most importantly, they'll know that God is loving, responsive, and always there for them too, not rejecting and distant. Not a despot.

And as an added bonus, when parents are there for the common, everyday interactions with their children, the kids learn how best to deal with their emotions and the emotions of others. They learn how to solve social problems and how to focus their efforts on worthwhile, meaningful goals.

We hope we're getting the point across that parenting is neither for the selfish nor the faint of heart, that its responsibilities are staggering and its rewards are sometimes dubious, at other times heavenly. And above all, we want to say that parenting is a high, maybe the highest, godly calling. One thing is sure—as a parent, you're always having an influence—either good or bad.

DOING WHAT SHOULD COME NATURALLY

As we describe attachment parenting in this chapter, our goal is simple—to help you see that in many ways, attachment parenting is just the natural order of things and comes easily to those with secure attachment styles. One parent, who considered but chose not to use a more "cookie-cutter" parenting approach with her newborn girl, put it this way: "It just doesn't seem right to let my baby cry and cry when she's hungry. She needs me to comfort her now, when she's little. It can't be healthy to just let her cry and thrash around in her crib at night. She needs me *to help her learn how to calm down.*"

In this chapter we'll show you why that mother is right in following her instincts. We'll walk you through what we call the T-factors, five critical ingredients in attachment-based parenting, ingredients we hope will become important techniques within your parenting repertoire. And they should. Because these five behaviors will help develop secure attachment styles in your children while helping you grow emotionally and spiritually as you use them. But before we get to the T-factors, we want to help you enter into the mind-set of attachment-based parenting.

This mind-set will help you focus on what's important and guide your behavior through the winding road of parenthood. An attachment-based parenting mind-set consists of four guiding principles: vision, training your child in the way of love, emotional learning, and sensitivity.

As principles, these guidelines help organize your parenting style. Eminent child psychologist Russell Barkley notes that a great advantage of principle-centered parenting is that "when you see the 'why' [of what you do as a parent], you are likely to do the 'how.'"[1] In other words, understanding why you should do certain things as a parent helps you do those things more effectively and efficiently.

Vision

We need to always parent with a vision, a goal, in mind. Such a vision organizes and directs our behavior even when we're beset by stress and turmoil. The Scriptures tell us, "Where there is no vision, the people perish" (Proverbs 29:18 KJV). As we've said, parenting is not for the faint of heart. It's stressful at best. It's not uncommon to feel absolutely lost at times, befuddled, confused, betrayed by standards and even by God. Even with the most well-behaved, easygoing kids, the normal transitions in life—from crawling to walking, from diapers to underpants, from preschool to elementary, from human to teen (just kidding!), from high school to college, from calm to unexpected storms—it's never easy to decipher what kids actually, truly, really need from you.

Through all these parenting times, vision helps you stay the course. Stephen Covey uses this kind of this analogy: If you're a pilot wanting to fly from Atlanta to San Francisco, simply wanting to get there isn't enough. You can't just hop in the pilot seat, take off, and hope you'll somehow mysteriously arrive. You need a detailed flight plan that specifies direction as well as altitudes and corresponding speeds. Once in the air, the plane may encounter unexpected atmospheric conditions, some of which may blow you completely off course. But even with the plane where it shouldn't be, the flight plan gives you reference points. These points allow you, or a computerized autopilot, to guide the plane back to the original flight plan.[2]

A coach's football game plan is another example of vision. It's like a blueprint for war. It describes, often in undecipherable shorthand, how the coach's team is going to decimate the other team. It details plays, plans, and what-if scenarios. And if something unexpected happens, if a key player is injured or an opposing team member comes up with the game of his career, there's enough planning and detail in the coach's game plan to help the coach react and get his team back on track.

Or, if football's not your thing, consider the good teacher. She doesn't just show up for class, hold her finger in the air, and based on wind direction, decide what to teach. She's got a lesson plan. Within that plan is a step-by-step overview of the topic, a breakdown of what each class meeting will cover, homework that'll be assigned, and teaching aids to be used. There might even be a list of students noted with each one's learning style. To put it succinctly, she's ready for just about anything.

But vision also has a broader perspective. It's not just about what you do in the present moment; it's also asking yourself, *How do I want my kids to remember me when I'm gone?* A college professor from our past had a cozy, book-lined office. We all found that office a fine, quiet place to work—except for one distracting thing: the human skull he kept on the second shelf right above his desk. You might ask why he kept a human skull where he could always see it? "It helps me remember what's really important," he would say.

You may not have such a decorative ornament to put on your mantel to remind you of what's really important, but you might try one of Stephen Covey's recommended exercises to accomplish the same thing: Imagine your own funeral. Then picture your child being asked to comment honestly about the kind of parent you were. What would you want your child to say?[3]

Training Your Child in the Way of Love

When the religious zealots of his day asked Jesus which commandment was the most important, Jesus replied, "Love the Lord your God with all your heart and with all your soul and with all your mind.' This is the first and greatest commandment. And the second is like it: 'Love your neighbor as yourself.' All the Law and the Prophets hang on these two commandments" (Matthew 22:37–40).

Attachment-based parenting prepares children to follow these two commandments. The scripture that says "train up a child in the way he should go" (Proverbs 22:6 NKJV) is about laying the foundation for our children to walk in the way of Christ, keeping His commandments. And as Jesus summed it up, the whole law rests on commandments of love: loving God and loving your neighbor as you love yourself. So training your children is about training them to love and to be loved.

Let's make this simple. In the course of helping your children love and be loved, they need to

- believe they are worthy of love—God's and yours
- believe relationships are warm, pleasurable, satisfying, and safe
- believe they can trust others to respond appropriately and promptly to their needs
- have the ability to regulate and manage their negative emotions
- have the ability to live within limits
- have the ability to deal with frustration, loss, and failures and to actually grow stronger from such experiences
- have the ability to solve social problems effectively, using words rather than aggressive behavior or social withdrawal

Emotional Learning

We hope these beliefs and abilities will become an integral part of your vision for your children and that you keep them in focus as you deal with your kids. As often as is practical, reflect on how you're relating to them and whether you're accomplishing these seven goals.

These reflections are particularly important during emotionally stressful moments. At times like those, guard against becoming *re*active and instead be *pro*active parents. And remember: The lessons we want our children to learn are often best taught during times of emotional intensity. It's relatively easy to teach kids about truth at an intellectual level during Sunday school class or in a kids' Bible study, but if the lesson is not reinforced during times of emotional intensity, it is probably not learned. Such a situation certainly answers the question, "Can your child behave in a balanced, emotionally healthy way when chaos and pressure break out?" It's primarily within the volcano of emotional stress where children really learn about themselves and others.

Sensitivity

As we often mentioned, sensitivity is the mother's milk of attachment parenting. Sensitive parents are *attuned,* or *keyed in to,* their children's needs—which might be quite different than the children's wants. Then those parents take the next step and *promptly and effectively respond to those needs.* And when they're not intuitive about their children's needs, they take the necessary time and energy to understand them. As best they can, sensitive parents get behind their children's eyes and see the world from their perspectives.

Developmental Awareness

It's important for sensitive parents to know that their children's needs change as they develop. A three-month-old infant needs different nurture and support than a one-year-old, which, in turn, is different from what's needed by a three-year-old. Sensitive parents understand that their children must learn how to do just about everything: how to calm themselves when upset, how to deal with frustration, how to delay gratification, how to handle social conflict, and how to motivate themselves to do what they just don't want to do. Children learn all this from their sensitive parents, and as they do, the sensitive parents coach them to work through and overcome the major challenges of life.

Creating a Comfortable Child

Sensitivity is about helping your child achieve comfort, whether it's physical, emotional, or spiritual. Patricia Crittenden, renowned expert in attachment theory and parental sensitivity, has produced a detailed manual that's used by scientists to identify both sensitive and insensitive parents of infants and toddlers. She says, "Adult sensitivity is any pattern of behavior that pleases the infant and increases the infant's comfort and reduces its distress."[4]

When a three-month-old is fussy, a sensitive parent responds in a way that helps the child reach a state of comfort. In contrast, insensitivity involves ignoring the child and letting him or her "cry it out." Sensitive parenting assumes children cry when they are uncomfortable and when they need soothing. These parents then respond promptly and appropriately, which helps children learn how to calm down and to believe that their felt needs are considered important. They learn they're valuable, worthy people and that others are responsive. They grow up believing, *I can trust others to be there for me in times of need.*

Insensitive parenting—also called "detachment parenting" by William Sears[5]— assumes that fussy children are just "misbehaving" or "manipulative" and just trying to get their own way. And, like a good behaviorist,[6] those parents decide the best way to eliminate bad behavior is to ignore or punish it. However, this parenting approach usually backfires. The children don't learn to calm down, and they become extremely vulnerable to negative moods later in life. Moreover, their view of themselves and others is generally negative. They might say, "There must be something wrong with me. I'm not worthy of love. And I can't count on others when I need them."

Children raised by insensitive parents are more likely to have behavioral problems, fewer intimate relationships with peers, and less than an intimate relationship with a future spouse. They are also more likely to turn for comfort to things—possibly resulting in addictions—rather than to people or, ultimately, to God.

The Zone: Finding Balance

In chapter 7, we discussed the zone of proximal development, a principle that says children need the right combination of support and challenge to help promote their healthy personality development. To achieve this, we believe good parenting is much like good coaching. A good coach works *with* you to help you build the necessary skills. He or she doesn't assume you possess the skill naturally and then criticize you when you mess up. A good coach supports your efforts then positively challenges you to do better: "Way to go! Now try doing a little more of this: Keep your eye on the ball. I'm going to throw it a little faster this time. Make a level swing. That's it. Go *through* the ball."

Insensitive parenting uses a one-size-fits-all mentality. For example, insensitive parents might require a rigid feeding schedule. Some children may adjust to this pretty quickly. However, if an infant doesn't eat enough and then gets hungry before the next scheduled feeding, it will probably spend some time crying. The insensitive parent may take this opportunity to teach the child natural consequences: If you don't eat, you go hungry. All the infant knows is that he's hungry and no one is feeding him. To him, his parents are unavailable.

What about Spoiling?

But if you respond to every little need children have, aren't you going to end up spoiling them? The answer is "No!" Sensitive parenting is not indulgent parenting. You're responding to your children's needs, not their wants. Discerning the difference between needs and wants becomes more difficult as children grow older. But as you promptly and appropriately respond to your baby's needs, your own sensitivity and awareness grow and mature.

Eventually a "dance" develops between the two of you.[7] You become so attuned to your children's needs, and so able to decipher your children's needs from their wants, that you respond naturally. In contrast, insensitive parents ignore intuition and replace it with rigid schedules, time clocks, and calendars. These parents typically lose touch with what their children really need. Over time, confusion over their needs and their wants intensifies, and in the end, both parents and baby become extremely frustrated with each other.

The "spoiling theory" is based on this assumption: If you are sensitive, warm, and responsive to babies, if you feed them on cue, hold them when they cry, and help provide comfort, you'll cause them to become clingy, dependent, moody, and demanding. Since no one wants this kind of children, the spoiling theorists have worked to replace sensitive parenting with detachment parenting. Of course they don't call it this. They even go so far as to use marketing schemes that imply their detached form of parenting is "wise" and Godendorsed. But we warn you that such detached parenting—replacing babies' feeding cues with rigid schedules, letting babies lie in their cribs for long periods trying to cry themselves to sleep, ignoring babies' cues to be held and interpreting such cues as manipulative attempts to get attention—is destructive to children.

This isn't just our opinion. The scientific literature teems with well-designed research studies that show parental insensitivity leads to insecurely attached kids—clingy, dependent, moody, irritable, demanding, and aggressive children. On the other hand, sensitively raised children become secure and are more independent and emotionally stable. They have better relationships, better academic performance, more obedient behavior, and are morally more sensitive.

What about the "Hovering Parent"?

People sometimes confuse sensitivity with "hovering." But those two approaches to parenting are quite dissimilar. Hovering parents (usually they're moms) confuse their own needs with the babies'. Such parents tightly control everything their babies do, from how they feed to how, when, where, and for how long they play. They often interfere with what the children are doing and may snatch them up and move them while they are in the middle of some activity. In essence, a hovering parent is "highly interfering, [having] little respect for her baby as a separate, active, and autonomous person whose wishes and activities have a validity of their own."[8]

Jennifer was a hovering mom, although she wouldn't have called it that. Mildly depressed and very irritable, she complained vigorously to us about her toddler, whom she described as irritable, clingy, and demanding. "Nothing satisfies him," she said, exasperated. "I try everything to please him, but nothing works." Her depression was, in part, due her frustration. Knowing we had to see mother and child together to help her, we invited her to bring Alex, her baby, with her.

We filmed them while they played together on the floor. And as they did, Jennifer tried to look happy, but her happiness seemed forced, a sweetness that lacked spontaneity or authenticity. But more importantly, her facial and vocal expressions ignored Alex's expressions. Jennifer treated him as if he was merely an extension of herself. She didn't attend to him as a distinct person who had moods, a will, and preferences. He did what she wanted him to do and how she wanted him to do it.

Nowhere were her efforts more visible than when she wanted him to play with blocks. She shoved them right into his face. When he pulled away, she grabbed his hand and tried to make him pick up and stack the blocks. Alex resisted. He had no desire to play with blocks, and the more he fought her, the more Jennifer's frustration mounted.

Finally, Alex turned away from Mom to explore other toys nearby. "Why are you trying to get away from me, Alex?" Jennifer complained. She grabbed his arm and pulled him onto her lap. "Come, sit in Mommy's lap, and let's play tickle. You always like that."

But Alex resisted and became even fussier. Defeated, Jennifer gave us a look of frustrated helplessness. "See?" she said. "I can't get him to do anything, and nothing makes him happy. Nothing!"

Our stomachs tightened. This was an uncomfortable scene. Although Jennifer thought she and Alex were just having a playtime, she, in fact, was taking an opportunity for mutual joy and turning it into a wrestling match as she imposed her will on a reluctant Alex. Unfortunately, Jennifer couldn't see what her intense need for control was doing to her relationship with her son.

In future sessions, we went over the film with Jennifer. Seeing herself working with Alex allowed her to be more objective and provided her with a powerful realization as we focused on short segments of their playtime. For example, we studied the block-playing section and the time when she pulled him up onto her lap to play tickle. "We know you're trying to be positive here. You genuinely want Alex to have fun. That's admirable. But even as young as he is, he's a person, just like you are, and he wants to do what he wants to do," we said. "He's not all that excited about being controlled and intruded upon."

We pointed out how Alex had tried to explore other toys and she had stopped him. "Jennifer," we asked, "what did you feel like Alex was trying to do here?"

"I don't know," she answered. "I guess he was trying to go off and do his own thing."

"And then you tried to pull him into your lap for a game of tickle, right?"

"Yea, I was hoping to get him interested in me."

"What would have happened if you had followed Alex over to those toys and just joined in with whatever he was doing?"

"I'm not sure. I guess that would have been fine. But I really didn't want to be going all over the room, chasing him around. I wanted to sit there and play a nice quiet game of blocks . . . or something fun."

"But what about Alex? What do you think he wanted?"

"Certainly not what I wanted. It's always like that. He drives me crazy!"

It took awhile before Jennifer completely understood. She was a controlling, hovering parent, and she just couldn't see how her behavior frustrated Alex. The more she controlled, the more he resisted, which led her to control him more. We tried to increase her awareness of Alex's feelings, desires, and intentions. But aware or not, she still mowed over him like weeds. They were hardly doing a dance of intimacy. Instead, one waltzed while the other oompah-oompah-pahed to a polka.

We had a breakthrough with Jennifer when we brought up her relationship with her own mother. It wasn't one of the best. She and her mom battled each other to a frazzle, doing their best to fill just about every waking moment together with anger and resentment. "One word describes my mom—meddlesome! Actually, two words—meddlesome and interfering. No, three words—meddlesome, interfering, and intrusive. Make that four words—meddlesome, interfering, intrusive, and prying. I couldn't get away from her. I still can't. Her hobby is to tell me how to live my life—where I should work, who my friends should be, how I should raise my kids. She drives me nuts. Now she's started on Alex's father. She hates his new job. But what's it to her? So what if we have to move out of town? Of course, then we wouldn't be at her beck and call."

We weren't all that surprised. Attachment styles pass from generation to generation like hair color, unless consciously and intentionally changed (again like hair color). Jennifer and Alex's relationship was the mirror image of

Jennifer's relationship with her mother. And it had been chaos between her and her mom for as long as Jennifer could remember. The anger and resentment generated by that friction became even hotter when it rubbed up against the frustration in her relationship with Alex. The way we finally helped her change her methods with Alex was to help her get in touch with her feelings toward her mom's intrusive control.

But that was no easy task. Jennifer was deeply wounded and angry. Her mother meant well, just as Jennifer did with Alex, but Jennifer's mother treated her as if her feelings didn't exist. Relating to Jennifer as if Jennifer only wanted what her mom wanted, her mom never took Jennifer's feelings into account, often just replacing them with her own.

Jennifer's anger—her real, legitimate, valid primary anger—was not difficult to access. Sadness and also a deep sense of loss were mixed in with the anger. She could easily see how much she wanted her mom to care about her feelings, her wishes, and her dreams. She wanted Mom to be there without being controlling and without intruding. "I want her to care about me, about the things I'm interested in, about what's good for me and my family—I know she really resents that I got married and moved away," she said.

As we helped Jennifer work through these thoughts and feelings, we had her bring Alex back in several more times, and we watched them play together again. We filmed each ten- to fifteen-minute play session then reviewed the film with Jennifer afterward. As time went on, she became more sensitive to Alex's feelings and learned to follow his leads. As she did, their playtimes together became more like a dance than a wrestling match. She learned to enjoy motherhood, and by her last session with us, Jennifer had taught us a lot about how parenting styles, whether good or bad, are frequently an extension of how we were parented.

How Your Attachment Style Affects Your Parenting Style

Attachment styles not only color our own lives but also some of the most important little people in our lives. Our attachment styles strongly influence how we parent our children. Research and our experience confirm that the most important parental influence concerns sensitivity. Let's see how.

Attachment-Based Parenting

Parents with Secure Attachment Styles

As we've said, parents with secure attachment styles are more apt to be sensitive to their children's needs. Starting right from birth, they respond quickly and appropriately to their children's cries for comfort. They know their babies aren't being manipulative or controlling. They just need whatever they need, and their tears merely signal discomfort.

As their children mature, the secure parents continue to respond. But even with all this good parenting going on, the kids, like all kids, get upset from time to time. And when they do, secure parents set limits on how the kids express those feelings, but they also coach the children on how to ultimately deal with their emotions. Secure parents also understand, and aren't threatened by, their children's need for autonomy. They actually encourage their kids' independence by, among other things, letting the youngsters take controlled risks, like going to a friend's house for the night or going roller-skating with a friend's family. But although they want the kids to grow up with a certain sense of independence, they also remember that their kids are still just children, and they remain available for them in case the going gets a little rough.

Parents with Avoidant Attachment Styles

Parents with insecure forms of attachment aren't quite so sensitive—in fact, they might lack sensitivity altogether. For example, parents with avoidant attachment styles are generally annoyed by their babies' bids for comfort. This annoyance often drives them to adopt parenting styles that prematurely encourage independence, even if their children end up crying for hours. Avoidant parents may hold their children only when there's some specific reason to do so, like when they're feeding them or changing diapers; they seldom get pleasure from cuddling and cooing with the little ones.

They may be controlling, especially over how emotions are expressed. And as their children mature, parents with avoidant attachment styles ignore, criticize, even reject their children's bids for comfort. They typically don't coach their children's emotions. And for good reason! To the avoidants, emotions aren't to be coached; they're to be repressed, or suppressed, and certainly not expressed. Negative feelings aren't allowed at all. Happiness is demanded. As someone once wisecracked, "The flogging will continue until morale improves." Around these parents, you've gotta be happy or nothing. Keep those negative feelings to yourself.

The children of avoidant parents learn that if they need comfort, they had better find a way to provide it themselves, because they certainly can't count on anyone else to be emotionally responsive to them. All this leads to the fact that avoidant parents really—and we mean *really*—want their children to be autonomous and independent. And probably because of this eagerness, they don't supply much of a secure base for the kids when the kids are upset and in need of comfort.

Parents with Ambivalent Attachment Styles

As you might expect, parents with ambivalent attachment styles are inconsistent. Sometimes they attend to the little munchkins, and sometimes they're aloof and unavailable. The children learn that to get Mom's attention they must be overly distressed or hugely dramatic. Ambivalent parents are also controlling, but not in the same way as parents with the avoidant attachment style. Instead of reining in their children's emotional expressions, ambivalent parents fence in their children's attempts at autonomy and independence.

These parents feel threatened when their children go off to do things on their own or with others; when they leave, Mom feels like she's being abandoned. So she reinforces their neediness and dependence and ignores or even punishes their attempts at independence. As a result, these children learn that the road to acceptance winds through the dismal gardens of helplessness and dependence. And Mom slams that kitchen door right in your face when you try to do anything without her.

Parents with Disorganized Attachment Styles

As we've already seen, people with disorganized attachment styles have a lot of unresolved loss or trauma in their lives. As parents, they may reject and control their children's negative emotions like avoidant parents do or, like parents with the ambivalent attachment style, they may be chaotic and fearful when their children behave independently. In either case, their trauma and loss usually intrude on their parenting behavior, leading to times when they just "lose it," exploding at their children, intimidating and frightening them.

Or these parents, particularly the moms, may immerse themselves in abusive relationships where the children might see them being threatened or beaten. In severe cases, disorganized-attachment parents may have been abused as children, either by their mothers or fathers. Unfortunately, those who have been abused as children and have deep and unresolved trauma tend to repeat this abuse in some way with their own children.

THE T-FACTORS

We've looked at the mind-sets of sensitive parents, discussed how parents' overarching goal should be to train their children to love and be loved, and we've reviewed how the attachment styles affect parents' relationships with their children. Now we want to get practical. That's what the T-factors are designed to do. T-Factors are simple concepts you use to help promote secure attachment patterns in your children. The nice things about them are that many of you probably already use these concepts naturally.

We've compiled these concepts not only from the professional and academic literature but also from our clinical observations of healthy, secure parents. If you're not yet a parent but you are looking forward to having children someday, we believe the T-factors will give you a sound, parenting framework. If you're already a parent and your children seem happy and well adjusted, the T-factors will help keep you and the kiddos on track. If you and your kids are struggling, the T-factors should help you work your way back to the path leading to a secure relationship.

T-Factor One: Temperament

Lori is a labor and delivery nurse. She can tell us from experience what we all know intuitively, that each child, right from birth, is different. She'll tell you that such differences are subtle but, to the trained eye, observable. As the days and months progress, these differences become more pronounced, and they reflect the formulation of the child's individual temperament.

Temperament reflects the most basic aspect of our personalities. It includes such elements as our activity level, our attention span, our ability to settle into patterns like eating and sleeping, our basic mood quality (whether we're laid-back and easygoing, uptight and tense, or fussy and irritable), our ability to adapt to new situations, and our tendency to stick with difficult projects.

Each child is born with a certain temperament, and by a very early age, most children can be classified into one of four temperament categories.

• *Easy kids* are pretty even tempered; they're laid-back. They get into easy feeding and sleeping patterns and adjust well to new situations. Their attention level is good, and they're not too bouncy. Plus, their mood is generally positive and stable.

• *Difficult kids* are often grumpy and fussy; they tend to retreat from novel situations, and they are hard to get onto a predicable schedule. They are easily distracted, and their activity is often too intense for the situation. Their mood is generally negative.

• *Slow-to-warm-up kids* are less active and have difficulty warming up to new situations and people. Their moods are usually negative, especially in those new situations, but when the situation finally becomes familiar, they can blossom into being more pleasant and engaged.

• *Mixed temperament.* Not all kids fit neatly into one of these three categories. Some have a unique blend of each.[9]

You may see yourself in one of these descriptions. That's because temperament involves lifelong traits. It's in our list of T-factors because it's important that you see how well your temperament matches your child's. Experts call this the goodness-of-fit model.[10] If you and your child are similar in temperaments, it makes for a "good fit." However, the more mismatched you are, the more easily difficulties arise.

"Oh no!" you suddenly cry. "My child and I are completely opposite. Now he's doomed to be insecurely attached."

Not so. Researchers have studied the link between temperament and attachment pretty intensely and have found that what *really* matters is how well parents adjust to their child's temperament. If you and your children have mismatched temperaments, or if you both have difficult temperaments, you can set behavioral limits and make sure your children always know you love them; in this situation, temperament seldom becomes a problem. However, if parents insist on changing their children's temperament through criticism, punishment, and rejection, problems hover on the horizon like midnight-black storm clouds.

Here's a quick example: A friend of ours, Terri, is the mother of five-year-old Jacob. Terri has a slow-to-warm-up temperament while Jacob has a mixed temperament. Morning finds him leaping out of bed, scrambling downstairs in a positive, upbeat mood, and displaying a whirlwind of goal-directed activity. Terri, on the other hand, needs three cups of strong, black coffee and a tombful of silence to get her brain jump-started. As Jacob swirls around her each morning, a whirling dervish of movement and chatter, it takes all the emotional muscle Terri can muster to keep her temper in check. A minute or two of his hyperactivity, and she wants to explode.

But she manages quite well. She desperately wants to criticize him for being too "wound up," too energetic, too chaotic. But she knows all this activity is just his temperament, just the way he is in the morning. The last thing Jacob wants is to anger Mommy, but he finds it very difficult to be anything but what he is. And Terri doesn't ask him to be. Instead, she accepts him for who he is.

Even when Terri's struggling her hardest in the morning, she cloaks her words in warmth and kindness, always aware of what her child needs and how he views his world. She, and all she is to him, are right at the center of it.

T-Factor Two: Time

For some, time is precious; they even liken it to money. Others, however, give little consideration to time, particularly to how they use it. Parents should be in the first group. For them, time is crucial. Why? Because parenting requires lots of love, and giving love takes lots of time. We tell parents that kids spell love T-I-M-E.

Some parents make a distinction between *quality* of time and *quantity* of time, and they say, "What kids really need is *quality* time." What they're really saying is, "I don't have much time for my children. But when I do, I want us to have lots of fun."

But relationships with children don't work that easily. No element of life does. Important, relationship-defining moments generally don't arrive on cue. They occur when they occur. To actually have quality time with your kids, you have to work your way through a lot of ordinary time with them, time when you develop trust, learn their language, and understand their ways.

It's just like gaining value from anything in life; you have to make an investment—you can't get something for nothing. Quality moments with your children come from building up many hours of little moments—talking over your children's day after school—their triumphs and their losses—dinnertime conversation, reading stories at bedtime, getting drinks of water in the middle of the night, listening to the stories of bad dreams the next morning.

Some of these moments may sound bland, but they're not. They mean so much to kids. And because these moments mean so much to them, they'll mean a lot to you. Especially when you take the time to really understand them—hear their words, watch their eyes, their smiles, their frowns, their joys and frustrations. And what heart could ever be immune to their laughter?

Let every word you say, every cock of your head, every movement of your brow, tell them, *I like you. In fact, I love you. And because I do, I care about every bit of you: curly hair, freckles, muscles, and all.* All of these little "bland" moments make possible the high-quality moments. Bottom line: Kids need *both* high-quality and high-quantity time. They need "you" in healthy doses. Big presents and extravagant escapades pale in comparison to you. Now take a moment and try to remember: When was the last time you shared an Easy-Bake cake or skipped a rock on the lake?

And when we say you need to be there for your kids, we mean it in more ways than one. Sometimes it's not enough to be there physically if your mind is a million miles away, or if your presence seems more judgmental than supportive. This lesson was brought home to us when a father came to see us with his grown son. The son was working through abandonment issues, and early in the session he told his father, "Dad, you were never really there for me."

Without a heartbeat's hesitation, his dad broadsided him: "That's not true! I came to every baseball game you ever had. I sat in those bleachers, burning under that hot sun. I watched every inning of every game. I even came to most of your practices too."

"Yeah," his son volleyed, "you were there physically, but your head was miles away. You were just filling a spot in the bleachers. You never talked to me about what I was doing—no, that's not true. You gave me a super hard time every time I messed up. But if I did well, you said nothing. And when *I* talked to *you* about the games, your brain was off wallowing in one of your business deals. Dad, I needed you, and you weren't there for me."

The moral of this story isn't all that subtle—listen when you spend time with your kids. You may think you can get away with only being physically present, but you can't. Kids know, just like you know when someone you're with is there in name only. You know that person is "out to lunch" when he or she has to ask you again and again to repeat what you've say. Or suddenly the person looks at you with blank eyes and says, "Oh, I'm sorry. Did you say something?"

And when you're not "all" there, kids tell themselves that you really don't care about them. They see you there, sitting in the stands with your cell phone jammed up to your ear as you peck away on your Palm Pilot, and they think, *I'm not as important to you as what you do. And since I'm not important to you, my parent, I must not be important to anyone.*

Of course, there is another side to this coin. Some parents get overly invested with their kids. Parents who were neglected as children might, for example, overcompensate with their own kids. They might feel the need to constantly entertain their children—keep a red Rudolph-the-reindeer nose and a rainbow-streaked shock wig around, and if the kids get bored, these parents see it as their responsibility to solve the problem.

Curiously enough, even though it's the parents themselves who create this situation, it's also the parents who eventually feel put upon and begin to resent their children. One such parent told us in a war-weary voice, "I feel like a play slave to my children. I can't get away from them. I really can't stand it any-more." But whenever she set boundaries with them and told them she was only available to play with them at certain times, she felt guilty. As a child she had often been left alone for hours at a time. This was bad enough, but to add to her guilt, she had no memory of her parents' ever playing with her or doing anything else with her that engaged her emotionally.

Gifts of time require boundaries, guiltless boundaries. All parents need "down time," away from their kids. They need to have conversations in their own home between themselves and with other adults without the kids inter-rupting. Now, the kids won't like this. Their natural tendency is to be the center of all activity, particularly those involving words. But don't let them interrupt. This is crucial, just like it's crucial to recharge a car battery. If you're going to have the physical and emotional energy to spend all the time needed to uncover your children's quality moments, you need time to charge your own batteries with other adults.

Each day, make time for just you and your spouse to talk, perhaps sitting at the kitchen table or in the living room. It's okay for the kids to be there, but tell them they can't interrupt. Stick firmly to this boundary. It'll take time to teach them this rule if they're used to intruding on your conversations, but they will learn in time. And as they learn, your time with your spouse will become increasingly meaningful and renewing.

Another battery-charging activity is a good old-fashioned date. Take that young hottie you're married to out to a movie, or a play, or miniature golfing, or bowling, or out on the lake, or wherever a good time is to be had, and *have* it—at least twice a month. And while you're out there knocking those pins down or taking in the silver screen, don't talk about the kids. Talk about them during the week, but not during your date night.

Finally, make time to take care of yourself. Exercise, read a good book, write in your journal, watch a good movie, enjoy a cup of coffee with a friend. A few minutes here could energize you to spend hours of good, solid time with the kids. And if you sense yourself struggling or find yourself losing control, use your quiet time to heal—with that good book or that cup of coffee shared with a friend.

Maybe you're trying very hard to do the right things with your kids. Perhaps you came from a difficult home life and truly want to make life far better for your children. But maybe you just don't know how to do it. Seek help. Don't be bashful; don't be self-conscious. Don't see getting help as a weakness. To know you need help is actually a strength, and the help you get is an investment—in your kids. What an incredible investment that is.

T-Factor Three: Touch

Human touch is powerful. Without it, infants literally wither away. Studies on the impact of chronically neglected kids suggest that their brains grow differently primarily because they don't receive enough touching. Severely disturbed kids we've counseled, many with insecure attachment styles, have no idea how to respond to touch. And yet they need it like a garden needs water. Your children need your soft, gentle touches too.

Kids need eleven touches a day. That's what we were taught in graduate school. As we have mentioned earlier, noted child psychiatrist Grace Ketterman told us she believed one hundred per day would be better.[11] We agree: from high-fives and wrestling matches to strokes of the hair, squeezes of the hands, and good-night kisses—find ways to get "in touch" with your kids. Those of you with babies, hold them, gently and lovingly, not just functionally. Snuggle them, rock them, soothe them with soft singing, and above all, enjoy them. It's within the safety and warmth of your arms that children are shown that relationships are nurturing and secure.

Of course, just like the other factors, the need to touch your children may be hampered by your attachment style. Perhaps you've got an avoidant attachment style, and you just don't care much for physical intimacy. If so, holding and nurturing your children will be a challenge. But it's critical to meet this challenge, because both you and your children need to learn the value of touch.

In contrast, those with the ambivalent attachment style may want to touch their kids all the time. If you're an ambivalent-attachment person, your need to touch and touch and touch may cause your children to pull away as they try to protect their private space. Respect that. Although it may be difficult, moderate how much touch you give them. Remember, physically touching your children should never be a substitute for hugs you ought to be getting from your spouse. Kids don't need to feel responsible for hugging you to make you feel better. It's very much the other way around.

Finally, some children are repulsed by certain kinds of physical touch, like rubbing their arms, tickling, or even hair tousling. It's not because of some deep-seated psychological problem; it's merely because of sensitive skin—a tactile hypersensitivity. If children suffer from this malady, attempts to snuggle and comfort them feel like they're being scraped by sandpaper. They naturally shrink away from it. Sensitive parents pay attention to their children's cues and adjust their behavior accordingly. Search for which type of touch feels good to your children and do it every chance you get.

T-Factor Four: Teaching

As we discussed in the time T-factor, kids need time for play and open expression. And they also need time for teaching. Deuteronomy 6:6–9 challenges all us parents to start with the truth locked deeply in our hearts so we can pass it on generation to generation. Truth harbors safety.

From an attachment perspective, one of the most important lessons children need is learning how to handle negative emotions. We discussed *emotion coaching* in chapter 7 and told you why it is important to learn how to cope with difficult situations and how to keep emotions from becoming overwhelming. For the same reasons, we need to teach our children to deal with emotions, not just ignore them or push them aside. Advice like "just get over it," or "you shouldn't feel that way," does little good. Instead, we need to set limits on how our children behave when they're upset and teach them ways to manage their feelings and effectively solve their problems. When we adopt this position, when we create a secure base from which our children can deal with negative emotions, a host of good things begin to happen.

For example, research shows that kids who have secure attachments with their parents and have learned how to deal with negative emotions form strong, positive relationships with other emotionally healthy kids.[12] These relationships help buffer them from academic, behavioral, and drug problems.

We have also seen that kids who can regulate their negative feelings are more open to the gospel and more willing to involve themselves in spiritual activities. Think about it: Most kids act up when they are overwhelmed with anger or depression. If you teach your children how to deal with negative feelings, you will prevent a large percentage of their behavioral problems.

T-Factor Five: Tenacity (Structure)

Tenacity is sticking to something; it's remaining persistent in the face of stress. Tenacity is the parenting glue. It's the unalterable commitment to being a good parent. You may fail at times, and glaringly so, but tenacity brings you back to your vision, your commitment, your heart-centered longing to see your children grow up right.

Tenacity helps create a resilient family structure, one that generates warmth with clear boundaries and realistic and constructive limits. Dr. Froma Walsh, a renowned expert in family resilience, has worked with and studied families for years. She's come up with the following important principles that help create a healthy, warm, and stable family environment:

1. *Commitment to a healthy belief system.* Help your children learn how to grow from adversity by seeing the positive side of negative events as they search for ways to become stronger persons. As Christians, we help our children see the world from what Gary Habermas calls a "top-down perspective."[13] By doing so, they see situations in light of the kingdom of heaven and believe this life is preparation for the life to come. That's the lesson Jesus taught during the Last Supper, as told in John 13. As He sensed His disciples' fear and concern for what was to come—the cross—He shared with them the wonderful reassurances recorded in John 14:1–6: Our hope is heaven, God's place of safety; a place where we are harbored in His love forever.

2. *Setting boundaries.* Boundaries concern rules and roles, the underlying structure of our families. Just like computer programs have a language that guides what the programs can and can't do, families have a hidden language too, and it guides the family members' behavior. This hidden language consists of rules and roles that create family boundaries.

Rules are the limits families set on behavior, rules that need to be firm, but not *too* rigid. The discipline factor, not punishment, is essential for healthy parenting and must be appropriate, immediate, consistent, and never done out of anger. Roles are about who does what: who washes the dishes, takes out the garbage, manages the finances, and makes discipline decisions. When boundaries become blurred, problems result. For example, if the rule is "Treat one another with respect," and then a parent screams irrationally at a child for spilling milk, the inconsistency creates a problem. Kids don't understand how the rule applies: Why do I have to be respectful and my parents don't?

Another boundary violation occurs when parents expect kids to meet their own emotional needs. This can be obvious, for example, when parents keep children home from school because they're lonely and depressed. Or it can be subtle—a parent not allowing her nine-year-old to verbally express anger or disappointment. One parent we worked with would actually tell the child she couldn't express her anger because "it puts me in a bad mood." When we explored this with the parent, she told us she expected her child to be upbeat all the time. We helped her see that this put the child in the parent's place. It was the parent's job to help her child learn how to express and cope with negative feelings. She was giving her child the message that it was the child's job to take care of her parent's moods.

3. *Open communication.* Family members need to feel comfortable talking with one another. This means talking about good stuff and difficult stuff. Healthy family communication is clear; it emphasizes understanding one another. This doesn't mean you always agree, but you do work to see things from each other's perspective. This helps

kids learn to empathize with others, which is a golden-rule building block.

Open communication also allows each family member to express negative feelings appropriately and facilitates the family's working together to solve problems, both within and outside the family. So, for example, if little Johnny and little Tammy are angry with one another, instead of packing them off to their separate rooms, you sit them down, help them express their feelings openly but respectfully, help them identify exactly what the problem is, come up with some reasonable solutions, and then try out the solution. If the solution doesn't work, the family comes back to the drawing board.[14]

The Most Important Thing . . . Isn't a Thing

What's really important to us is the family—our core relationships. Sadly, much is working against this God-ordained institution in today's world. But one thing is certain—God gave you that child, and He wants to work through you to make that child more like Him. God has a neat plan for each of your kids. Be an instrument and an agent of hope in your child's life journey and don't provoke him or her to wrath (see Ephesians 6:4).

To a sensitive, secure parent, success is that little nose pressed up against the windowpane waiting for you to come home, or that smile that comes from centerfield when your eyes make contact from your spot in the stands.

P.S. Cody's dad was there.

12

BREAKING FREE!

An Attachment Prescription for Changes That Heal

Never give up!
—WINSTON CHURCHILL

Yogi Berra once said, "When you come to a fork in the road, take it." Well, life has a nasty habit of presenting us with forks in our emotional roads. They're crossroads, really, times when we come nose to nose with hard choices: Either we continue on as before, or we make changes that are sometimes painful, always frightening. These can also be times when all the lights go on, when we suddenly see things very differently. Ever been there?

These fork-in-the-road choices can be life changing, tumultuously so, even when they seem to come suddenly, out of the blue. Sam's came when his father died and he realized he'd never made peace with the man. Johnny's came one day when his wife, Julie, screamed at him, "I'm leaving you! This time for good." Bob stepped up to his when he awoke one morning to realize he really didn't know his wife, Maria, who had slept there next to him for years. And Tammy came eye to eye with hers when she held the gun her young daughter had used to commit suicide.

When these life-changing experiences come, when we approach these moments—these crossroads—the choice may not be just a choice between behaviors; it is more likely a choice between the pathway to healing and the pathway to continued pain.

Ed was forty-five when he approached his crossroad. He chose to continue on in pain. In need of open-heart surgery to prevent the inevitable, he rejected his wife and his children's pleas and decided not to have it. Awhile before, he'd seen his brother, sore and wired back together, right after his open-heart surgery, and Ed had vowed never to subject himself to the same ordeal. Two years later, at forty-seven, Ed died from of a massive, preventable heart attack.

The nearer Sally got to her fork in the road, the greater the pain at the center of her heart. Years before her father had passed away, and immediately afterward her invalid mother had demanded every minute of her time. But now her mother had been moved into a nursing home, and for the first time in years, Sally had time to think and feel. When she thought about her mother and father, she felt a mixture of guilt and anger. And the more she thought, the more guilt and anger she felt. She wanted to hide, just to run somewhere—to the mountains, the seashore, some faraway place where she wouldn't be reminded of what she saw as *her failure*.

But then a concerned neighbor told her about Jesus, and she immediately understood that His warm, open arms were waiting to comfort her and take her burdens. At that moment, she courageously decided to confront her pain, her feelings of guilt and failure. Accompanying the neighbor to church, she was quickly directed to a support group for those suffering unresolved loss. Within a month Sally began experiencing God's love and comfort and bathed herself in Christ's warm, infinite fount of grace.

Have you recently come to one of life's forks, when life has just stopped you stone cold in your tracks? Maybe you're facing a situation demanding that you make a life-changing decision, like Johnny did when Julie said she wanted to leave him. Or do you face one now, like Bob, who suddenly realized his wife was more a stranger than a lover? Our prayer is that your crossroad isn't like Tammy's as she held the revolver her daughter had used.

If you haven't come to one of these life-changing forks in the road, we can almost guarantee that you will. How are you going to respond? What process can you use to decide how you'll respond?

May we suggest the first step? As Shakespeare said, "Know thyself." The difficulty with that thought is how threatening and tough it is to face the truth about who you are. It's far easier to live in denial, to just go on with life as it is. But the first step to knowing which prong of the fork to take is to face the absolute truth about ourselves and what brought us to where we are. It's time to stop and take an inventory. To get honest sets the stage for us to be set free—free to know God's peace and contentment deep in our souls, free to fulfill our destiny, to mature into all that God and life hold for us, and free to love and be loved again. That is what this chapter is all about.

Soul Hunger

In many of us, the hunger for change is enormous right now. The awareness of our personal, spiritual poverty in the midst of our comfortable, plentiful lifestyles feeds a deeper hunger than money and things can satisfy. But there is good news! The Bible says God is willing to change us so thoroughly that everything becomes new. Nothing is the same anymore. The old life is gone, and a new life has begun (see 2 Corinthians 5:17).

Think about it for a moment. *Everything* becomes new. Everything. And foremost is a fresh relationship with the Creator, the eternal God of love, who yearns to plant the Spirit of the Savior deep within our hearts and souls. With Christ in our hearts, our perspective is also reborn. We begin to see life in a redemptive light, understanding that evil and injustice, pain and suffering are far from the final word. Instead we believe God will, in time, turn all our lemons to lemonade. We also suddenly possess a new source of hope and power, learning to live by faith and continually inviting the power of God to shine, share, and shape a life for us that will never end.

Isn't the freedom that springs from God's healing touch what we all hunger for? Doesn't the peace of God lovingly poured out by the God of peace fill the hole in our souls with gifts that satisfy and truly last? Isn't this the beating heart of all that matters, the very thing the apostle Paul pointed to when He proclaimed, "Godliness with contentment is great gain" (1 Timothy 6:6)? Isn't this the everlasting treasure that never rusts and can never be stolen, unlike the world's wealth, about which Paul wrote, "People who want to get rich fall into temptation and a trap and into many foolish and harmful desires that plunge men into ruin and destruction" (v. 9)?

Of course, life's big deception is that we can achieve all this freedom, peace, and contentment apart from a personal relationship with God through Jesus

Christ. So we cram our lives with everything we think might give us purpose, value, and meaning, like money, sex, power, the exercise of influence, shopping, sports, retirement dreams, costly toys, clothes, diamonds, insurance policies and annuities, and friends who sparkle when they walk. And we foolishly believe these possessions and behaviors tell us we're on the right track. Yet those who honestly evaluate their lives and face life's great crossroads with perceptive eyes often admit how empty, shallow, and purposeless life is when lived selfishly and alone.

Sooner or later, life trashes our trophies. Sometimes painfully, we find out our trophies, our promotions, our big house in the suburbs, our speedboats, swimming pools, hot tubs, and big-screen TVs don't do what we *really* want them to; they don't grant us peace, spiritual comfort, and satisfaction.

When wisdom finally takes root, we discover that what really matters is *who* we love and who loves us, both vertically, you and God, and horizontally, you and at least one significant other. You see, eventually we all face tragedy and loss, and with it comes a pain that shakes us to the core. No one goes untouched. Such loss hits all of us. And when it does, the crisis that follows propels us inexorably to that life-changing crossroads and causes us to challenge our most fundamental beliefs. Some invite God into this crisis and work through it as they rest in His blessed freedom. Others, tragically, hunker down, cloak themselves in denial, and drive themselves deeper into the deception, their lives all but lost. You've seen it happen.

So ask yourself: Isn't it time I prepared myself to choose the right path when tragedy hits my life? Have I been trapped for too long in the pain of my past? Isn't it time to make peace with a past I regret? Isn't it time to move on? What choice am I about to make right now—to live and to heal or to continue in pain and eventually die? Will the path I'm about to choose lead to freedom and renewed life? Or will it lead to bitter loneliness and death?

Can you hear God's whisper deep in the stillness of your soul? Can you sense His presence, beckoning to you? Do you hear Him promising a way out? Do you want to find and experience His haven of safety, His sheltered harbor for your heart? If so, choose life—and let's get on with it!

Breaking Free!

Finding the Freedom to Love and Be Loved

We met Sam at the top of the chapter and saw that he confronted his crossroad soon after his father died. His dad was a vigorous man who still ran a small hardware store well into his seventies. Maybe he was a bit too vigorous, because his heart failed him one day as he stacked his store's shelves. The entire family was stunned by his death, so much so that it took them several months to finally absorb its affects. It took Sam a little longer.

Sam was the eldest son, having recently turned fifty, and he'd had a long history of run-ins with his dad. Their disagreements over the years had run the gamut: Vietnam, drug use, politics, career choices, religious commitments, and finally, how Sam chose to raise his children.

His dad always demanded that Sam adhere to some pretty high standards of behavior, and Sam had never seemed to measure up. As Sam got older, the emotional wound caused by the antagonism between them grew, and because neither Sam nor his dad initiated the crucial talks necessary to aid healing, the wound festered and became excruciating. One method Sam employed to deal with the pain was to deny the rift existed; another was to fill his life with possessions and experiences he figured would eventually salve the nagging ache in his soul—his soul wound.

It wasn't that Sam and his dad never talked. They did—about sports, local business, and hunting; they even went golfing together. But even though they spent hours on the links together, they both adhered to an unspoken but powerful family rule: Thou shalt *not* talk about issues that hurt. To bring up any subject that touched their personal wounds or ignited family conflict or made anyone in the family uncomfortable was just not done. So their discussions glossed over all the pain, the anger, and the feelings of resentments that had piled up over the years. They pretended buried feelings didn't exist. And they fashioned a family myth: If we don't talk about issues, they just go away.

In chapter 6, we said that untold stories are bound to be repeated. We leave home determined to raise our kids differently than we were raised. We set our jaws and commit to a different path, one that won't emotionally wound our children. But somehow history repeats itself; the old anger resurfaces, and old habits take over. And when we become aware of them, which is probably much later than we'd like, we're instantly consumed by confusion and frustration.

That's what happened to Sam. Determined that his kids would have a different life than he'd had, Sam found himself battling a tide of emotional anguish when he realized the same rift that had separated him and his dad now separated him from his seventeen-year-old son, Jason. And when he tried to reconnect with Jason, he was rebuffed. Jason was just not interested in a father-son relationship. After all, Jason saw his dad as someone who really wasn't "in touch" with what was happening in his life, and anyway, now he had relationships with all the guys at school, relationships energized by all those pressures to look good and act cool. He also had relationships with just about as many girls at school, relationships that required even more attention than those with the guys. To add a desperate father to the "to do" list was just more hassle than this young man wanted to bear.

Sam took stock of Jason's anger and the guilt he felt about his son, and he wondered if there ever would be a close connection between the two of them. The more Sam examined this issue in his life, the more he realized that he had always had trouble with relationships. Not just with his deceased father and closed-off son, but with everyone. Sam came to see that he was intimate with no one; there wasn't a single person he trusted without hesitation. He immediately blamed himself, feeling completely ashamed and worthless. Although he usually made fun of those who went to see counselors, Sam decided to do just that. He was finally going to tell his story, his whole story.

FINDING A NEW LIFE:
THE CORRECTIVE EMOTIONAL AND RELATIONAL EXPERIENCE

Thankfully, Sam found a new life and now enjoys new intimacy in his relationships. This love has set him free to finally experience peace about his dad and to love his son the way he'd always wanted to. Sam's journey to healing involved a *corrective emotional and relational experience,* a journey at the center of which God lives and works. Over the course of our work with Sam, we've seen some amazing transformations in him.

And no wonder. This experience is designed to bring God-imbued healing into our injured souls and apply an emotionally therapeutic salve to the wounds in our hearts. It helps us work through powerful, long-buried feelings within warm, safe, supportive relationships. And as we process these feelings, we revise our relationship rules, those core beliefs we hold about ourselves and others.

These revised relationship rules replace our old ones so that now our relationship behaviors promote closeness and intimacy. And as we grow closer to one another, we move closer to God and begin to live our faith in new, more courageous ways. We learn to stop hiding; we give up on isolation. Instead we learn to break out of our fantasy world and live totally in the present, in the now—not in the past or future, but right here and right now.[1]

You can take the same journey Sam did, because, as it turns out, the corrective emotional and relational experience consists of a series of well-defined steps. And there's nothing particularly new about them. They lie along a well-traveled path, one trod by a great many people over the centuries. As a result of our own clinical experience, affirmed by the work of quite a few pioneers in the field,[2] we've defined a pathway with five distinct steppingstones, and it leads right to healing. These steps are applicable to nearly any person who has experienced an attachment wound, and that's just about everybody.[3]

Step One: Remember Your Story

To remember history can be a great blessing—or a great curse. Today's Jews certainly call it both. When referring to the Nazi Holocaust they darkly but sincerely chant, "Never forget!" To forget invites repetition. However, remembering this tragedy in their history bathes the Jew with bitter images and devastating pain, both of which can erode the spirit and scar the psyche yet again.

We want to take George Santayana's famous phrase to heart: "Those who forget the past are doomed to repeat it." And G. K Chesterton's observation, as well: "We are destined to misunderstand the story we find ourselves in." So we want to remember our stories.

You may be thinking just the opposite: *I can't get it out of my mind. I don't want to keep dwelling on what happened.* We don't want you to dwell on what happened, either; we want you to talk about it to a trusted other and get it out in the open. In doing so, the experience moves from being pictures in your mind to pictures with a story. Ironically, this kind of remembering is empowering. It's the type of personal recollection that has a corrective nature all its own.

As you formulate your story, do the following:

• *Recall the facts.* Describe, in play-by-play fashion, specific painful events. If you're angry because your father "let you down," describe the specific events that typified what he did. How old were you? Where were you? What was the situation? Who was there? How did the situation unfold? What exactly did he do that hurt you? What resulted from the hurt? How long ago did this event occur? How did the situation end? Describe it factually, much like a newspaper reporter would.

• *Retrace the path of the pain.* By describing the facts, the past comes alive in the present. Of course, it's always been alive—covered up, but alive. How so? Your past hasn't really passed if you still carry its pain. As you describe the wound, this confrontation may become tangled with emotion and discussed in the present tense, as if the situation were ongoing; you may tell the story with flushed face, raised voice, and exaggerated behavior. But once the painful events are released into words, it's possible to heal the soul wound. The wounded self is no longer cloaked in denial.

Now complete the story. Access and remember the feelings that burst to the surface during the episode. Were you angry? If so, what about? Were you afraid? How afraid? Terrified, maybe? What did you think was actually going on? What did it mean to you? What did you want to happen that didn't? How did you respond? How did you want to respond? How did you feel as you responded? How did others respond? How did this incident affect you? How does the incident affect you now? How do you feel, right now, as you relive the event?

Answer these questions and your whole story begins to emerge. And as you translate your life experience into a story, you externalize it, you place it in the open air so those who are helping you heal can better understand you and what brought you there. Using words to describe what happened to you also helps you gain control of the event. Once it's told as a story, the thing that happened to you has a beginning and an end and words with finite meanings describing it. It's no longer some unrestrained, giant, all-consuming, never-ceasing turmoil you could never hope to deal with in a million years. It's now bounded by meaningful words, and you can now begin to deal with it.

The goal for a healing participant or a helper during this process is quite simple: *Help facilitate the story* and encourage it along when the person is hesitant or fearful.

Step Two: Recognize Your Pain and the Need for Healing

Professional counselors often say, "You can't treat what you don't see." These first two steps, remember your story and recognize your pain, have been defined to help heighten your awareness of the pain that plagues your soul. But why experience that pain all over again? We think you'll see why this step is necessary as we guide you through this part of the process.

• *See purpose in the pain.* Pain has a purpose. In fact, the pain we feel as we talk about our story has several important ones. As we described in chapter 9 when we talked about taming emotional storms, accepting primary pain is validating. Up to this point, your emotional life may have been shrouded in guilt and shame as the result of believing yourself wrong for feeling as you did. Giving yourself permission to feel primary pain tells you that you were right to feel as you did.

In addition, when we acknowledge our pain and vulnerability, we become more aware of our need for God. Jesus said, "Come to me, all you who are weary and burdened, and I will give you rest" (Matthew 11:28). To come to Him with our burden first requires us to acknowledge that we have one, and that we're weary and anguished from carrying it. And as we lay it at the cross, we quickly find He's our soul's great Comforter, our refuge from life's storms.

In 2 Corinthians 12:8–10, Paul described his struggle with personal weakness, weakness he saw with divine purpose. God told him, "My grace is sufficient for you, for my power is made perfect in weakness." Paul then decided he would "boast" in his weakness, "so that Christ's power may rest on me."

It follows then that when we disavow our raw emotions, we deny that Christ is powerful enough to help us deal with them honestly. Our denial pushes Him away. Soon, if we push Him away enough, we experience Him as a distant, uninvolved, even uncaring Engineer of the universe. We become *emotional atheists,* denying the reality of God's ability to touch our hearts and heal our deepest wounds.

• *Validate your anger and mourn your losses.* When you have been wounded by attachment injuries, anger swells. And as we've discussed in previous chapters, this anger is appropriate. But you want to get past it, and the best way to do so is to first own it and then validate it. You can say to yourself, *I was wronged, and it's okay for me to be steamed about it. I needed you to be there for me and you weren't.* Attachment injuries create a sense of loss. So give yourself permission to grieve, to feel sorrow, to cry, and then cry out to God, who will come and be a great consolation. True sorrow is an aspect of spiritual brokenness that especially attracts the comfort of the Holy Spirit, who comes into the life of the sufferer with considerable power and effect.

Step Three: Reframe the Meaning of Your Story

Attachment injuries trigger intense, painful emotions. And in previous chapters, we've described how people deal with this pain by burying it. As a result, these emotions and the beliefs they foster about self and others are frozen, mummified. We become locked into negative, rigid views of how relationships work and how we should behave.

For example, Sam's anger toward his father left him feeling wronged and victimized. He had difficulty achieving intimacy with his own son—and with others—because he feared being misunderstood and criticized. So he kept himself distant. But no matter how far away he put himself, he was always right there *with* himself, and he was his own worst critic. He would constantly berate himself for even the slightest shortcoming or failure. And to outdistance the sound of that internal voice, he pushed himself unmercifully to always do more, earn more, achieve more. But, as you can imagine, he was never satisfied with how much he did, earned, or achieved. He never heard the voice say, *Enough. You're okay!* And whose words did he use to flog himself? His father's, of course. He carried the part of his father he resented most right there with him everywhere he went.

When Sam found himself with a son of his own, he overcompensated. He refused to push Josh at all. Unfortunately, Sam spent so much time trying to satisfy the endless demands of his own internal critic, he had little time or emotional energy for Josh. Which resulted in Josh's growing apart from his father. After all, he'd been wounded too; he felt his dad didn't love him. He believed he could do nothing that would interest his father, so, for emotional support, he learned to depend on himself, just like his dad. In spite of all Sam's good intentions, his story had repeated itself in his relationship with Josh.

For Sam, *reframing* involved understanding his story from a new perspective. He could see he was a workaholic, that he struggled to connect with others, especially his wife and children. He could see his anger toward his father and how he had internalized his dad's harsh, self-directed criticism. But while these aspects of his life were true, he could now see *why* he behaved the way he did. After all, Sam could have turned against his dad, but he didn't. Instead, he turned the anger on himself and, in a perverse way, the strategy worked. It preserved the relationship with his dad. His dad would have never understood Sam's anger. He would've seen it as rebellion, as weakness. So Sam held in his anger as a way of maintaining some kind of closeness with his dad. The price of this denial, however, was that the anger became like a snapping dog, constantly barking, criticizing, and never satisfied.

By reframing his story, Sam could see that his response to his dad's chronic disapproval was his way of adapting, at the time, to a difficult situation. And, as we said, it worked. In spite of the anguish and frustration, Sam was married with children. He had a good job, and he was successful at it. His heart was in the right place. He *wanted* to connect; he wanted to be a successful parent and a loving husband. In a way, it wasn't his fault that he had no idea how to break free from the bonds of the past and make it happen.

The objective of reframing your story is to see yourself, and your past, in a different light. Where before you generally saw just your weakness and frail-ties, now you're able to see your strengths as well, along with your tenacity, your will to survive, and your desire to thrive. More importantly, if you look, you'll begin to see how God has worked in your pain to woo you closer to Himself and to bring healing moments throughout your journey. He works in every nook and cranny of our lives to win our hearts, to show us how safe we are with Him.

As you tell your story, ask yourself questions. For instance, How did I react to the pain of my past? Did my reaction to it work at the time? Did my way of dealing with it back then get me through? How has what I've gone through made me a different person, perhaps even a stronger, wiser person? How has God revealed himself to me during these times of turmoil? Did I turn away from Him? If so, why? What kept me from turning back to Him, or turning to Him in the first place? Is God calling me now? Or, a better question, How is God calling to me now? Do I still want to turn away? Or do I want to change my life? Is my fear a sign of weakness or an element of self-preservation?

These questions and others like them set the stage for change. They help us see that our present situation is largely a reaction to fear and hurt. And while what we used as a strategy worked then, *we need to admit openly that it doesn't work now.* For example, Sam's protective self decided that when he hurt, his only option was to look to himself for comfort. We all agree that this isn't a healthy relationship style, but as children believing there's nowhere else to turn, if we've been conditioned by a difficult parent to believe we're essentially unlovable and unworthy, the only available comfort we see is self-provided. Or we may have learned the only way to find someone to love us is to take the doormat position; we allow others to take advantage of us, and we mold our-selves to meet their expectations. This may have worked for us as children, keeping us from getting hurt too badly. But now it's time for a change. We want to break free.

Reframing lets us see the healthy strivings that lie just beneath the surface of our unsuccessful behaviors.[4] Sam could see that his distancing from Jason was, in part, rooted in a healthy desire not to harm Jason as his dad had harmed him. But his method, distancing, wasn't the best way to get what he wanted. In fact, it produced the outcome he wanted to avoid. But now that Sam can see his healthy goal, he can explore healthier options. He can begin to break free from the shackles of his past as he repairs his story.

Some might say that reframing your life's story is just an exercise in denial via positive thinking. There certainly is positive thinking involved (finally!), but there's no denial. Instead, effective reframing only begins once you've broken through the denial. It looks past the pain and leads you to understand how you've matured and what you've gained through your experience.

Remember Joseph of the Old Testament and how he classically reframed the abuse he had suffered at the hands of his brothers? Many years later he looked his brothers in the eyes and told them, "You meant evil against me, but God meant it for good" (Genesis 50:20 NKJV). You may not be able to say anything this positive about the harmful incident(s) in your past, but you need to identify the gains you've experienced because of having gone through that painful life-passage.

Part Four: Repair Your Story—and Your Damaged Relationships and Emotions

Now comes the longest and most involved of the five steps. To repair means to restore by putting together or fixing something that's been broken or torn. Is your story working—the way Sam's story worked? If it is, your story is broken!

A broken story is one that doesn't work. Like Sam's didn't work. Insecure attachment styles are broken stories. They may have worked in the past, as you might have discovered in the reframing part of the healing process. But now, your story only creates more pain—over and over again.

• *Understand and halt the vicious cycles.* You've heard the old saying: If at first you don't succeed, try, try again. It's good advice, of course, but what happens if what you "try, try again" keeps making matters worse? Well, then you fire up a different saying: The definition of insanity is doing the same thing over and over and over again and wishing for a different result.

Okay, we're not going to call a broken story insanity, but we *are* going to call it the perfect definition of the vicious cycle and the madness it provokes. Here's another example of a vicious cycle. Gary Sibcy had cancer in his mid-twenties, and fighting it included removal of the lymph nodes along his spinal cord. The operation left a stomach scar from his sternum down past his belly button. The surgeons needed every inch of that opening. Through it they removed all his intestines to get to the lymph nodes; then, when the cutting was done, they stuffed them back inside and sewed him up. By all measures the operation was a success. But there was pain. A lot of it. So the doctors gave him a pain reliever with codeine to help soothe it.

He wasn't home for more than a couple hours before the pain returned, but this time it was more severe. He called the doctor, who told him to take more of the pain reliever. Which Gary did. But again, when the pain returned it was far worse than it had been before. And now he was getting increasingly nauseated. Within a couple of days, he landed back in the hospital. Why? The drug was designed to deaden his pain, but the doctors found that the codeine was causing his intestines to shut down—which caused *more* pain! So the more he took, the worse he felt. A vicious cycle.

In the same way, our insecure attachment styles are designed to protect us from pain in our youth. But when these styles are played out in our adult relationships, they can cause more pain, unnecessary pain. The repair process involves breaking these vicious cycles. To do so requires two important steps in repairing your story. You begin by identifying the elements of your story that are broken.

For example, if you have an avoidant attachment style, your relationship story's vicious cycle probably goes something like this: (1) You believe others are basically inept at meeting your emotional needs. (2) You believe you can take care of yourself, that you really don't need anyone else, especially to provide comfort and support during times of distress. (3) You deny your feelings of vulnerability and your longing for connection. (4) Your philosophy is "suck it up, quit whining, and pull yourself up by your own bootstraps."

Sure, this formula has worked for you in the past, but now it's wearing thin. The broken part is that your loved ones are angry with you. They complain that you are uninvolved and consumed with work. The more they complain, the more pain you feel—pain you deny. You deny your longing for their support and feel angry and resentful when criticized. Instead, you say to yourself, *That just proves I can't rely on people to be there for me.*" So you pull away more and more to retreat into fantasy, work, success, or possessions—your addictions. This brings you back full circle. And the broken story becomes a vicious cycle, a self-defeating pattern of behavior.

We saw this cycle at work in Leah, a woman who came to us for help with her feelings of depression and anxiety. Her insecure attachment pattern played itself out in a number of her close relationships. One was with Marisa, a friend at church. In an unusual step for Leah, she and Marisa talked about everything, even some of her deepest feelings about her childhood, her children, and her marriage.

What made this intimacy with Marisa so unusual was that Leah had come out of a childhood that promoted a more insecure relating style. Leah had a fairly strong relationship with her father, a sensitive and warm man. But he was a passive influence on her life and allowed Leah's mom to rule the roost. A stern, humorless woman, her mother was far too busy to listen to her children discuss something as insignificant as feelings.

Leah's mother prided herself on being practical about every aspect of life, and she looked at the world through calculating eyes. Leah learned an important relationship rule from Mom that she applied to other relationships with women: *Don't get too close, and when you're upset, don't talk about your feelings. It will only cause trouble. People, especially women, don't need to hear about your pain. They have enough to do without having to listen to you whine.*

The exception to this rule seemed to be Marisa. Leah saw that relationship as going quite well. But for persons with attachment issues, even good relationships don't go well for long. Leah's friendship with Marisa ran into difficulty when stress crept into Leah's home life. Her husband, a successful businessman, began to travel out of town more than she liked. Her parents lived eight hours away, and she had no other family in town who could help. This left Leah at home with their four children, feeling abandoned and resentful—and ashamed and guilty. Why ashamed and guilty? Because she was embarrassed about feeling abandoned and resentful at her husband. After all, he was just trying to earn a living, a living she and the four kids needed.

It didn't take much for Marisa to sense her friend's distress, and she offered to help. But surprisingly, Leah refused her help. Unable to believe that anyone could possibly be truly concerned about her well-being, Leah was sure Marisa's offer originated only from a desire to fulfill some warped sense of "Christian duty."

Rightfully feeling snubbed, Marisa found herself getting angry with Leah. Especially when Leah, warned by caller ID, stopped taking Marisa's calls altogether. Leah just didn't want anyone feeling sorry for her. Instead, she decided to feel sorry for herself. She withdrew into her own world, lying on the couch all day while the kids were in school, her head buried under a quilt.

After Leah's husband's business returned to normal and Leah's home world settled back into its familiar groove, she called Marisa. Well, guess what? The instant Marisa realized who she was talking to, her voice developed a thick, icy crust. She was clearly upset, and she probably had a reason to be. Leah had cut off her gestures of friendship without warning or explanation, and there are unwritten rules among friends about behavior like that.

Now Leah was at a crossroad. She had a choice to make here: She could have simply said, "You sound upset. Did I do something?" And Marisa would have told her what the problem was, and Leah would have managed an explanation and apologized and their relationship would have had the breath of life breathed into it. Unfortunately (and predictably, we might add) Leah's attachment style took over, as it does in times of stress, and interpreted her friend's attitude as yet another billboard in her life that flashed: REJECTION-REJECTION-REJECTION. She said to herself, *See what happens when I get close to other women? They dump me every time. Why do I even try?*

Leah had no idea why Marisa was upset. Which is interesting, because Leah had actually done to Marisa exactly what Leah interpreted Marisa as having done to her. But Leah's attachment pattern refused to allow Leah to consider that possibility. Instead, the only alternative it allowed to filter through was that Marisa was angry because Leah had had a bad week and her less-than-attractive emotions had seeped to the surface.

Breaking this vicious cycle involves two important steps: revising relationship rules and replacing defensive behavior with courageous loving.

• *Revising relationship rules.* As we explained earlier, relationship rules are core beliefs about ourselves and others. Although these beliefs aren't always fully conscious, they have a powerful influence over our behavior. For example, Sam's relationship rules included that he couldn't really trust others and that he had to depend on himself for support and comfort. As you can imagine, his rules had a negative influence on his behavior, resulting in chronic work so that he could completely control his environment, high self-criticism because he constantly had to be above reproach, and a retreat from intimacy—because how can you be intimate with someone you don't trust?

At a fully conscious level, all Sam knew was that others were hostile toward him and that he received very little satisfaction from relationships. But as he worked his way through the steps we've outlined so far, he saw how his distancing and excessive devotion to work triggered that resentment from others. He then was able to see the rules governing his previous behaviors and understand how they directly influenced how he related.

Likewise, Leah's relationship rules affected how she related to her female companions, especially when she was under stress. In session, we asked, "Leah, why do you think Marisa was so cold and distant when you talked to her?"

"I don't know. I guess because she just doesn't like me anymore."

"Any idea why she would just stop liking you?"

"Well, I've been in a bad mood lately. Nobody likes me when I get upset; it's best I just stay to myself when I get like that."

You can see Leah's relationship rules at work here. They clearly shaped her conclusion that Marisa didn't like her because she was upset, even though Marisa had had no way of knowing why Marisa was distressed and retreating. We're happy to report that Leah, like Sam, walked the steppingstones we've outlined and finally saw how she interpreted the present through the lens of the past.

Now that both Sam and Leah could see their relationship rules at work, the task was to help change them, to revise their faulty assumptions about others and to help them see how they are prone to distort the reality of the present to fit the experiences of the past.

Change is what we call an *iterative process:* two steps forward, one step back. And it winds through the garden of our lives for the full extent of them. And as we change, we transfer much of how we build and maintain relationships from the emotional sphere to the intellectual. This isn't a quick, direct jog from point A to point B. It's a real, tedious, and often times painful journey.

- *Replace defensive behavior with courageous loving.* Genuine, godly love is not for the faint of heart. It requires courage; vulnerability always does. In fact, it was your vulnerability, those many years ago, that got you hurt in the first place. And that's why you may have developed an insecure attachment style way back then—for defense, to minimize your vulnerability. So that the ones you loved and who claimed to love you wouldn't hurt you again.

But now that you've learned about attachment patterns and behaviors, our hope for you is that if, in the past, you saw relationships as nonessential parts of your life or as just too risky to get involved in, that now you've changed and you realize that healthy relationships are not only crucial to a happy, vital existence but that they are possible for you. And if you belief this, then you probably want to change the way you relate, right? This change requires courageous loving, a change in those defensive behaviors, perhaps even doing away with them altogether. It requires that you become vulnerable again and risk being rejected, criticized, and used. We don't mean that you lie down and become a doormat but that you learn to love honestly and boldly.

In Sam's case, we asked him to increase the time he spent with his family—to just be with them, listening, watching, and understanding. Sam started by spending the first thirty minutes after he got home from work talking to his wife about his day. He touched on the high points and the low ones. Before long he was talking about his hopes for work, for promotion, how he wanted to change things there. He told her about his boss and some of the people he worked with. Before long, his wife started opening up. Vulnerability breeds vulnerability as trust breeds trust. Soon they were both talking about their feelings—what they liked and what they didn't. They began to talk about themselves as a couple. They talked about their future, their hopes, and their dreams.

Fortunately, hoping this would happen, we'd also worked with Sam to help him actively listen to his wife. In his old attachment style he had had the bad habit of tuning her out, believing that the elements of his life—his career, for instance—were always more important that her petty little issues. After all, he dealt with issues that meant the life and death of his family—money issues.

But he didn't tune her out anymore. He tried to understand her, and when he didn't, he asked questions. Not the kinds of questions that smacked with criticism; instead he really wanted to understand. And as he listened, he found her interesting. Even funny. It was truly delightful the first time they laughed together. It had been so long, yet it felt so comfortable.

For Sam, the hardest part of being vulnerable and embracing that same vulnerability in his wife was learning that to understand the way she felt did not mean he had to fix her problems or even give her advice. "If she wants help, she'll ask for it," we'd told him. "Mostly she just wants you to listen. She wants to be important enough to you that you make the effort to know what she really means." He needed to learn the value of listening to others and allowing others to listen to him.

By connecting in this way to his wife and others, Sam's relationship belief that only he could provide himself comfort and support began to change. That half-hour after work became increasingly important to him. He found that the more he understood his wife, the more she understood him, and when she didn't, she asked questions until she did.

And the more she understood, the less she criticized him. In fact, she began to encourage him. Even when he did what she hated most, left his underwear on the bathroom floor, she picked it up. She only mentioned it that night when they finally fell into bed. "You seem preoccupied tonight," she told him. "You've been pretty good about throwing your dirty clothes in the hamper, but you didn't tonight. Is something wrong? Is there something you'd like to talk about?"

Yes, there *was* something wrong. There were rumors of layoffs at work, and Sam was feeling scared. As he told her his worries, she placed a warm, reassuring hand on his arm and just smiled at him. That was all. No words, but he felt at the moment absolutely safe. Not safe from bad things happening but safe because he knew, at that moment, that no matter what happened, they'd get through it together. At that moment, the cycle had been broken. Sam had taken the first big step toward repairing his story.

Step Five: Reconnecting

As we wrote at the beginning of this book, we believe God created people for relationships, for attachments to those they hold dearest. Thus, the ultimate destination in this healing journey is to build better, more enduring relationships— relationships that are rich, satisfying, and intimate, that help you grow stronger, that fill you with a sense of purpose and meaning, that inspire you to act with grace and mercy to the world around you, and that strengthen your spiritual awareness and enhance your ultimate relationship: your relationship with God.

Of course, such relationships have conflict and even smatterings of pain. But healthy relationships ultimately grow from and through conflict. In fact, the participants in the relationship actually begin to see conflict as an opportunity for growth. They certainly don't see conflict as the thundering, lightning-sparked hooves of the approaching Four Horsemen of the Apocalypse.

Attachment injuries and soul wounds break the ties that bind those relationships together. They erode our willingness to trust others. In some cases, where the offender is repentant, has sincerely apologized for his or her wrongdoing, and has promised to turn from his or her damaging ways, reconciliation and forgiveness are possible. But when repentance doesn't occur and reconciliation isn't possible, our forgiveness still should be given. In this section, we want to suggest that reconnecting starts with forgiveness.[5]

When we've been betrayed by someone close to us, someone we trusted to make our needs a priority, an attachment injury forms, a wound that bleeds anger and oozes resentment directed toward the offender or oneself. To move on and grow, to forgive, we need to work through these feelings. David Stoop, an expert on forgiveness, describes three paths to forgiveness. Two are destructive, while only one actually leads to resolution and reconnection.

The first destructive path is *denial* or *self-blame*. On this path we do one of two things: We tell ourselves the injury didn't really happen, or we acknowledge that it happened but blame ourselves for the injury. For example, if your parents were unavailable to you as a child, you might tell yourself and others that they were really great parents. Like Arnold did back in chapter 4. For years he denied he even had any attachment injuries. He dealt with the pain through an addiction to possessions, success, and power. Ultimately, because he buried his story, he repeated it with his own family. Others, as a result of burying their stories, might fall into emotional numbness and depression.

Where denial paves over the wound and pretends it doesn't exist, self-blame says there is a wound but *I'm at fault*. Someone might say, "My parents were never there for me, but if I had a kid like me, I wouldn't be there for him either. I was very hard to live with." In both cases, denial and self-blame, the wounded person can't bear to place the blame where it belongs. Self-blame comes with the added burden of responsibility, a burden that can be a real anchor to drag along.

The second destructive path is *bitterness*. Here our emotional feet get mired in the event; no matter how hard we try, we can't move on from it. We keep reliving the event, continually asking ourselves, "Why me?" This incessant search for an answer that never comes only leads to intense anger and smoldering resentment. Replaying the event comes from our need to understand the world we live in, and from a need for justice. However, since there's no acceptable reason for someone to hurt you, and there's no godly way for you to seek justice, you're left trapped in the past. Just like the path of *denial,* the path of bitterness eventually leaves you feeling hopeless and depressed.

In some ways, we believe these two false pathways to forgiveness mirror two forms of insecure attachment: The avoidant attachment style is rooted in *denial,* and the ambivalent attachment style is stuck in *bitterness.*

The third, and constructive, path to forgiveness consists of eight steps:

1. *Place blame appropriately.* You don't act like the injury didn't occur, you don't blame yourself, and you don't make excuses for the offender. You're honest about what happened and how it hurt you.

2. *Grieve.* When you grieve, you appreciate what was lost. For instance, you might grieve for your lost ability to trust. Then you allow yourself to experience the feelings that result. Though grief includes sadness and loss, it also includes anger and protest. You acknowledge what you wanted and needed and how the injury let you down. In grieving there is usually vacillation between anger and sadness; both are important to the grieving process.

3. *Empathize.* Empathy is the ability to see the world from another person's perspective. As an emotion, it helps us to cooperate, to act with compassion and mercy, and to restrain aggressive impulses. Empathy is critical to forgiveness because it helps us look at offenders in a different light. We try to understand their history, background, and life experiences, not to give them excuses or to let them off the hook, but simply to try and understand what could have motivated them to do what they did.

Our work with Sam, for example, included helping him explore his father's background. Sam's father's father also had died young, when Sam's dad was only thirteen. As the oldest son, it had fallen to him to keep the family business going and to protect the family. He had risen to the occasion, but in doing so, he had never had the time or the support to grieve his father's passing. His feelings probably only got in the way. He was one hardworking youngster, but he was always hard on himself. This attitude kept his nose to the grindstone, but it got him through.

By understanding his dad's own history, Sam was able to see the world from his father's perspective. His dad wasn't just a mean ol' grump who incessantly pressured Sam to perform. He was a hardened man who had come from a hard life, doing a hard job for which he was ill prepared. And he did it the only way he knew how, always pushing himself harder. He had done the same with his son.

Keep in mind that there's another side to empathy. As you come to understand the background behind the other person's "sin," you realize that you have sinned against others too. Maybe not in the same way, but you *have* wronged others. Which means there are others out there who deserve to be angry with *you.* You're not pure. Self-righteousness is hard to maintain when you're not as righteous as you originally thought. You need to be forgiven too. Denying this reality puts you in the same class as the unforgiving servant in one of Jesus' parables (see Matthew 18:23–35). The king forgave this servant an enormous debt. But then the servant demanded from one of *his* servants the immediate repayment of a relatively small debt. His servant begged for mercy but received none. The unforgiving servant refused to grant mercy and had his servant cast into prison. Obviously the unforgiving servant lacked empathy. He refused to see what it was like to be unforgiven, so he could not extend forgiveness to his debtor.

Empathy was a powerful experience for Sam as he studied his relationship with his son. Sam desperately wanted his son's forgiveness. He could see how he had hurt him, and seeing this hurt allowed him to understand the anger and resentment that had built up over the years. This understanding, in turn, helped him see how his own dad, if he were alive today, would want and need Sam's forgiveness. Sam wept bitterly. He felt differently toward his dad. He'd found compassion.

4. *Forgive.* There are two acts of forgiveness. The first is being willing to partake in the forgiveness process, to go through the pain, to take the steps necessary to achieve a forgiving heart. The second act is to extend forgiveness—which may be easier said than done. Several roadblocks can prevent it. And each is rooted in a misconception about forgiveness.

The three most common misconceptions about forgiveness are: (1) "If I forgive, it means that I'm condoning the act." No. Forgiveness begins with righteous anger, an acknowledgment that the offense was wrong and that it hurt you. (2) "To forgive means I must forget—and I can never forget." This is also false. Forgiveness does not mean you forget anything. You just give up the right to replay the event, and you stop wishing for revenge. (3) "If I forgive, I become a doormat; I'm saying it's okay for people to walk over me." This is blatantly false. While you don't hold the injury against the offender any longer, forgiveness does not mean you give him or her, or anyone else, a license to walk all over you. As we will see, to forgive is different from reconciling.

5. *Consider reconciliation.* Forgiveness is a one-way process. It requires you to give up your anger and your desire for revenge. Reconciliation, on the other hand, is a two-way process in which the other person is willing to apologize for his or her wrongdoing and to commit to not doing wrong again. Even so, you want to be cautious until trust is earned.

6. *Make peace with yourself.* Unyielding rage toward someone not only leaves you bitter and resentful, it also locks you into a chronic pattern of self-doubt and self-criticism. Forgiving others frees you to forgive yourself. You learn to care about yourself in an honest and genuine way, and you learn to trust yourself and your ability to love others.

7. *Learn to trust again.* Attachment injuries and soul wounds shatter our

ability to openly trust others and lead to isolation and emotional defensiveness or to excessive clinginess. Forgiveness helps free us up emotionally so we can face closeness again. Since we're no longer so afraid of being hurt, we become more courageous and willing to try again. This isn't a speedy process by any means, but it is a potentially rewarding one.

8. *Reconnect.* The final step comes when you plug back into the world of relationships. You allow yourself to love and be loved. If you're a parent, you reconnect with your children, honestly acknowledging your shortcomings, your distance, your criticism. You make a commitment to connect deeply and warmly. Your message to your loved ones is simple: *Above everything else, I love you.* If you are a spouse, you recommit to your marriage. You consciously love your spouse, and you become very intentional about taking the necessary steps to improve the quality of your marriage. If you are single or divorced, you commit yourself to no longer being isolated but to reconnecting with others—healthy people who are able to love you in return.

WORKING YOUR WAY TO THAT
MORE WONDERFULLY FULFILLING PLACE

Well, you're here. You've reached the end. We've worked hard to give you a good look at relationships and the attachment styles governing them. Our hope is that you've seen your own style within these pages and that if your style isn't secure you've decided to change. To help you, in this last chapter we've given you a map that defines the pathway to healing and helps you construct a platform from which to launch yourself. We hope you take advantage of both.

If you feel comfortable working on your own, good. But if you don't, please seek help right away from your pastor or a professional Christian counselor. If you're not sure how to find one, give the American Association of Christian Counselors a call at 1-800-526-8673, or visit our website at www.aacc.net and we'll help you find someone you feel comfortable with.

As you work your way to that more wonderfully fulfilling place, don't forget: God created us for relationships. Why? Maybe so that we'd have enough practice in them that we would yearn for a healthy, intimate relationship with

Him. It's upon that relationship, our relationship with God, that every good element of our lives, especially all our other relationships, is based. Which means that concentrating on that relationship should be the principle focus of our lives.

Thankfully, if our relationship with God is healthy and intimate, if it compels us to love others in godly, selfless ways, it will also help us fashion healthy, intimate earthly relationships, particularly with our husbands and wives. And when our relationships are in order, they bring us fulfillment, safety, and comfort, and they fill our cup to overflowing with love and contentment. They also act as a firm foundation from which we can launch ourselves into the other aspects of our lives—our jobs, our churches, our hobbies, and our friends.

If you take on the challenge of change, you'll never regret that decision. Life is short. We hope you've decided to start changing your life the instant this page is turned. May God be with you every step of the way!

Acknowledgments

Although excitement fuels the beginning of most books, exhaustion often comes with the ending. That is only partly true with this book, however. We are both very pleased with this labor and thankful to God for the wisdom and strength He granted us to complete it.

Furthermore, the conclusion of this book brings a deeper friendship and respect between us, a greater love and appreciation for our wives and children and our extended families, and a heightened respect for all those who interacted with and assisted us in this project.

We especially want to thank our editor, Sue Ann Jones, with whom we've had a delightful collaboration, and Integrity Publishers president Byron Williamson and publisher Joey Paul for supporting and believing in this work. Sealy Yates and John Eames have stood with us as agents and friends from the beginning when this book was just a dream—we anticipate a long-term and deepening friendship together.

Heidi Brizendine, Shannon Miller, and the entire American Association of Christian Counselors team was very patient and labored many hours to help keep us encouraged, organized, and focused.

Our friends and colleagues George Ohlschlager and Sharon Hart Morris are also passionate about this topic, helping us think through its many applications, and sharing with us in the writing of two chapters.

Doris Woodie, Ellen Hendricks, Brian and Donna Ratliff, Ron Hawkins, and Gary Habermas asked many good questions and gave many helpful insights along the way.

A huge thank-you goes to Bill Kritlow, a master storyteller who walked through this book with us, helping us tell our stories and express our thoughts more vividly and clearly.

Our solemn prayer is that God will be glorified in and through all we do. He is our safe place.

Notes

Chapter 1. The Heart of the Matter: Attachments in Everyday Living

1. Ernest Becker, *The Denial of Death* (New York: Free Press, 1973).
2. Russell A. Barkley, *Defiant Children: A Clinician's Manual for Assessment and Parent Training,* 2d ed. (New York: Guilford Press, 1997).

Chapter 2. Shaping Our View of Ourselves and Those We Hold Dearest

1. For a dynamic review of the history of attachment theory, see I. Bretherton, "The Origins of Attachment Theory: John Bowlby and Mary Ainsworth," *Developmental Psychology* 28 (1992): 759–75, and R. Karen, *Becoming Attached: First Relationships and How They Shape Our Capacity to Love* (Oxford, England: Oxford University Press, 1994).
2. John Bowlby, *Attachment and Loss,* vol. 1, *Attachment* (New York: Basic Books, 1969).
3. Adapted from J. Holmes, *John Bowlby and Attachment Theory* (New York: Routledge, 1993).

4. We realize that children are not actually asking questions in a verbal fashion. But they act as if they are. The point is that attachment is so basic that it develops even before our language systems develop.

5. Bowlby, *Attachment and Loss,* vol. 1, *Attachment.*

6. This grid is adapted from K. Bartholomew, "Avoidance of Intimacy: An Attachment Perspective," *Journal of Social and Personal Relationships 7* (1990): 147–178.

7. While we use the term *disorganized* attachment style, other researchers refer to it as the *fearful* style.

8. Mary Ainsworth, M. C. Blehar, E. Waters, and W. Wall, *Patterns of Attachment: A Psychological Study of the Strange Situation* (Hillsdale, N. J.: Erlbaum, 1978).

9. Mary Main and E. Hess, "Parents' Unresolved Traumatic Experiences Are Related to Infant Disorganized Attachment Status: Is Frightened and/or Frightening Parental Behavior the Linking Mechanism?" in M. T. Greenberg, D. Cicchetti, E. M. Cummings, eds., *Attachment in the Preschool Years: Theory, Research, and Intervention* (Chicago: University of Chicago Press, 1990), 161–82, and M. Main and J. Solomon, "Procedures for Identifying Infants As Disorganized/Disoriented During the Ainsworth Strange Situation," in Greenberg, Cicchetti, and Cummings, *Attachment in the Preschool Years,* 121–60.

10. G. Habermas and Gary Sibcy, "Religious Doubt and Negative Emotionality: The Development of the Religious Doubt Scale," 2001. Manuscript is currently under review in the *Journal of Psychology and Theology.*

‡ W. Pollack, *Real Boys* (New York: Henry Holt, 1998), 113.

Chapter 3. Soul Wounds

1. Mary D. S. Ainsworth, "Attachments across the Life Span," *Bulletin of the New York Academy of Medicine* 61 (1985): 792–812.

2. Susan Johnson, J. A. Makinen, and J. W. Milikin, "Attachment Injuries

in Couple Relationships: A New Perspective on Impasses in Couples Therapy," *Journal of Marital and Family Therapy* 27 (2001): 145–55.

3. John Bowlby, *Attachment and Loss,* vol. 2, *Separation: Anxiety and Anger* (New York: Basic Books, 1973), 246.

4. Ibid., 249.

5. John Gottman, *The Marriage Clinic: A Scientifically Based Marital Therapy* (New York: W.W. Norton, 1999).

6. David Olson, "Circumplex Model of Marital and Family Systems: Assessing Family Functioning," in Froma Walsh, ed., *Normal Family Processes,* 2d ed. (New York: Guilford Press, 1993).

Chapter 4. The Hardened Heart

1. Pollack, *Real Boys.*

2. C. S. Carter, "Oxytocin and Sexual Behavior," *Neuroscience and Biobehavioral Reviews* 100 (1992): 204–32. and C. Hazan and D. Zeifman, "Pair Bonds As Attachment: Evaluating the Evidence," in J. Cassidy and P. R. Shaver, eds., *Handbook of Attachment: Theory, Research, and Clinical Applications* (New York: Guilford Press, 1999).

3. G. D. Nass and M. P. Fisher, *Sexuality Today* (Boston: Jones and Bartlett, 1988).

4. E. Hess, "The Adult Attachment Interview: Historical and Current Perspectives," in J. Cassidy and P. R. Shaver, eds., *Handbook of Attachment: Theory, Research, and Clinical Applications* (New York: Guilford Press, 1999), 395–433.

5. L. Sandler, "Issues in Early Mother-Child Interaction," *Journal of the American Academy of Child Psychiatry* 1 (1962): 141–66. This is a classic article on parent-child interaction.

6. R. Bell and M. D. S. Ainsworth, "Infant Crying and Maternal Responsiveness," *Child Development* 43 (1972): 1171–90.

7. Ibid., 118.

8. A. N. Shore, "The Effects of a Secure Attachment Relationship on Right Brain Development, Affect Regulation, and Infant Mental Health,"

Infant Mental Health Journal 22 (2001): 7–66, and D. Siegel, *The Developing Mind: Toward a Neurobiology of Interpersonal Experience* (New York: Guilford Press, 1999).

9. N. Weinfield, L. Sroufe, B. Egeland, and E. Carlson, "The Nature of Individual Differences in Infant-Caregiver Attachment," in Cassidy and Shaver, eds., *Handbook of Attachment* (New York: Guilford, 1999), 68–88.

10. J. F. Masterson, *The Search for the Real Self: Unmasking the Personality Disorders of Our Age* (New York: Free Press, 1988), 90.

11. J. F. Masterson and R. Klein, eds., *Disorders of the Self: New Therapeutic Horizons: The Masterson Approach* (New York: Brunner/Mazel, 1995).

12. This aspect of the exiled self is true of those who actually come in for therapy. There is a subgroup of individuals who fit the criteria for schizoid personality disorder in the *DSM-IV* (*The Diagnostic and Statistical Manual of Mental Disorders,* 4th ed., published by the American Psychiatric Association). This subgroup is more emotionally hollow and interpersonally withdrawn than the folks we refer to as the exiled-self group. Because those in the *DSM-IV* group are more impaired, they are less likely to identify with a desire to connect with others and are consequently less likely to respond favorably to any type of therapy.

13. For an overview of the characteristics of obsessive-compulsive personality disorder see D. Robinson, *Personality Disorders: Explained* (Port Huron, Mich.: Rapid Psychler Press, 2000).

14. See chapter 3, "Soul Wounds."

15. Habermas and Sibcy, "Religious Doubt and Negative Emotionality."

16. Gary Habermas, personal communication, 2000.

Chapter 5. Don't Abandon Me!

1. I. Yalom, *Existential Psychotherapy* (New York: Basic Books, 1980).

2. A. Beck, A. Freeman, and associates, *Cognitive Therapy of Personality Disorders* (New York: Guilford Press, 1990).

3. S. Shea, *Psychiatric Interviewing: The Art of Understanding* (Philadelphia: W. B. Saunders, 1988), 355.

4. D. G. Perry, L. C. Perry, and P. Rasmussen, "Cognitive and Social Learning Mediators of Aggression," *Child Development* 57 (1995): 700–711, and Robinson, *Personality Disorders: Explained.* Both of these resources provide a helpful overview of the *DSM-IV* personality disorders. Keep in mind that personality disorders are maladaptive extensions of personality styles.

5. L. Benjamin, *Interpersonal Diagnosis and Treatment of Personality Disorders* (New York: Guilford, 1993).

6. Fredrick Firestone, *Combating Self-Destructive Thought Processes: Voice Therapy and Separation Theory* (New York: Sage, 1997).

7. T. Millon, *Disorder of Personality: DSM-IV and Beyond* (New York: John Wiley & Sons, 1996).

8. Shea, *Psychiatric Interviewing,* 358.

9. Gary Sibcy, "Self-Reported Attachment Styles and Psychopathology in a Clinical Population" (doctoral diss., Union Institute and University's School of Clinical and Professional Psychology, Cincinnati, Ohio, 2000).

10. Beck, Freeman, and associates, *Cognitive Therapy of Personality Disorders.*

11. L. Greenberg and S. Paivio, *Working with Emotions in Psychotherapy* (New York: Guilford Press, 1997).

12. For a distinction between criticism and contempt in marital communication see J. M. Gottman, *The Marriage Clinic: A Scientifically Based Marital Therapy* (New York: W. W. Norton, 1999).

Chapter 6. The Grass Is Always Dead on Both Sides of the Fence

1. Mary Main and E. Hess, "Parents' Unresolved Traumatic Experiences Are Related to Infant Disorganized Attachment Status: Is Frightened and/or Frightening Parental Behavior the Linking Mechanism?" 163.

2. Louis Breger, *From Instinct to Identity: The Development of Personality* (Englewood Cliffs: Prentice-Hall, 1974), 211.

3. C. H. Kempe, F. N. Silverman, B. F. Steele, W. Droegmuller, and H. K. Silver, "The Battered-Child Syndrome," *Journal of the American Medical Association* 181 (1962): 17–24.

4. H. I. Kaplan, A. M. Freedman, and B. J. Sadock, eds., *Comprehensive Textbook of Psychiatry*, 2 vols. (Baltimore: Williams & Wilkins, 1980).

5. Bruce Perry, "Violence and Childhood: How Persisting Fear Can Alter the Developing Child's Brain, a special Child Trauma Academy website version of the neurodevelopmental impact of violence in childhood" (http://www.childtrauma.org/vio_child.htm). This information is also included in D. Schetky and E. Benedek, eds., *Textbook of Child and Adolescent Forensic Psychiatry* (Washington, D.C.: American Psychiatric Press, 2001), 221–38.

6. We are not proposing a new legal definition of abuse that would mean if you yell at your child one day you need to call social services and turn yourself in. But we want to make a strong statement about how destructive certain kinds of parenting can be, and we want to help educate parents to be mindful of how they can prevent themselves from treating their children in these ways.

7. William Bernet, "Child Maltreatment," in H. I. Kaplan and B. J. Sadock, eds., *Comprehensive Textbook of Psychiatry*, 7th ed., vol. 2 (New York: Lippincott, Williams and Wilkins: 2000), 2878–89.

8. David Finkelhor, *Sexually Victimized Children* (New York: Free Press, 1979).

9. John N. Briere, *Child Abuse Trauma: Theory and Treatment of the Lasting Effects* (Thousand Oaks, Calif.: Sage Publications, 1992).

10. Ibid.

11. Stephanie Brown, *Treating Adult Children of Alcoholics: A Developmental Perspective* (New York: John Wiley, 1988), 27.

12. Breger, *From Instinct to Identity*, 198.

13. Basal van der Kolk, "Trauma and Memory," in Basal A. van der Kolk, A. C. McFarlane, and L. Weisaeth, eds., *Traumatic Stress: The Effects of Overwhelming Experience on Mind, Body, and Society* (New York: Guilford, 1996).

14. Basal van der Kolk, "The Complexity of Adaptation to Trauma Self-Regulation, Stimulus Discrimination, and Characterological Development," in van der Kolk, McFarlane, and Weisaeth, *Traumatic Stress,* 193.

15. Ibid.

16. Basal van der Kolk, "The Compulsion to Repeat the Trauma: Re-enactment, revictimization, and Masochism," *Psychiatric Clinics of North America* 12 (1989): 389–411. Also posted on the Internet at http://www.cirp.org/library/psych/vanderkolk/

17. R. Pitman, S. Orr, D. Laforque, et al., "Psychophysiology of PTSD Imagery in Vietnam Combat Veterans," *Archives of General Psychiatry* 44 (1987): 940–76.

18. We don't want to imply that all victims of trauma are addicted to tragedy and go searching for ways to get beat up or raped. But research shows that victims of childhood trauma are more likely to experience traumatic relationships and events during adulthood.

19. Firestone, *Combating Self-Destructive Thought Processes,* 56–57.

20. Bruno Bettelheim, "Individual and Mass Behavior in Extreme Situations," in *Surviving and Other Essays* (New York: Knopf, 1979), 48–83. Original works published in 1943.

21. A. Miller, *Thou Shalt Not Be Aware* (New York: Farrar, Straus, & Giroux, 1984).

22. R. Firestone and Joyce Catlett, *The Fear of Intimacy* (New York: American Psychological Association, 1999).

Chapter 7. Equipped to Face Challenges and Take Risks

1. Bowlby, *Attachment and Loss,* vol. 2, *Separation: Anxiety and Anger,* 246.

2. Greenberg and Paivio, *Working with Emotions in Psychotherapy.*

3. L. S. Vygotzky, *Mind in Society: The Development of Higher Psychological Processes* (Cambridge, Mass.: Harvard University Press, 1978).

4. John Gottman, *Raising an Emotionally Intelligent Child: The Heart of Parenting* (New York: Simon and Schuster, 1997), and John Gottman,

L. F. Katz, and C. Hooven, "Parental Meta-Emotion Philosophy and the Emotional Life of Families: Theoretical Models and Preliminary Data," *Journal of Family Psychology* 10 (1996): 243–68.

5. See Gottman et al., "Parental Meta-Emotion Philosophy."

6. For a review of this concept, see D. K. Silverman, "The Tie That Binds: Affect Regulation, Attachment, and Psychoanalysis," *Psychoanalytic Psychology* 15 (1998): 187–212.

7. Richard Foster, *Prayer: Finding the Heart's True Home* (San Francisco: HarperSanFrancisco, 1992).

8. M. Scott Peck, *The Road Less Traveled* (New York: Simon and Schuster, 1978).

9. Bowlby, *Attachment and Loss,* vol. 2, *Separation: Anxiety and Anger,* 208.

10. Viktor Frankl, *Man's Search for Meaning: An Introduciton to Logotherapy* (New York: Simon & Schuster, 1963, 1984).

11. Gary Habermas, personal communication, 2002.

12. J. Holmes, *John Bowlby and Attachment Theory* (New York: Routledge, 1993).

13. J. L. Pearson, D. A. Cohn, P. A. Cowan, and C. P. Cowan, "Earned- and Continuous-Security in Adult Attachment: Relation to Depressive Symptomatology and Parenting Style," *Development and Psychopathology* 6 (1994): 359–73, and J. L. Phelps, J. Belsky, and K. Crnic, "Earned Security, Daily Stress, and Parenting: A Comparison of Five Alternative Models," *Development and Psychopathology* 10 (1998): 21–38.

Chapter 8. God and You—with George Ohlschlager

1. Irvin Yalom, *Existential Psychotherapy* (New York: Basic Books, 1980).

2. Peter Kreft, *Love Is Stronger Than Death* (San Francisco: St. Ignatius Press, 1992).

3. F. Firestone, *Combating Self-Destructive Thought Processes: Voice Therapy and Separation Theory* (New York: Sage, 1997), 258.

4. Otto Rank, *Will Therapy and Truth and Reality* (New York: Alfred A. Knopf, 1945).

5. Dallas Willard, *The Spirit of the Disciplines: Understanding How God Changes Lives* (San Francisco: Harper & Row, 1988), 98.
6. Ibid., 9.
7. Ibid., 156.
8. Ibid., 163.
9. Ibid., 172.
10. Richard Foster, *Prayer: Finding the Heart's True Home* (San Francisco: Harper, 1992). This is only one of many types of prayer that Richard Foster so eloquently elaborates on in this classic book. We believe that all types of prayer facilitate our attachment with God. We discuss simple prayer because we believe it is the steppingstone to other types of prayer. And also, simple prayer seems to most closely parallel the dynamics of an attachment relationship because in it we learn to immediately turn to God.
11. Ibid., 11–12.
12. Søren Kierkegaard, quoted in Foster, *Prayer,* 39.

Chapter 9. Taming Emotional Storms

1. Greenberg and Paivio, *Working with Emotions in Psychotherapy,* 21.
2. We adapted these triggers from G. Klerman, M. Weissman, B. Rounsaville, and E. Cheveron, *Interpersonal Psychotherapy of Depression* (New York: Basic Books, 1984). This book is a classic and is a must-read for any serious therapist treating depression and emotional disorders.
3. Gottman, *The Marriage Clinic.*
4. Becker, *The Denial of Death.*
5. David Burns, *The Feeling Good Handbook: Using the New Mood Therapy in Everyday Life* (New York: W. Morrow, 1989).
6. In Dallas Willard's new book, *Renovation of the Heart: Putting on the Character of Christ* (Colorado Springs: Navpress, 2002), he identifies three crucial elements involved in change: vision, intentionality, and means. We also believe a fourth element is crucial, and that is courage.
7. This technique is based on the most recent research on treating depression. It seems that people do change from the outside in. By getting

depressed people active, their minds seem to be more open to new ways of thinking, and their self-esteem begins to snap back. See J. B. Persons, *Essential Components of Cognitive-Behavior Therapy for Depression* (Washington, D.C.: American Psychological Association, 2000).

Chapter 10. Love, Sex, and Marriage with Sharon Hart Morris, Ph.D.

1. John Gottman, *Why Marriages Fail* (New York: Simon and Schuster, 1994).
2. Sharon Hart Morris, "Conceptualization and Development of 'Haven of Safety' Marital Assessment Scale" (doctoral diss., Fuller Graduate School of Psychology, Pasadena, Calif., 2000).
3. A word of caution: In abusive relationships, risking to trust again can be dangerous. Evaluate the emotional and physical safety of your relationship. If your relationship is peppered with emotional, physical, or sexual abuse, seek professional help. We would not ask you to risk your heart with a spouse who is abusive. On the other hand, sometimes a hurt heart can feel like it has been abused. Seek counseling to discern the difference.
4. John Gottman, *The Relationship Cure* (New York: Crown, 2001).

Chapter 11. Attachment-Based Parenting

1. Russell Barkely, *Taking Charge of ADHD: The Complete, Authoritative Guide for Parents,* 2d ed. (New York, Guilford Press, 2000), 6.
2. Stephen Covey, *How to Develop a Family Mission Statement,* audiotape (Provo, Utah: Covey Leadership Center, 1996).
3. Stephen Covey, *The Seven Habits of Highly Effective People: Restoring the Character Ethic* (New York: Simon and Schuster, 1989).
4. Patricia Crittenden, *CARE-INDEX Coding Manual* (Miami: Family Relations Institute, 2001).
5. William Sears and Martha Sears, *The Attachment Parenting Book* (London: Little Brown, 2002).
6. Some recent parenting programs call for a highly structured parent-

centered approach to raising infants and toddlers. But the real origin of this approach began with the radical behaviorists of the 1940s and 50s. Such individuals as B. F. Skinner and J. B. Watson were not at all friendly to Christianity and to the belief in God. They believed that children came into this world as blank slates—with no previous learning in the womb plus no genetic hardwiring. So they claimed that an infant's cry was merely a learned behavior, not a God-programmed behavior designed to cue parents into its needs. The goal of the behaviorist was to manufacture children who were precociously independent and autonomous. Since crying ran counter to these goals, behaviorists assumed it to be a negative behavior that needed to be extinguished. Picking up the crying child and feeding it would reinforce the behavior and lead to a spoiled child, they said. Such a philosophy has been scientifically proven to be woefully inadequate and even harmful to kids.

7. Ainsworth, Blehar, Waters, and Wall, *Patterns of Attachment.*

8. Mary D. S. Ainsworth, "Maternal Sensitivity Scales," a mimeographed report (Baltimore: Johns Hopkins University, 1969), now available through a State University of New York at Stony Brook website: http://www.psychology.sunysb.edu/edu/ewaters/measures/senscoop.htp

9. S. Chess and A. Thomas, *Know Your Child* (New York: Basic Books, 1987), and A. Thomas and S. Chess, *Temperament and Development* (New York: Bruner-Mazel, 1977).

10. Thomas and Chess, *Temperament and Development.*

11. Dr. Grace Ketterman, personal communication, 2000.

12. J. M. Contrera, K. A. Kerns, B. L. Weimer, A. L. Gentzler, and P. L. Tomich, "Emotion Regulation As a Mediator of Associations Between Mother-Child Attachment and Peer Relationships in Middle Childhood," *Journal of Family Psychology* 14 (2000): 111–24.

13. Gary Habermas, personal communication, 2000.

14. Froma Walsh, *Strengthening Family Resilience* (New York: Guilford Press, 1998).

Chapter 12. Breaking Free!

1. Living *in* the now should not be confused with living *for* the now. To live *in* the now is to accept your experiences and appreciate what you have. It heightens your sense of responsibility and helps you make effective choices. Living *for* the now is self-centered and impulsive. It actually causes you to feel a lack of responsibility and leads to poor choices.

2. Our thoughts on this subject have been influced by Dan Allender, Larry Crabb, John Gottman, Leslie Greenberg, Susan Johnson, and Donald Meichenbaum.

3. Keep in mind, just because you don't feel like you have been wounded, doesn't mean you haven't been. Many people come from families where the rule is not only do you not talk about painful events but you also do not remember them.

4. D. B. Waters and E. C. Lawrence, *Competence, Courage, and Change: An Approach to Family Therapy* (New York: W.W. Norton, 1993).

5. David Stoop, *Real Solutions for Forgiving the Unforgivable* (Ann Arbor, Mich.: Servant, 2001).

Bibliography

Ainsworth, Mary D. S., M. C. Blehar, E. Waters, and S. Wall. *Patterns of Attachment: A Psychological Study of the Strange Situation.* Hillsdale, N.J.: Erlbaum, 1978.

Barkley, R., *Defiant Children: A Clinician's Manual for Assessment and Parent Training,* 2d ed. New York: Guilford Press, 1997.

Bartholomew, K. "Avoidance of Intimacy: An Attachment Perspective." *Journal of Social and Personal Relationships* 7 (1990): 147–78.

Beck, A., and A. Freeman and associates. *Cognitive Therapy of Personality Disorders.* New York: Guilford Press, 1990.

Becker, E. *The Denial of Death.* New York: Free Press, 1973.

Bell, R., and M. D. S. Ainsworth. "Infant Crying and Maternal Responsiveness." *Child Development* 43 (1972): 1171–90.

Benjamin, L. *Interpersonal Diagnosis and Treatment of Personality Disorders.* New York: Guilford, 1993.

Bettelheim, B. "Individual and Mass Behavior in Extreme Situations," in *Surviving and Other Essays.* New York: Knopf, 1979. (Original works published in 1943.)

Bowlby, J. *Attachment and Loss.* Vol. 1, *Attachment.* New York: Basic Books, 1969.

———. *Attachment and Loss*. Vol. 2, *Separation: Anxiety and Anger.* New York: Basic Books, 1973.

———. *Attachment and Loss*. Vol. 3, *Loss*. New York: Basic Books, 1980.

Breger, L. *From Instinct to Identity: The Development of Personality.* Englewood Cliffs: Prentice-Hall, 1974.

Brennan, K. A., and J. K. Bosson. "Attachment-Style Differences in Attitudes Toward and Reactions to Feedback from Romantic Partners: An Exploration of the Relational Bases of Self-Esteem." *Personality and Social Psychology Bulletin* 24 (1998): 699–714.

Bretherton, I. "The Origins of Attachment Theory: John Bowlby and Mary Ainsworth." *Developmental Psychology* 28 (1992): 759–75.

Briere, J. N. *Child Abuse Trauma: Theory and Treatment of the Lasting Effects.* Newbury Park: Sage Publications, 1992.

Brown, Stephanie. *Treating Adult Children of Alcoholics: A Developmental Perspective.* New York: John Wiley, 1988.

Carter, C. S. "Oxytocin and Sexual Behavior." *Neuroscience and Biobehavioral Reviews* 100 (1992): 204–32.

Dodge, K. A. "Social Cognition and Children's Aggressive Behavior." *Child Development* 51 (1980): 162–70.

Dodge, K. A. "Attributional Bias in Aggressive Children" in P. C. Kendall, ed., *Advances in Cognitive-Behavioral Research and Therapy.* Vol. 4. New York: Academic Press, 1985.

Dodge, K. A., and C. L. Frame, "Social Cognitive Biases and Deficits in Aggressive Boys." *Child Development* 53 (1982): 620–35.

Drossman, D. A. "Physical and Sexual Abuse and Gastrointestinal Illness: What Is the Link?" *American Journal of Medicine* 97 (1994): 105–107.

Drossman, D. A. "Chronic Functional Abdominal Pain." *American Journal of Gastroenterology* 91, no. 11 (1996): 2270–81.

Bibliography

Finkelhor, D. (1979). *Sexually Victimized Children.* New York: Free Press, 1979.

Firestone, R., and Joyce Catlett. *Combating Self-Destructive Thought Processes: Voice Therapy and Separation Theory.* New York: Sage, 1997.

Firestone, F. *The Fear of Intimacy.* New York: American Psychological Association, 1999.

Fonagy, P. "Attachment in Infancy and the Problem of Conduct Disorders in Adolesence: The Role of Reflective Function." Plenary address to the International Association of Adolescent Psychiatry, San Francisco, 2000.

———. "Attachment, Reflective Function, Conduct Disorders, and Violence." Paper presented to the American Academy of Child and Adolescent Psychiatry's Mid-Year Institute on Integrating Psychotherapy and Psychopharmacology in the Treatment of Children and Adolescents: A Practical Approach. Puerto Vallarta, Mexico, 2000.

Fonagy, P., M. Steele, H. Steele, G. S. Moran, and A. C. Higgitt. "The Capacity for Understanding Mental States: The Reflective Self in Parent and Child and Its Significance for Security of Attachment." *Infant Mental Health Journal* 12 (1991): 211–24.

Fraiberg, S., E. Adelson, and V. Shapiro. "Ghosts in the Nursery: A Psychoanalytic Approach to the Problems of Impaired Infant-Mother Relationships." *Journal of the American Academy of Child Psychiatry* 14 (1970): 387–421.

Frankl, Viktor. *Man's Search for Meaning.* Boston: Beacon Press, 1963.

Gottman, J. M. (1997). *Raising an Emotionally Intelligent Child: The Heart of Parenting.* New York: Simon and Schuster, 1997.

———. *The Marriage Clinic: A Scientifically Based Marital Therapy.* New York: W. W. Norton, 1999.

Gottman, J. M., L. F. Katz, and C. Hooven. "Parental Meta-Emotion Philosophy and the Emotional Life of Families: Theoretical Models and Preliminary Data." *Journal of Family Psychology* 10 (1996): 243–68.

BIBLIOGRAPHY

Greenberg, L., and S. Paivio. *Working with Emotions in Psychotherapy.* New York: Guilford Press, 1997.

Habermas, G., and Gary Sibcy. "Religious Doubt and Negative Emotionality: The Development of the Religious Doubt Scale." (2001) Manuscript is currently under review by the *Journal of Psychology and Theology.*

Hazan, C., and D. Zeifman. "Pair Bonds As Attachment: Evaluating the Evidence," in J. Cassidy, P. R. Shaver, eds., *Handbook of Attachment: Theory, Research, and Clinical Applications.* New York: Guilford Press, 1999.

Hess, E. "The Adult Attachment Interview: Historical and Current Perspectives." J. Cassidy, P. R. Shaver, eds., *Handbook of Attachment: Theory, Research, and Clinical Applications.* New York: Guilford Press, 1999, 395–433.

Holmes, J. *John Bowlby and Attachment Theory.* New York: Routledge, 1993.

Johnson, S. M., J. A. Makinen, and J. W. Milikin. "Attachment Injuries in Couple Relationships: A New Perspective on Impasses in Couples Therapy. *Journal of Marital and Family Therapy* (2001).

Kaplan, H. I., A. M. Freedman, and B. J. Sadock, eds. *Comprehensive Textbook of Psychiatry.* 2 vols. Baltimore: Williams & Wilkins, 1980.

Karen, R. *Becoming Attached: First Relationships and How They Shape Our Capacity to Love.* Oxford, England: Oxford University Press, 1994.

Kempe, C.H., F. N. Silverman, B. F. Steele, W. Droegmuller, and H. K. Silver. "The Battered-Child Syndrome," *Journal of the American Medical Association* 181 (1962): 17–24.

Lochman, J. E., and L. B. Lampron. "Situational Social Problem-Solving Skills and Self-Esteem of Aggressive and Nonaggressive Boys." *Journal of Abnormal Child Psychology* 14 (1986): 605–17.

Lyons-Ruth, K., and D. Jacobvitz. "Attachment Disorganization: Unresolved Loss, Relational Violence, and Lapses in Behavioral and Attentional Strategies," in J. Cassidy and P. R. Shaver, eds., *Handbook of Attachment:*

Theory, Research, and Clinical Applications. New York: Guilford Press, 1999.

Main, M., and J. Solomon. "Procedures for Identifying Infants As Disorganized/Disoriented During the Ainsworth Strange Situation." In M. T. Greenberg, D. Cicchetti, E. M. Cummings, eds., *Attachment in the Preschool Years: Theory, Research, and Interventions.* Chicago: University of Chicago Press, 1990.

Main, M., and E. Hess. "Parents' Unresolved Traumatic Experiences Are Related to Infant Disorganized Attachment Status: Is Frightened and/or Frightening Parental Behavior the Linking Mechanism?" in M. T. Greenberg, D. Cicchetti, and E. M. Cummings, eds, *Attachment in the Preschool Years: Theory, Research, and Intervention.* Chicago: University of Chicago Press, 1990.

Masterson, J. F. *The Search for the Real Self: Unmasking the Personality Disorders of Our Age.* New York: Free Press, 1988.

Masterson, J. F., and R. Klein, eds. *Disorders of the Self: New Therapeutic Horizons: The Masterson Approach.* New York: Brunner/Mazel, 1995.

Miller, A. *Thou Shalt Not Be Aware.* New York: Farrar, Straus, & Giroux, 1984.

Millon, T. *Disorder of Personality: DSM-IV and Beyond.* New York: John Wiley & Sons, 1996.

Nass, G. D., and M. P. Fisher. *Sexuality Today.* Boston: Jones and Bartlett, 1988.

Olson, D. H. "Circumplex Model of Marital and Family Systems: Assessing Family Functioning." In Froma Walsh, ed., *Normal Family Processes,* 2d ed. New York: Guildford, 1993.

Pearson, J. L., D. A. Cohn, P. A. Cowan, and C. P. Cowan. "Earned- and Continuous-Security in Adult Attachment: Relation to Depressive Symptomatology and Parenting Style." *Development and Psychopathology 6* (1994): 359–73.

Peck, M. Scott. *The Road Less Traveled.* New York: Simon and Schuster, 1978.

Perry, D. G., L. C. Perry, and P. Rasmussen. "Cognitive and Social Learning Mediators of Aggression," *Child Development* 57 (1986): 700–711.

Phelps, J. L., J. Belsky, K. Crnic. "Earned Security, Daily Stress, and Parenting: A Comparison of Five Alternative Models. *Development and Psychopathology* 10 (1998): 21–38.

Robinson, D. *Personality Disorders: Explained.* Port Huron, Mich.: Rapid Psychler Press, 2000.

Rosenfeld, A. A., C. C. Nadelson, and M. Krieger. *Journal of the American Academy of Child Psychiatry* 136 (1979): 791–95.

Sandler, L. "Issues in Early Mother-Child Interaction." *Journal of the American Academy of Child Psychiatry* 1 (1962): 141–66.

Shea, S. *Psychiatric Interviewing: The Art of Understanding.* Philadelphia: W. B. Saunders, 1988.

Shore, A. N. "The Effects of a Secure Attachment Relationship on Right Brain Development, Affect Regulation, and Infant Mental Health." *Infant Mental Health Journal* 22 (2001): 7–66.

Sibcy, Gary. "Self-Report Attachment Styles and Psychopathology in a Clinical Population." Doctoral diss., The Union Institute and University's School of Clinical and Professional Psychology, Cincinnati, Ohio, 2000.

Siegel, D. *The Developing Mind: Toward a Neurobiology of Interpersonal Experience.* New York: Guilford Press, 1999.

Silverman, D. K. "The Tie That Binds: Affect Regulation, Attachment, and Psychoanalysis." *Psychoanalytic Psychology* 15 (1988): 187–212.

Slaby, R.G., and N. G. Guerra. "Cognitive Mediators of Aggression in Adolescent Offenders: 1. Assessment." *Developmental Psychology* 24, no. 4 (1988): 580–88.

Bibliography

Sperry, L. *Handbook of Diagnosis and Treatment of DSM-IV Personality Disorders.* New York: Brunner/Mazel, 1995.

Stoop, David. *Real Solutions for Forgiving the Unforgivable.* Ann Arbor, Mich.: Servant, 2001.

van der Kolk, B. A. "The Body Keeps the Score: the Psychobiology of Traumatic Experiences." In B. A. van der Kolk, A. C. McFarlane, and L. Weisaeth, eds., *Traumatic Stress: The Effects of Overwhelming Experience on Mind, Body, and Society.* New York: Guilford, 1996.

————. "The Complexity of Adaptation to Trauma Self-Regulation, Stimulus Discrimination, and Characterological Development." In van der Kolk, McFarlane, and Weisaeth, eds., *Traumatic Stress.* New York: Guilford, 1996.

————. "The Compulsion to the Trauma: Re-enactment, Revictimization, and Masochism." *Psychiatric Clinics of North America* 12 (1989): 389–411.

————. "Trauma and memory." In van der Kolk, McFarlane, and Weisaeth, eds., *Traumatic Stress.*

Vygotzky, L. S. *Mind in Society: The Development of Higher Psychological Processes.* Cambridge, Mass.: Harvard University Press, 1978.

Waters, D. B., and E. C. Lawrence. *Competence, Courage, and Change: An Approach to Family Therapy.* New York: W.W. Norton, 1993.

Weinfield, N., L. Sroufe, B. Egeland, and E. Carlson. "The nature of individual differences in infant-caregiver attachment." In J. Cassidy and P. Shaver, eds., *Handbook of Attachment: Theory, Research, and Clinical Applications.* New York: Guilford Press, 1999.

Willard, D. *The Spirit of the Disciplines: Understanding How God Changes Lives.* San Francisco: Harper and Row, 1988.

Yalom, I. *Existential Psychotherapy.* New York: Basic Books, 1980.